A GENEROUS PRESENCE

A GENEROUS PRESENCE

Spiritual Leadership and the
Art of Coaching

Rochelle Melander

THE
ALBAN
INSTITUTE

Herndon, Virginia
www.alban.org

The Alban Institute
2121 Cooperative Way, Suite 100
Herndon, VA 20171

Scripture quotations, unless otherwise noted, are from the New Revised Standard Version of the Bible, © 1989, Division of Christian Education of the National Council of Churches of Christ in the United States of America, and are used by permission.

Revised Standard Version of the Bible, copyright 1952 [2nd edition, 1971] by the Division of Christian Education of the National Council of the Churches of Christ in the United States of America. Used by permission. All rights reserved.

The Madeline L'Engle poem on page 29 is reprinted from *The Ordering of Love.* Copyright © 2005 by Crosswicks, Ltd. Used by permission of WaterBrook Press, Colorado Springs, CO. All rights reserved.

The excerpts of poems by Rumi on pages 283, 288, and 289 are used by permission of Coleman Barks, translator.

Cover design by OffPisteDesign, Inc.

Library of Congress Cataloging-in-Publication Data

Melander, Rochelle.
  A generous presence : spiritual leadership and the art of coaching / Rochelle Melander.
      p. cm.
  Includes bibliographical references.
  ISBN-13: 978-1-56699-325-8
  ISBN-10: 1-56699-325-3
  1. Church work. 2. Personal coaching. 3. Christian leadership. I. Title.

  BV4400.M445 2006
  253.5—dc22
                          2006019275

        06   07   08   09   VG   4   3   2   1

For my dear daughter Elly,
the princess of generous presence.

❀ Contents

Part 3 THE COACHING CORE
Acting for Change

✸ Acknowledgments

Great is Thy faithfulness! Great is Thy faithfulness!
Morning by morning new mercies I see;
All I have needed Thy hand hath provided
Great is Thy Faithfulness, Lord unto me.

Thomas Chisholm, 1866-1960

I thank the Lord there's people out there like you.

Bernie Taupin, Honky Chateau

Writing a book requires more than a computer and a room of one's own. It takes a village, the generous prayers of the villagers, and the mercy of God. Without these gifts, this book would not be.

A Generous Presence emerged from conversations with my friend, colleague, and editor, Beth Gaede. She encouraged me through the challenging process of getting my ideas and imaginings onto paper and then guided me in shaping those words into a book. When the manuscript was finished, Andrea Lee smoothed the rough edges with artistry and grace.

I am deeply grateful to my amazing clients. Their generous sharing of stories, suggestions, and successes are the heart and soul of this book. In addition, many of the ideas in this book surfaced from dialogues with my teachers, therapists, coaches, and colleagues in both ministry and coaching. A huge thanks to all of you for the insights, advice, and encouragement that support me, my coaching practice, and my writing life, especially Irene Cunningham, Judy Feld, Carol Gerrish, Susan Luff, Gloria McDowell, Caroline Miller, Joelyn Olen, Tim Pearson, Bishop Peter Rogness, Bishop Paul Stumme-Diers, my colleagues at Christos Ministries, the faculty members at The Center for Family Process, and my instructors at Coach U.

Several people offered their wisdom about contemporary music and culture. I thank Micah Stumme-Diers, Jenn Thiel, Ken Kinard, and Evan Boyd.

The generous welcome and prayerful presence of the community at Hephatha Lutheran Church has revived and deepened my faith. This book was inspired and informed by the sermons of Hephatha's pastor, Mary Martha Kannass, and my ministry colleagues at Hephatha, Joseph and Joyce Ellwanger, Richard and Betty Warber, Doris Gant, Erica Johnson, and Louise Meyer.

As an Ash Wednesday girl in a Mardi Gras world, I am reminded by my dear friends that life is about delight as well as discipline. Their generous presence and our fierce conversations widen my world and enlarge my soul. You all have my deep gratitude and love: Maureen Bezold, Siiri Branstrom-Peters, Debbie Brenegan, Holly and Mike Carlson, Jan Ewing, Gretchen Froh, Barbara and John Horner-Ibler, Marty Hultgren, Jeanette Hurt, Kathy Kannass, Mary Martha Kannass, Minerva Kannass, Kathy Kastilahn, Sue Lang, Andrea Lee, Sarah Lutter, Ellen Meissgeier, Donnita Moeller, Karen Natterstad, Diane Olson, Bonnie Peterson, Dawn Pomento, Amy Reumann, Jeannee Sacken, Bob Sitze, Norene Smith, Laurie Stumme-Diers, Holly Toensing, Nancy Toensing, Peggy Tromblay, Joan and Chuck Van Norman, Jan Veseth-Rogers.

My family has generously helped me keep body and soul together in the writing months. My parents, Diane and Dick Melander, watched the children over many weekends. My siblings and sisters-in-law provided support and encouragement—Mary Jo Melander, Chris and Denise Melander, Rebekah Eppley, and Carmen Cortez. My husband, Harold Eppley, made sure I ate and slept. My dear children, Sam and Elly, kept me sane by sharing hugs, laughs, movies, and plenty of treats. All three of you make life delicious. You have my love and thanks!

⊛ Introduction

We sing this African-American spiritual in church:

> I know I've been changed,
> I know I've been changed,
> I know I've been changed.
> The angels in heaven done change my name.[1]

The song reminds me of Jacob wrestling with God. Roman Catholic nun and spirituality writer Joan Chittister says this about Jacob's experience: "Jacob is alone when the struggle begins. There is not a soul around to whom he can talk about it. There is no one who can even give him comfort, let alone aid. He's in this alone. And that is the point. It is the isolation of struggle that wears us down. If we show our pain, we may be mocked for it, or gloated over because of it. If we fail to show our pain, it stands to smother us even as we go on smiling."[2]

We cannot do life alone: it will do us in.

Rabbi Marc Gafni identifies the purpose of life as "overcoming loneliness and moving to connection, to union."[3] In the Judeo-Christian creation story, God declared that it is not good for humans to be alone. Humans need one another. According to Gafni, "As long as the human being is lonely, all of the good of creation cannot sate him. As long as the human being has no one with whom to share her experiences, as long as the human being feels alienated, separate from, and empty, then all of the objective goods of the universe will be irrelevant. That is the experience of loneliness—to feel apart from, severed from, alienated, and empty."[4]

According to Gafni, the combination of the two phrases "It is not good" (*lo tov*) and "alone" or "lonely" (*levado*) only appears in two places in the Hebrew Bible: in the creation story and when Jethro coaches Moses to train a company of leaders (Exod. 18).[5] Moses was exhausted from the relentless work of leading people through the wilderness, settling disputes, and explaining God. Jethro, Moses's father-in-law, said something like, "It is not good that you judge all the people alone." (See Exod. 18:18.) Jethro advised Moses to no longer work alone, feeling lonely, but to lead in community with other leaders. Jethro advised a companionship model of leadership—where leading happens in conversation with one another.

God said it in the beginning: it is not good for humans to be alone.

Jethro knew leading alone was unwise.

Jesus told his disciples to lean on and love one another. Even on the cross Jesus was connecting people, telling his mother, "Woman, here is your son" (John 19:26). Jesus made companions and family members out of acquaintances.

Jesus Transforms

Following Jesus's command can be difficult. We're better at keeping our distance—even with our own family members! How can we imagine loving strangers or our enemies? Emory University liturgy professor Don Saliers has said that in this culture of denial and defensiveness, we need to lay down our fists, to be vulnerable to one another. The story of Jesus and Zacchaeus from Luke 19 teaches us what laying down our fists might look like. If anyone had reason to be defensive or to deny his sins, Zacchaeus did. As a chief tax collector for the Romans he would have been despised by his fellow Jewish people and guilty of defrauding many of them. On Jesus's way through Jericho, he saw the rich chief tax collector Zacchaeus and went to his house to share a meal. It appears that Zacchaeus made himself vulnerable to Jesus and, as a result, decided to give half of what he owned to the poor and pay back fourfold those he had defrauded. When we studied this story at my church, my pastor remarked, "I've never known anyone to change so much in one meal. It might make us afraid to eat with Jesus."[6] Indeed. Connecting with Jesus has the power to transform us, to make us more of who we are. Look at what happened with Mary, Joseph, the shepherds, Peter, and Mary Magdalene. Jesus encountered these ordinary people and they become extraordinary. As my pastor says: "When God comes, the regular, the common is made holy—holy as in set apart for God."[7]

Fortunately, we do not need to wait for God to show up at our dinner table to be transformed. In this world, we embody Jesus for one another and walk with each other into more whole and holy ways of being. We set aside our competitiveness and put on a willingness to be vulnerable. When we are vulnerable, we become more open to one another, able both to offer and to receive care. In such connecting, we have the opportunity to transcend and transform the pain of loneliness. I saw this embodied on Ash Wednesday 2006. My daughter has a seizure disorder. Her medicine makes her crabby and tired. By the time we got to church for the evening service, she was snarling like a cornered cat. Shortly after we arrived, Elly saw Johanna, a friend of ours who has AIDS. Elly and I had been corresponding with Johanna through our pastor, but Johanna and Elly had not met. Because of her illness, this was Johanna's first venture to church in many months. Within minutes of their meeting, Elly crawled into Johanna's lap and laid her head on Johanna's chest. Johanna wrapped her arms around Elly, and they settled into one another. The encounter transformed these two people. Elly calmed down and Johanna seemed stronger. A holy moment.

Why I Wrote This Book

I went into the ministry because I sought the sort of holy, transforming moments I witnessed between my daughter and Johanna. But I rarely saw such moments—a truth that I realized in a brief exchange with a friend, which went something like this:

"I'm jealous of you," my friend said.

"Why?" I asked.

"You're a pastor; you get to talk about God all day."

I laughed and said, "Is that what you think I do?"

When I started out in ministry, I also thought I'd be pondering God all day. I was wrong. I thought I'd be a prophet, inspiring and challenging the people. Wrong again. I thought I'd be spending my life inside a deeply spiritual community, appreciating mutual support, prayer, and love and witnessing holy moments. That didn't happen either.

Instead of talking about God all day, I listened to stories of pain, abuse, and illness. Instead of being prophet, I faced the challenge of a conflicted parish that resisted my calls for unity. Our time together was often filled with arguments and disagreements. The deep spiritual relationships did not always appear. Though I knew God was in the midst of all of this, I experienced frustration: wasn't ministry supposed to be rewarding? The members of my congregation were coping with challenging life experiences: job loss, alcoholism, abusive spouses, chronic and catastrophic physical illnesses, and mental illness. I felt powerless to support these people in confronting their challenges and changing their lives. I also felt very alone.

Then one day I heard a word of hope. Years after I left my first parish, while working as an interim minister, I heard Thomas Leonard, the founder of modern coaching, talk about the profession. Leonard, who died in 2003, was a visionary. He saw possibilities in everything. He didn't worry about roadblocks or problems. He taught us coaching techniques that supported change. He spoke about some of his coaching relationships—and how the conversations transformed clients. I was hooked. I signed up to learn more about this new profession.

The coaching relationship calls people to accountability, asking that they take responsibility for living healthy, holistic lives of integrity. In the companionship of coaching, we connect in ways that strengthen and stretch our souls and our relationship with one another. The transformation is mutual. Coach and client, teacher and learner, host and guest enter the relationship knowing that the conversation can and will renew and transform them. The companionship I found in the intentional coaching relationships brought both dramatic and ongoing changes to my life. Coaching gave me a grab bag of skills and solutions to expand the way I function in my daily responsibilities and relationships. These skills also support me in difficult moments. For this, I am deeply grateful.

This book emerged from that gratitude and a desire to care for my younger self. I recently heard that scientists are very close to realizing time travel. It made me long to go back to visit my 26-year-old self, to give her some advice about how intentionally connecting with others can be transformative, even holy. I cannot do that. Until I can, I have to settle for supporting the people who face challenges similar to the ones I faced in ministry. This book is my way of doing this.

Spiritual Leaders and Coaching

I have written this book for spiritual leaders. Although many of the book's examples are about congregational leaders, I understand and apply the term spiritual leader to include anyone who leads from a spiritual perspective. This includes but is not limited to ordained and lay members of the faith community, therapists, physicians, teachers, public servants, leaders of nonprofit businesses, other helping professionals, and professional coaches. I define the term "professional coach" rather narrowly, limiting it to individuals who have been properly trained through an International Coach Federation accredited school or an equivalent process and are certified or are working toward certification in the field of coaching. This book is designed to support all spiritual leaders in deepening and enriching their personal and professional relationships by teaching concrete coaching tools. Using these skills will not turn a spiritual leader into a professional coach. They will improve the leader's ability to understand self and relate to other people.

One way to image how spiritual leaders use coaching skills is to compare it to the way a friend of mine relates to my daughter. As my child's friend and "honorary auntie," she uses parenting skills in relating to my daughter, telling her, "Be careful, sweetie" or "Stop running." But using parenting skills cannot be equated with being a parent. My friend is very clear that she's *not* the parent. She often tells me, "I will not be the bad cop." (As the mom, *I* get to do that job!) That means my friend will not be the one to pick up my daughter from the floor in the middle of a temper tantrum or make her eat green beans. Spiritual leaders who use coaching skills are not coaches, just as friends who use parenting skills are not necessarily parents.

Perhaps the main difference between a coach and a spiritual leader is the purpose for their interactions. Clients hire coaches and, for the most part, the coach works solely for the client. Spiritual leaders work on behalf of a community—for example, a congregation, school, or board. When a member of the community approaches a leader for support, the leader is serving not only the needs of the individual but also the larger community. Because the spiritual leader is responsible to a whole cadre of people, he or she cannot take on the responsibility of intensely coaching or counseling just a few people.

How to Use This Book

Perhaps the best use of this book is to support your own growth. Ordinary encounters remind us that we need to heal ourselves before we can care for other people. After following a friend's car out of a movie theater, I noticed that she was driving a smidgen too fast. I called her home answering machine and razzed her for speeding without a license plate (hers had been stolen). "That's a sure way to get a ticket," I laughed. About thirty minutes later as I sped toward home, a police officer stopped *me* for speeding. All I could think of was, "Physician, heal yourself" (Luke 4:23 RSV).

You can use this book to

- strengthen and grow your definitions for healthy living and relating;
- raise your awareness about your own life and relationship skills;
- support yourself in making personal lifestyle changes;
- improve your skills in relating to individuals and groups;
- explore your call to become a professional coach.

This book will also be helpful in the work you do with other people, including

- supporting you in communicating about healthy relationships and community;
- teaching basic relationship skills such as listening, asking helpful questions, and offering comfort;
- helping other people do the core work of coaching—accepting the past, creating a strong foundation, assessing assets, creating a life vision, setting goals.

Finally, if you are a coach in training, this book can also be used in conjunction with your training program. If you are already a coach, this book can be used alone or with colleagues to strengthen your coaching skills and to add to your toolbox of skills.

About This Book

This book is a collection of story-driven essays about the philosophy, tools, and work of coaching. Each essay includes one or more exercises, titled "Try," and discussion tools, titled "Talk." The book is divided into three sections, each one having multiple chapters. The first part, "The Coaching Collage," explores some of the key theological, psychological, and sociological concepts that surround and support the coaching relationship. Like every profession, coaching has its own lens through which coaches view the world. Part 2, "The Coaching Toolbox," collects skills and solutions from coaching for you to use in your work as a spiritual leader. Using these skills will not make you a professional coach. They will improve how you relate to yourself and other people. People often ask me, "What do you *do* in a coaching session?" "The Coaching Core," part 3, answers that query, reviewing common coaching situations and providing a stash of strategies for addressing them. As you read this book, you may decide that you want to hire a coach or become a professional coach. You may want to read more about coaching. An appendix of frequently asked questions and a resource list provides information for you find answers to all of these questions. This section provides sources for more information on coaching.

ASSUMPTIONS

This book is far from an objective or systematic approach to coaching. It's based on my own assumptions and approaches to life. Knowing some of these assumptions may be helpful as you read and use the tools here.

STORY AND TRUTH

Professor Don Saliers has said, "The deepest things we know are found in the form of defining affections and passions. A person or a society is better known through what is feared, loved, grieved over, and hoped for than through its factually stated ideas and thoughts."[8] We access these "defining affections and passions" through story. As Madeleine L'Engle has said, "Stories, no matter how simple, can be vehicles of truth; can be, in fact, icons. . . . Stories are able to help us become more whole, to become Named."[9]

We construct narratives around our experiences. These stories help us to convey what we believe to be true and hope to accomplish. In constructing this book, I have relied heavily on stories. However we define truth, we communicate truth through our narratives—about God, ourselves, and the world!

SYSTEMS

I do talk about systems, but I do not believe that there is one objective structure, system, or collection of values that defines health or truth. The health of every family or individual cannot be measured by one systemic theory, such as Bowen's multigenerational family systems theory. Instead, we construct healthy lives, families, communities, and institutions in many ways. This book is designed to suggest ideas and tools for living and relating in healthy ways no matter what system you call home.

PROCESS AND OUTCOME

Brother Martin rushed to find the prior. "Brother Ben has run away!"

The prior looked up from his book, "Run away? Why?"

"He didn't like it here."

The Prior answered, "*Like it*? Who says you have to *like* it?"

Coaches do! In coaching, liking the process matters as much as achieving a good outcome. Coaching is designed to support people in living the lives God has called them to. It's important to me that coach and client enjoy the journey as much as the destination. I'm not looking to get my clients from point A to point B no matter the cost. Nor do I want to listen to people whine for years on end without seeing them move forward. But coaching cannot be reduced to mere outcomes—numbers on a chart measuring satisfaction or personal growth. The value of coaching is deeper and broader than that. The value comes from the blessing of connecting with one another in a deep and powerful way—as soul friends (*anamcara*). In the context of the faith community, this connecting carries with it the power of God's presence, dwelling in the midst of what we do. God transforms the people who connect, making the relationship a holy place.

Some Final Words about Using this Book

Ultimately, you get to decide how to use this book! Coaching values the needs and agenda of the client—not the coach. Here are a few tips to help you set your own agenda:

CONVERSATION

Because coaching is about conversation, this book will probably be most helpful if used in community! As spiritual leaders, we can easily become isolated from others. But we cannot learn to relate well with others when we are in a room by ourselves. Ideally, you will work through this book with either a partner or a group of colleagues.

PROPER ORDER

The book is presented from the ground up—coaching philosophy and skills, then coaching situations and exercises. In an ideal, academic world, you might start reading this book at the beginning and build your skill set chapter by chapter until you reach the end. In the real world, each of us enters a book with our own agendas. You face a particular set of ministry challenges. Read the chapters that relate to your areas of interest. The only proper order is the order that's proper for you and your colleague group.

PRACTICE

In coaching school, much of my training was practical. From the first moment of the first class, the instructors urged us to get coaching! A key element of learning to coach is practicing coaching. I encourage you to do the same. These tools are practical, not theoretical. Invite your partner, colleague group, family, and friends to work with you in practicing the skills.

PLAY

"Who wants to play?" In coaching, conversation is often called "play." Thinking about our talk as play removes our anxiety. Consider how young children get into roles as they play house or store. They don't worry about what to say or how to act—they dive in and do it! It's the same with the skills presented in this book: dive in. Don't worry about getting it right. Don't agonize over every word you say. Try to grasp the concept and then play with it. Take risks. Have fun. Play.

HOLY WORK

We don't often think about our conversations as holy work. But every human exchange—even our chatter with strangers—links us together, reminding us of our connection to the body of Christ. Words carry great power to affect the life of another person. God works through our words. Our conversations with one another bless, inspire, support, comfort, and challenge. Of course, our words can also cause great pain and hurt. Even as we enter into our talks with courage, taking risks, we pray that God will guide our words, using them to bless and not to hurt. As you use this book, remember that God is in the midst—in, with, and under—your conversations. This isn't idle chatter but holy work!

THE STRENGTH WITHIN YOU

In the New Testament, Jesus went to Jerusalem, to a pool called Beth-zatha, where many invalids laid. The text says that one man had been there for 38 years. Jesus asked him, "Do you want to be made well?" (John 5:6). The man answered with excuses: "Sir, I have no one to put me into the pool when the water is stirred up; and while I am making my way, someone else steps down ahead of me" (v. 7). Jesus said, "Stand up, take your mat and walk" (v. 8). The man was made well; he walked. As I read this text, I get the impression that this man had access to this healing power for 38 years and did not know it! There was always some reason not to get healed. He couldn't get to the water. Someone cut in line. The water wasn't stirred up enough. Excuses! A poolside pity party! It took an encounter with Jesus for this man to know and experience healing.

Most of us have more resources than we can imagine. Sometimes it takes an encounter with Jesus—usually with the Jesus we meet in one another—to transform us. My hope is that this book and the work you do with one another will help you recognize the strength within you and the tools that surround you. Expect miracles!

 # PART 1

THE COACHING COLLAGE
Essential Facets of Intentional Relationships

❀ Introduction

In Greek the word "*to follow*" not only means
"*to walk in the footsteps*" of a master
but also *to accompany*, to *be with*.

> Jean Vanier, *Drawn into the Mystery of*
> *Jesus through the Gospel of John*

I was wandering lost through the streets of Cadiz, thanks to my acute
sense of disorientation, when a good man rescued me. He instructed
me on how to get to the old market, and to any other destination in
the wide world:

"Let the road lead you."

> Eduardo Galeano, "The Upside-Down World"

My daughter Elly has an older brother but yearns with all of her heart
to be a big sister. In place of real siblings, Elly has a wooden statue and
a rag doll, named Santa and Princess Anne, respectively. If anyone
asks her about her family, she will talk about these two siblings, totally forgetting her flesh-and-blood brother. One morning, as I prepared
to leave for my errands, my daughter tugged at my sleeve and thrust
her favorite picture book at me. It was open to an artist's drawing of
four children playing in the yard. "Mommy, you need this." "Why do I
need this, Elly?" I asked. "It will help you find my little brother and
sister. This is what they look like."

The picture of these four children was my reference point for Elly's
task: finding new siblings. (Oh, how I wish it were that easy! We're still
searching.) This section of the book, "The Coaching Collage," functions as a sort of reference point, too. As such, you can refer to it as
you build your own ideas about the coaching process and its relationship to the work you do as a spiritual leader. As a reference point, this

philosophy is not a photograph or representational painting. It's also not a map or a system or a comprehensive modality. My philosophy of coaching is most like a collage—a collection of ideas, unequal in weight and depth and texture, that together image the coaching relationship. The goal of the coaching relationship—like all intentional relationships—is to support both participants in becoming more whole and centered. When we are living in integrity, we act in a way that is compatible with our values. Our insides and outsides line up.

In the Bible, the word *integrity* appears only in the Hebrew Bible. Integrity (*tom*) carries with it the sense of wholeness, fullness, completeness, and soundness. By far, the majority of verses talk about walking in integrity, such as, "I walk in my integrity" (Ps. 26:11). (See also Ps. 101:2; Prov. 10:9; 19:1; 20:7; 28:6; 28:18; Mal. 2:6.) I once heard someone say, "We have to be walking somewhere or else we're just wandering." We build lives of integrity by walking with and following Jesus. As Doris Gant, the neighborhood minister at my church, said, "Only when we follow Christ can we know our true selves." We follow Jesus when we accompany one another on this life journey. We connect with those whom Jesus loved—the people who society typically casts out. Jesus cared for the people who were poor, sick, blind, lame, sinful, demon possessed, or oppressed—and calls us to do the same. We follow Jesus together and in this way grow and deepen our own integrity. We cannot do integrity on our own.

When we seek the people who need care, we start by looking in the mirror. As leaders, coaches, or helping professionals, we are more like the ones Jesus chose in his ministry than we might like to believe. Knowing this frees us to see that the people we care for also sustain us as our teachers, coaches, and supporters. In coaching and in life, we learn from those whom we serve. As recovering alcoholic and motivational speaker Karen Casey said, "Even our most mundane interactions are sacred, each one contributing a necessary thread to the tapestry that is becoming our life. And none is more significant than another. I have learned the lesson well: No one wanders our way by accident. We don't have to understand why they have come, nor do we need to understand what they may be seeking from us. Our one and only assignment is to respond to every person who crosses our path as a holy companion—and one who is likewise on assignment."[1]

We are holy companions to one another—set apart for God's purposes. It may be tempting to judge our companionship against external or internal ideas of right and wrong. My daughter often plays the judge, measuring my words and actions against her vision of truth. When I say something that pleases her, she rewards me by saying, "Click. Right answer." Sometimes she will even throw her arms in the air and proclaim, "You're a genius." Mostly, though, my daughter tells me how I have done her wrong. Usually I hear, "Click. Wrong answer." This collection of ideas, my "philosophy of coaching," has become right for me in my work with people. But these ideas are not the only right answers; neither are they comprehensive or definitive. In the practice of relating well, a whole bunch of right answers exist. Some you will find here. Other right answers will emerge from the holy companions you encounter as you follow Jesus though this life.

1 ✸ A Safe Space

[Jesus said,] "Very truly, I tell you, I am the gate for the sheep."

John 10:7

Frodo was now safe in the Last Homely House east of the Sea. That house was, as Bilbo had long ago reported, "a perfect house, whether you like food or sleep or story-telling or singing, or just sitting and thinking best, or a pleasant mixture of them all." Merely to be there was a cure for weariness, fear, and sadness.

J. R. R. Tolkien, *The Fellowship of the Ring*

A friend told me that her college apartment served as a sort of "warming station" for weary travelers. We attended college in a place where the temperatures were often too cold for even the shortest walks. She and her roommates welcomed freezing college students into their home to warm up before continuing their trek to their own apartments farther away from campus. Thinking back on those days, I remember a friend whose dorm room always served as a safe place for me and mine for her. We never had to ask or wait to be invited. The knock at the door would begin a ritual of welcome—lighting candles, turning on classical music, and making Russian tea. In that safe space, much like at the Last Homely House East of the Sea, we could share our scariest stories and deepest dreams.

When I became an ordained minister, it was hard to find safe spaces in the parish I served. I didn't know who I could and should trust with my struggles and doubts. I took the advice of the deodorant commercial to heart, "Never let them see you sweat." I didn't. Colleague groups seemed no better. We all had so much to prove. We wanted to look and sound professional to one another. Some of my pastor friends started talking about their worship numbers and other successes. It was tough to find a safe place to tell hard stories and get good support.

I know I'm not alone. Now that I am coaching spiritual leaders, many of my clients express this same struggle. "It's like we're all pretending it's okay when it's not," one said to me, speaking about a colleague group. Another said, "I just don't know who I can talk to that won't gossip to others."

In the New Testament, most of the texts about hospitality refer to welcoming one another inside the Christian community. That surprised me. I expected the early Christians to be more concerned with welcoming outsiders, growing their numbers. I wondered if it was xenophobia—fear of strangers—that confined the writer's statements about hospitality to welcoming those people within the community of faith. After a bit of time in the church, I now think that the early church writers spoke so much about welcome within the community because their communities were conflicted. They needed to be told to love and welcome one another because they weren't doing it. How could they welcome strangers when they could barely tolerate one another?

We're no different. My pastor recently preached about the passage from the Gospel of John about Jesus protecting the sheep from the thieves. She said, "Jesus keeps us together with other sheep because no one but no one can stand up to the wolves out there alone. I do not care what wolf it is, cocaine or cancer, abuse or financial problems: no sheep, no lamb, must ever go out there alone to face the wolves by herself, to conquer his demons on his own. Jesus keeps us near him and near one another, trusting that we will not devour one another."[1] Unfortunately, *devouring one another* is all too often what we do. We gnaw at each other with destructive words. We tear apart trust with our gossip. We exclude people, act with spite, or let jealousy drive our actions—and in doing so, we nibble away at the community. We crush people with our unkind actions. Our behaviors strip the church of its role as a safe haven, leaving us searching for a place and a group of people that we can trust.

The coaching relationship provides a safe space for clients. In the coaching relationship, clients are with other sheep—not wolves or thieves. Together they protect and care for one another. I belong to a unique coaching group. Four of us meet monthly to coach one another toward our individual goals and dreams. In the midst of a difficult time in my life, all I had to offer was the story of some challenging days. I had not accomplished my homework. I could not think enough to be supportive to the others. No matter. I spoke about what happened. They supported me. No one attacked me for not having done my work. No one tried to fix me. I could say things that others may have felt were disloyal or unprofessional. No one berated me for these words. Here was safe space, safe people who welcomed me.

In the early nineties, churches were asked to designate themselves as safe spaces for children to go to when they experienced difficulty. Currently, some Christian and Jewish congregations choose to define themselves as being safe spaces for people who identify as being gay, lesbian, bisexual, or transgendered. Shelters offer safe spaces for people who are homeless or who are being abused in their homes. All of these movements express their understanding of "safe space." The following qualities of safe spaces need to be present in the coaching relationship. Although the language below refers primarily to coach and client, the same qualities create safety in the relationships we have within the community of faith.

- Acceptance. People are accepted for who they are. They do not need to create a persona in order to relate within the relationship or community. They do not need to hide parts of themselves to look more successful or be acceptable. They do not need to fear that who they are or what they say will be judged.
- Respect. The people within the relationship treat each other as credible and worth a "second look." They honor each other's choices and words.
- Confidentiality. The interaction within the coaching relationship stays there unless the client chooses to share it. Clients are never the topic of gossip with colleagues or other clients.
- Clear boundaries. The coach and client agree to clear boundaries and keep them. The client does not have to worry about offending the coach or tripping over hidden rules or agendas.
- Healthy conflict. The coach and client work to have a healthy, whole relationship. In that spirit, the coach invites the client to talk about anything that isn't working or does not feel right. The goal of the conversation is to make it right.
- Openness. The coach is not reactive but open to whatever the client needs to bring to the coaching conversation. This means that the client does not need to fear that the coach will be

shocked, fearful, hurt, or disgusted by the content of the
conversation.

- Integrity. The coach and client promise to be honest with one
  another.
- Unique. The coach is open to each client's unique needs for
  safety within the relationship. Clients who have experienced
  emotional, verbal, or physical abuse may have more difficulty
  feeling safe inside any relationship. Coaching does what it can
  to create a safe space. Some clients will need to pursue therapy
  to heal this issue.
- Client driven. The client sets the agenda for the relationship.
  The coach does not impose his or her agenda or program on
  the client.

The above list expresses an ideal safe space. It often takes time
and conversation for a relationship to feel safe to both coach and client. And, coaches and clients are human. Mistakes and misunderstandings will happen. As soon as a challenge appears, coach and client
need to talk about it and work to repair the relationship. For whatever
reason, some coaching relationships will not feel safe for one or the
other party. That is okay. It has been helpful for me to acknowledge
that I cannot be the right coach for everyone. Then, when a relationship doesn't work, I can release the client without resentment or hurt.
I wish them only the best in finding a coaching relationship that is
safe for them.[2]

We all need safe spaces. In John's Gospel, Jesus is the gate who
provides a safe space and good pasture for the sheep. Jesus the gate
protects the sheep from the danger of wolves. Jesus the gate sends
the sheep to good pasture. We do Jesus's work when we, too, become
the gate—keeping out the wolves and pointing the sheep toward good
pasture. We do Jesus's work when we create safe spaces for the people
we encounter in this life—family, friends, fellow members of the community of faith, and the strangers in our midst.

Try

Consider your relationships. Which ones are safe? Which ones
are not? What is the difference between the two? What might

be done to make the unsafe relationships safe for you? Do what is necessary to make one of your relationships more safe this week.

Talk

1. Look at the list of qualities for a safe space. What others do you believe to be necessary for a safe space? What qualities might be specific to a religious institution?
2. The image of Jesus as shepherd and gate is one way of thinking about how Jesus keeps us safe. What other biblical stories come to mind?
3. In what ways does the experience of safe space lay the groundwork for risk taking? In what ways might the practice of making safe spaces limit or stifle people?
4. What can you do (or not do) to create safe spaces for those you encounter?

---

2 ❈ A Place for Questions

I want to beg you, as much as I can, dear sir, to be patient toward all that is unresolved in your heart and to try to love the *questions themselves* like locked rooms and like books that are written in a very foreign tongue. Do not now seek the answers, which cannot be given to you because you would not be able to live them. And the point is, to live everything. *Live* the questions now. Perhaps you will then gradually, without noticing it, live along some distant day into the answer.

Rainier Maria Rilke, *Letters to a Young Poet*

And as we grow in faith, we will start to see that following Jesus doesn't give us all the right answers. It teaches us to ask the right questions.

Rochelle Melander and
Harold Eppley, *Dancing in the Aisle*

My son asks questions. All day, every day he throws questions at me. He demands answers, too. Real ones. Facts, he calls them. He wants the facts, not just my opinion. According to his standards, I shouldn't even think about answering a question with a question. But that's just what I did. All he wanted was a simple answer to his question, "What happens after the farmer takes a wife?" He was referring to the song, "The Farmer in the Dell." The farmer takes a wife who takes a child who takes a nurse and on it goes until the cheese stands alone. Instead of just answering him, I asked my son a series of questions: "What if the farmer is a woman? What if the farmer wants another farmer so that they can work together? What if the child wants a dog?" My son laughed at my questions because they suggested that the song's world could change. According to my son, "It is how it is." For him, there is always a right answer. But maybe there isn't, I prodded. What if the farmer wants a horse instead of a wife?

I understand my son's point of view. It's easier to hold onto what we know, to seek the right answers, the facts. But some questions do not have a right answer. Instead, these questions challenge the status quo. They open us to new ways of thinking and living. When we ask, "What if?" or "Why?" or "Why not?"—we may risk security and flirt with mystery. And yet, this leap of wonder is how every creative, imaginative act begins. Someone says, "What if?" And another person says, "Why not?" Someone asked, "What if we could build a machine that would make multiple copies of written material?" "Why not?" The printing press was born. "What if we could build a machine that puts oxygen in the blood?" "Why not?" The heart-lung machine was invented.

Those of us in the community of faith know that life is more mystery than certainty. As people who participate in a faith tradition, we may hold certain beliefs and doctrines. Still, our experiences teach us how little we know. Our faith is not provable by theorems and facts but rather, "the assurance of things hoped for, the conviction of things not seen" (Heb. 11:1).

We may go to the community of faith for answers. We may also see the faith community as the place where we wrestle with life's deepest questions. These are the questions that help us ponder our faith and the way we live our lives. The phrase "Living the Questions" comes from Rilke's quote above, "*Live* the questions now." It is also a small group study program for Christians.[1] The process invites participants to ask hard questions about God, the Bible, theology, and their own lives. The "Living the Questions" process depends on seeing the community of faith as the proper place for questions that do not have a right answer, questions like "What if?" or "Why?" or "Why not?" We may feel frightened by these types of questions because of their effect on the beliefs and practices we have come to depend on. These questions may open dialogue that challenges church doctrine, church tradition, and the Bible. They may push us beyond accepting the status quo as the only or preferred reality. They may persuade us to change the way we live our lives.

Spiritual leaders are often under pressure (internal or external) to preserve the theological and biblical traditions of their denomination. This may mean that spiritual leaders seem more interested in proclaiming truth than wrestling with questions. Questioners in these communities may be seen as doubters or, worse, heretics. Unfortunately, when the faith community presumes that there are a few right answers, we limit the potential for honest dialogue and the possibility of true growth.

The coaching relationship, as an expression of intentional community, seeks to be a place where people consider life's deep and difficult questions. Who am I? Why am I here? What has God called me to be and do in this world? This is not the place for what Quaker memoirist Heidi Hart calls "tidy answers to life's most perplexing questions."[2] The coaching relationship allows for the possibility of sitting with ambiguity until clarity appears. We ask questions that have many answers and questions that have no answers. We ask questions that have no right answers. We ask questions that challenge us to change our definitions of ourselves, our colleagues, and the people and institutions we relate to. Some questions work; others don't. Some questions have answers that come quickly, from our guts. Other questions have answers that take weeks or even years to be discovered. This is the place where we can live the questions and hope someday to live into the answers, propelling our lives forward.

Try

One way to keep any conversation open to questions is to pretend that you don't have the answer (even if you do). In your conversations this week, turn the questions back to the asker, "I don't know. What do you think?" If the questioner persists or says, "I don't know," ask: "If you did know, what would you say?"

Talk

1. What do you think it means to "live the questions"?
2. Talk about your beliefs about questions and answers. In what situations do you want an answer? In what situations do you feel compelled to give questioners a "right" answer? Give examples of each.
3. How do your conversations change when you refuse to give answers?

---

3   ❀   Truth Telling

At the core of all the pressures to abandon the self is the temptation to lie about what we really think, feel, and believe.

Martha Beck, *Breaking Point*

I'll tell you a strange thing. I lie quite a lot, because when I do people believe me. It's when I try to tell the truth that things go wrong for me.

Marilynne Robinson, *Gilead*

And you will know the truth, and the truth will make you free.

John 8:32

I love mystery novels. In the small world of the mystery novel, truth always triumphs. Like a fiber artist, a good author weaves in the loose ends—solving all the lies and half-truths—so that nothing will unravel. Recently, in the middle of reading a particularly slow mystery novel, it occurred to me that the whole book would be over much quicker if the characters would just tell the truth! Then the detective wouldn't have to waste so much of his or her (and my) time looking for it. But, of course, even in a mystery novel, people don't tell the truth. It's hard enough to tell the truth in real life.

An authentic relationship is built on truth. At the deepest level, this means that we tell the truth about who we are—what we think, feel, believe, and desire. An authentic relationship also means we are willing to accept the truths other people reveal about themselves. Without this commitment to be honest—with and about ourselves and other people—our relationships become false. Like counterfeit money, they may have many of the aspects of the real thing, but they do not hold the same value.

All of us have difficulty telling the truth at times. We feel pressure to look good to other people. We want to please both those we love and those we hope to impress. We fear that telling the truth might cost us the love, respect, and admiration of other people. The church is not immune to this. At a recent conference, the pastor of a large suburban parish said, "We do not tell the truth at my church. We present the face we want others to see. It's like a big cocktail party—with everyone posturing for each other." Virginia Ramey Mollenkott, Christian writer and professor emeritus of English at the William Paterson University, Wayne, New Jersey, described this phenomenon in her childhood church, "In our Plymouth Brethren Assembly, every family tried to look prosperous and trouble-free because that in turn would imply their 'rightness' before God. People did not talk about their deepest fears, their shame, or their painful emotions; and seeking psychotherapy was such a failure of faith that if anyone succumbed, nobody mentioned it. So for me it was a revelation to discover genuine community, places where people could be frank about their failing without risking loss of respect and frank about their disagreements without jeopardizing their relationship."[1]

Telling the truth means we need to take responsibility for our feelings, thoughts, beliefs, and desires. When we cannot face the truth—or fear others will reject us because of it—we tell little lies. We lie to ourselves. We lie to those we love. We lie to strangers. We get so used to lying that we no longer know truth from falsehood. Our lies do not have to be big to get in the way of having an authentic relationship. Here are some of the small lies that we tell every day:

"I'm feeling fine, thank you."

"Oh no, I don't mind."

"Of course I'm not angry."

"I don't need anything."

"I'd love to."

"It was great for me, too."

"I'd be glad to do that for you."

"I don't want anything."

"It doesn't bother me."

"Sure, go right ahead."[2]

Life coach and author Martha Beck, who compiled the list above in her book, *Breaking Point: Why Women Fall Apart and How They Can Re-Create Their Lives*, decided to do her own truth-telling experiment:

> On New Year's Day, 1992, I made just one resolution: I wouldn't lie, not once, for the entire year. A few months later, when I desperately sought out a therapist to help me cope with the fact that my life had exploded, she told me my problem was that I kept my New Year's resolution. She was joking, but she was right. My little truth-telling commitment had set me on a course that would lead me away from almost everything I thought defined me: my job, my profession, my religion, my home, and pretty much every relationship I'd ever formed before the age of about twenty.[3]

Telling the truth—or refusing to lie, as Martha Beck did—may mean that we have to let go of the relationships and commitments that contradict who we are. This can be scary—terrifying, even. We have grown used to the lies we have told ourselves. We find comfort—even some reward—in living from this false self.

The first step in learning how to tell the truth is recognizing it. At one point in my life, working hard to live the truth, I entered therapy. My therapist asked me a question that I carry with me to this day. She said, "What do you know?" I ask myself this question whenever I have a decision to make—especially when I am tempted to act out of my need to earn favor from another person. I often answer the question by completing this novel and song title, "I know this much is true . . ."[4] My therapist's question—*What do you know?*—reminds us that we do know the truth. The novel title teaches us that we do not need to know or admit the whole truth, only "this much." We only need to connect with a small portion of the truth to understand the right thing to do.

The second part of learning to tell the truth is the harder part—actually telling it. Know that telling the truth does not always mean telling everything, telling the whole truth. It may mean not lying, not saying anything that is untrue. Even so, when we tell the truth we do take risks. The truth can be hard to hear. When we begin to tell the truth in a relationship or institution committed to a culture of posturing, we may be rejected. Of course, without this truth telling, we risk not knowing the richness of having an authentic relationship—with ourselves and one another.

The thing about the truth is this—no matter how much we try to hide it or run from it, God knows the truth about us. God knows us intimately. As my pastor said in a sermon, "God knows you in and out, left and right, through and through, up and down. God knows you more than you know yourself. And this God who knows you so well loves you even more than you can know."[5] We may fear facing the truth about ourselves. Even more than confronting our truth, we may fear sharing it with other people. In the midst of our fear—in the midst of our lying—it helps to know that God sees the truth and loves us still.

Try

1. In your journal, complete the following sentence as many times as is helpful.

   • I know this much is true . . .

2. Martha Beck spent an entire year not telling lies. Can you do it for one day this week? Try to pick a day that is more social than reflective. When the day is over, reflect on the following questions:

   • What was difficult about this exercise? Why?
   • Who did you have an easy time being truthful with? Who did you have a difficult time being truthful with? What does this tell you about your relationships?

- How did not lying change the way you related to other people?

Talk

1. Discuss how lying or telling half-truths can be less threatening in your work than telling the truth.
2. Share an experience of how telling the truth—or not lying—created the foundation for an authentic relationship.
3. What biblical passages or quotations encourage you to be truthful?

---

4 ❋ Acceptance

In acceptance there is nothing "wrong" that needs to be changed, fixed, worked on, or otherwise improved.

Cheri Huber, *There Is Nothing Wrong with You*

When my daughter was two, we often walked around the block in our neighborhood. One day Elly spotted a yard filled with bright yellow dandelions. She exclaimed, "Flowers! Pretty flowers!" I didn't tell her the truth—this particular bloom is a weed that people both curse and obliterate. Instead, I accepted her declaration. I knelt down next to her and said, "Yes sweetie, that *is* a beautiful flower."

Elly's exclamation made me wonder: who decides? Who decides when a bloom is a flower and when it's a weed? For a child, the dandelion is as lovely as the daffodil (and more so, because within the dandelion seeds lie wishes, waiting for the breath of a dreamer to give them life). So who cursed the bold dandelion? For that matter, who decides who is beautiful or ugly, in or out, welcome or disdained, accepted or cast aside? We do. When we see a woman who is, as I once heard novelist Alexander McCall Smith say, traditionally built, we make assumptions about her. When we see a dark-skinned man with baggy trousers walk toward us, we think we know what he's about. We meet new people and within moments we have categorized them with our label-making minds as "one of those people" or "just like me." In either case, we are wrong. A little label cannot reveal the magnificence of a person. A person's tender complexities will always spill over the lines of our definitions. But we may not see this. Our labels and pre-judgments can hide what's inside a person, hampering the relation-ship. As author Madeleine L'Engle wrote:

> Because you're not what I would have you be
> I blind myself to who, in truth, you are.
> Seeking mirage where desert blooms, I mar
> Your *you*. Aaah, I would like to see
> Past all delusion to reality:
> Then I would see God's image in your face.[1]

In an authentic relationship, we seek God's image in the other person. Accepting the truth of another person—and seeing him or her as a reflection of God's goodness—is foundational to authentic, respectful relationships. When we do not see this truth, we simply have L'Engle's mirage—our vision (or delusion) of who we imagine the other person to be. We cannot build an authentic relationship on a mirage. Like a shadow boxer, we are attempting to relate to someone who is no more than our own shadow. In doing so, we dismiss the flesh-and-blood person before us.

Most relationships move through this shadowboxing stage. In the beginning, desperately wanting to like and be liked, we project our own feelings and desires on the people we encounter. We see and hear only what we want, dismissing anything that does not fit with our mi-rage of who this person should be. In order for an authentic relation-ship to develop, the partners in the relationship need to define themselves and remain connected with one another. This ability to define and connect, to accept one another in spite of differences, is crucial to forming an authentic relationship.

When we accept other people, we try to accept who they are (in-stead of who we desire them to be). We do not label or judge one another. We do not squeeze each other into categories or roles. We do not look to the other to be a mirror of ourselves. Instead, we look for the beauty that blooms inside of each person we encounter.

Jesus did this. When the blind men asked Jesus for mercy in Matthew's Gospel, the crowd ordered them to be quiet. Jesus heard their second plea for mercy and was "moved with compassion" (Matt.

20:33). He saw the bloom, men who sought healing from him, instead of the mirage, just more sick people getting in the way of his work. We see this same compassion in Jesus's embrace of the woman with the twelve-year flow of blood. He might have seen her through the eyes of Jewish law. This bleeding woman was unclean, and her touch made Jesus unclean. Jesus did not mention this to the unnamed woman. Instead, he healed her. Then, he gave her a blessing that announced her place in the family of God: "*Daughter*, your faith has made you well; go in peace, and be healed of your disease" (Mark 5:34, emphasis added). Jesus saw the bloom, a daughter of God, instead of the mirage, an unclean woman.

When we accept and befriend the real person before us, we enter into an authentic relationship. Our relationship has a chance to grow, to mature into something rich and true. In that place, we no longer care what other people think. We no longer see the person we are connected to and think "weed" or "flower." We simply see one of God's precious and beautiful children.

Try

This week approach the people in your life with openness and compassion. Pay attention to your automatic judgments and labels of people and events. Listen and ask questions that will help you get to know people in a deeper way.

Talk

1. How do you use categories and labels in your work and life? In what ways have they been helpful to you? In what ways do they hinder your ability to see or know other people?
2. What are ways you can use acceptance to make your relationships more authentic, respectful connections?
3. Talk about how approaching people with openness and compassion changed the quality of your relationships. How did it change you?

5 ⊛ A Client-Centered Relationship

So I no longer have many theories about people. I don't diagnose them or decide what their problem is. I simply meet with them and listen. As we sit together, I don't even have an agenda, but I know that something will emerge from our conversation over time that is a part of a larger coherent pattern that neither of us can fully see at this moment. So I sit with them and wait.

Rachel Naomi Remen, *My Grandfather's Blessings*

It's all about me.

T-shirt saying

I seem to have started a prayer-bead ministry. A client told me about the prayer beads she makes for her parishioners. I liked the idea—beads strung on a circle of wire or silk to be held while praying for self and community. Making prayer beads seemed to be something I could do at night to relax. I found a pattern online, purchased supplies, and began to bead. As I grew more confident, I varied the initial pattern. Each time I sit down to make a set of prayer beads, I am praying for the person who will hold them. I use his or her favorite color and ask God to guide me to create a set that is just right. After making beads for many of my family members and friends, I worried that I wouldn't have any more to make. I needn't have. As I wander through my days, names pop into my head—clients, people at church, neighbors. I hear the clear message—this person needs prayer beads. So I ask about favorite colors and get to work. After only a few weeks, word has gotten around. I made a set for a woman at church whose son was killed in front of her home. A young boy whose family was going through a difficult time saw them and asked if I could make a set for him. I did. He then asked if I'd make another set for his godmother. I always say the same thing, "Of course. But it will take time." It takes time because each set has to be created anew, crafted to reflect the personality and prayers of the person who will hold them.

The coaching relationship is also crafted to reflect the unique needs of the client. It is designed to offer value—to be meaningful and useful—to the person who receives it. The focus, content, and style of the coaching relationship reflect an intentional design.

Focus

At a recent coaching session, my client stopped in the middle of telling me a story about her life and said, "Where are my manners? I need to hear about *you*! What have you been up to?" I laughed. It's typical for new clients—especially ones who work in the helping professions—to want to be attentive to the needs of the coach. These people have kindness coursing through their blood. They want to be helpful. And the years of caring for other people have made some of them a wee bit uncomfortable with having the spotlight shining brightly on their life. I explained to my client that this time was about her—not me. In the coaching relationship, coach and client focus on the client's life.

This makes the coaching relationship different from a friendship, where two people take turns sharing the spotlight and the work of supporting one another. In coaching, the spotlight rests brightly and firmly on the client. This is not to say that mutuality does not exist in the coaching relationship; it does. Because, as coaches, we acknowledge our humanness, there will be times when the relationship shifts for a moment, and the client offers support for the coach. For example, when my daughter became suddenly ill with seizures, I needed to cancel several coaching sessions to be with her at the hospital. One of my clients called a few days later to see how I was. She promised to pray for our family both alone and at her congregation. She also offered the help of her husband, a physician who was willing to answer any medical questions I might have. I appreciated this great kindness. At our next session, the roles shifted back. After a brief assurance that my daughter was doing better, the spotlight settled on her again.

Content

In the coaching relationship, clients set the agenda. They decide what they want to get out of the session. The client articulates the content of the session—the topics to address. For example, I will often begin the coaching conversation with the question, "What do you want to discuss today?" I then ask, "What do you want to accomplish as a result of this session?" Clients quickly learn to spend time before each session planning what issues they will want to work with in the session.

In this way, coaching differs from other helping professions. In recent years, as coaching has gained popularity, people have used the coaching moniker to define anything from consulting to the work of a human resources department. In most other helping professions and in much of the work that institutional representatives such as human resource professionals and managers do, the professional sets the agenda. Consultants interact with the client based on their specific area of expertise. A church-growth consultant will be most interested in offering the client advice and direction based on the current church-growth theory. Therapists approach a client from one or more therapeutic modalities as well as the goal of connecting the client's story with a diagnosis. For example, a family-systems therapist may have the agenda of looking for triangles and other patterns outlined in multigenerational family-systems theory. A human resources professional follows the agenda of his or her employer. A denominational executive might be able to offer some coaching around career issues but will also be thinking about the particular needs of the geographic area he or she serves. All of these professionals offer valuable services—but they are not coaching. In coaching, the client has the opportunity to direct the conversation.

Style

The term *style* in the coaching relationship refers to the way coach and client relate to one another. It includes both the pace and the tone of the conversation. Some conversations will be paced quickly with a light tone. Other interactions will have a more somber character. Both coach and client will bring their own unique relating styles to the conversation. They quickly settle into a style of relating that works for the relationship. As the client moves in and out of various life issues, the character of the relationship will shift. For example, many of the clients I work with are self-directed professionals who have no trouble setting goals and achieving them. The style of our conversations is brisk; often we include lively dialogue and jokes. From time to time, these men and women encounter frustrations and challenges. In those times, the pace of our conversations slow way down to embrace whatever they are expressing at the moment—perhaps sadness or discomfort. As with focus and content, the style of the conversation depends on the client. Coaches will tend to follow the lead of the client, matching his or her mood.

For You

We all need to be seen and known, named and loved. When I first became a pastor, I moved to a place where I knew no one. I would sometimes go for days and even weeks without hearing my own name. On days off, I would wander anonymously from store to store at a local mall. It was a lonely time for me. I longed to simply be recognized by someone, to be welcomed and named and loved. As a coach, I hope to offer this welcome to the people I serve.

During communion at the church I attend, the pastor will press the bread into our hands and say our names and then that this bread of Christ is, "for you" or "for your life." That part of the service always reminds me of Jesus's particular love for me. For a moment, even on days when I am feeling more anonymous than known, I have a name and someone who loves me. I often imagine that the woman at the well, the woman with the twelve-year flow of blood, and the children who surrounded Jesus all felt this particular love when Jesus connected with them. As people of faith, we offer this kind of care to one another, a sense that knowing names and who people are matters—to us, to Jesus, and to the world.

Try

One of the best ways to learn how to focus on another is to spend time with a young child. Arrange to spend two or three hours with someone between the ages of two and four. Let the child set the agenda for the time together. If possible, allow the child to engage you in dialogue. Try to imitate his or her ways of talking and relating. Afterwards, think about how this experience might change the way you relate to adults.

Talk

1. In what ways do you see Jesus offering a ministry that focuses on other people instead of on his agenda?

2. As spiritual leaders, what are some of the ways you communicate particular care for the individuals you minister with and to?

3. At what times is it difficult to let go of your agenda? What tools have you used to do this?

---

6 ❀ Asset-Based Thinking

How did you account for an ensemble's improvement, she wondered, after months of not playing together? Was it that they'd each gone off in pursuit of their own improvement, and then come together again as more complete and satisfied people?

Peggy Benoit in *Rookery Blues*

I discovered the power of asset-based thinking in the summer of 2003. My husband had lost his job and we were without income for more than two months. I was working as a copyeditor to earn money. The project I received—by God's good grace and humor—was the book *The Power of Asset Mapping* by Luther Snow. I hated copyediting. I grumped about it. I dwelled in the badness of my life. All I could see was the worst-case scenario and I believed I was living it! But Luther Snow's ideas about assets began to break apart my negativity. I kept reading these words:

- What is your cup half-full of?
- What do you have to be thankful for?

When I started to look at my assets instead of my deficits, my life looked very different. Suddenly I could see solutions where before there were only problems. Luther says it this way:

We live in a society that surrounds us with a need-based, fixed-sum way of thinking and acting. We have developed personal strategies and approaches, competing with each other over supposedly fixed resources. We play the scarcity game even though we know that we are blessed with many gifts.

When we recognize and appreciate our assets, we transform our thinking. Instead of seeing needs and deficiencies, we see gifts and strengths. We transform negatives into positives. We see our cup as half-full.[1]

Common wisdom will often say:

- Each person can become competent in any task or skill.
- We have the greatest capacity for growth in our areas of greatest weakness.

This common wisdom results in a sort of "be all things to all people" mentality. We forget that each of us is specifically gifted and instead believe that any of us can do any job with the right sort of training and good support. In my ministry experience, I have seen this kind of thinking serve as a justification for accepting positions that don't quite fit who we are and what we do well. Despite the church's interest in talking about the individual's gifts for ministry and service, we sometimes are offered and accept ministry situations that do not make the best use of the unique assets that God has given us. When we don't do as well as we'd like in our ministries, we get discouraged. We spend time and money learning to develop the skills we lack—and have little passion for.

We seek help as a way of shoring up our weaknesses. The poor preacher is sent to the seminary to learn how to communicate without causing the gathered to fall fast asleep. The board president hands the shy leader a copy of *Networking for Dummies*. The explosive young activist is sent to anger-management training so that he can do a better job of communicating to his large exurban parish. There's a place for resolving our problems and improving our skills. When we focus only on fixing what's wrong; however, we unfortunately may lose track of the passions that pulled us into ministry in the first place. Our time might be better spent working with the tasks and ideas that give us joy.

Research tells us how important it is for us to use our gifts. When we work from our assets instead of our weaknesses, we are happier and more productive. The Gallup organization asked the following question of 198,000 employees working in almost 8,000 business units in 36 companies: "At work do you have the opportunity to do what you do best every day?" The response to that question was compared to the performance of the business unit. The researchers discovered that when the employees answered, "strongly agree" to the question, they were

- 50 percent more likely to work in business units with lower employee turnover;
- 38 percent more likely to work in more productive business units;
- and 44 percent more likely to work in business units with higher customer satisfaction scores.[2]

According to this study, those of us who use our assets or work from our strengths will stick with the work longer and do a better job. In addition, focusing on our assets is just a heck of a lot more fun and energizing than solving problems and fixing our shortcomings. Who wouldn't want to spend time talking about the things that make their eyes light up?

Coaching is about discovering and working from one's assets. Clients may initially seek (or be encouraged to seek) coaching as a way of fixing a problem. The presenting issue might be anything from excess weight to a difficult working relationship. In the first coaching session, client and coach aim to, as Luther Snow would say, "find the assets inside needs."[3] For example, we may look at what the client's difficult relationship teaches him about his strengths and passions. Each session—in fact, the entire coaching relationship—is about strengths and assets. The coaching client works to recognize and use his or her assets—to multiply them a hundredfold and more.[4]

We don't have to make a huge leap to imagine that when Jesus told his disciples the parable of the talents, he was talking about more than just money (Matt. 25:14-30). He wanted them to use their lives, to take risks even, to serve in the community of God. This is the same Jesus who wanted his disciples to be like salt: "You are the salt of the earth; but if salt has lost its taste, how can its saltiness be restored? It is no longer good for anything, but is thrown out and trampled under foot" (Matt. 5:13). Salt cannot learn to be sugar or garlic—salt can only be salt! Imagine making sugar cookies with salt—yuck! Or cinnamon-salt rolls. Goodness no. But salt seems perfect for a fried potato or a piece of steak. When we are like salt, we are true to who we are—in such a way that others can recognize our saltiness. Jesus had other images for his disciples: yeast, light, and fishers of people, to name a few. One imagines that Jesus did not expect each disciple to be good at each image—to be both salt and yeast. Instead, Jesus wanted each disciple to be the best salt or yeast that he or she could be. We need both, after all, to make a good loaf of bread!

Try

This week, hunt for assets. Look for the assets in every encounter, place, and experience. Pay special attention to finding assets inside problems, needs, challenges, and crisis. Keep an asset notebook and record your findings in it either as you go or at the end of the day.

Talk

1. With your partner, take turns complaining to each other for 45 seconds. Next, take turns naming your assets to your partner for 45 seconds. Reflect on the following questions:

   - Which felt better?
   - Which went faster?
   - Why do you think that's so?

2. How do you recognize and name the assets of others as part of your role as a spiritual leader?
3. Reflect on your experience of asset hunting. How did searching for assets change how you thought about the encounters and experiences of your week?
4. What biblical passages reflect asset-based thinking for you?

7 ❀ Experts and Seekers

> I mean, the way I see it is, one of the basic jobs parents have is to tell you what you already know.
>
> Parker in *What Do Fish Have to Do with Anything?*

Kristin sunk into the sofa at the campus ministry center. "Tell me what to do with my life!"

Pastor Jen sat on the opposite sofa. "Not my job, Kristin! It's your life!"

"Wimp!" whined Kristin. "No really, Pastor Jen. You have all that training. I'm just a college student. You can *at least* give me your professional opinion."

"Kristin, the only life that I'm any kind of an expert on is my own. I can listen. I can ask questions. But I can't tell you what to do."

Our society traditionally has viewed helping professionals, such as spiritual leaders, medical practitioners, educators, psychotherapists, and other highly trained professionals, such as lawyers and financial planners, as experts. An expert is someone who possesses special skill or knowledge. The people who seek the help of experts are called seekers. When we're sick, we want a doctor to use his or her expertise to cure us. When we face a moral dilemma or personal life crisis, we want our spiritual leader to tell us what we *should* do. When we experience an emotional crisis, we want a psychotherapist to tell us what's wrong and how to fix it. This expert-seeker model spills over into our whole life, dividing our world into a new kind of haves and have nots—those who have expertise and those who lack or seek it.

Before I began coaching, I worked as a visioning consultant in congregations. At first, I believed my work was about bringing my *expertise* to *help* the members of a faith community envision a better future. It didn't take long to learn that I was not the expert in the room. The members of the congregation were the experts on everything from their shared faith history to the many dreams they held for their community's future. I simply brought a process that supported them in accessing their expertise and using it to imagine their future.

In the coaching relationship, both the coach and the person being coached are experts. The coach brings his or her training to the relationship as well as a rich array of work and life experience. The client is *at least* the expert on his or her own life. Clients also bring an array of other assets—training, life experience, and reflection—that are a part of their expertise. Each person in the relationship has something valuable to give to the other. In many ways, coaching uses what has become known as the accompaniment model of mission work. In the old models of mission work, the missionaries brought their expertise on everything from medicine to Jesus to help the indigenous people. In the accompaniment model, the missionaries walk beside the people they work with. They learn from one another. In the coaching relationship, accompaniment means that the coach does not always take the lead—directing the conversation and giving advice. Instead, the coach walks with the client. We teach and learn from one another. We are more companions on the spiritual journey than teacher and student, spiritual leader and seeker, coach and client.

In missionary work, the accompaniment model gives every person in the mission relationship responsibility for the success of the relationship and the relationship's joint projects. It is the same in coaching. Both the coach and the client bring expertise to the working relationship. Both bear responsibility for the success of the relationship. Ultimately, though, the client is responsible for his or her own life success. The client must do the work that leads to growth.

Such work applies to congregations, too. I've noticed that many churches have begun to add a new line to the list of staff in each Sunday's bulletin: Ministers—the people of this congregation. This acknowledgment affirms what theologians call the priesthood of all believers. The writer of 1 Peter said it like this: "But you are a chosen race, a royal priesthood, a holy nation, God's own people, in order that you may proclaim the mighty acts of him who called you out of darkness into his marvelous light" (1 Pet. 2:9). All who have been baptized, who participate in the community of faith, bear responsibility for proclaiming their faith. According to 1 Peter, this proclamation includes the care and tending of the community and its people. The writer said, "Above all, maintain constant love for one another, for love covers a multitude of sins. Be hospitable to one another without complaining. Like good stewards of the manifold grace of God, serve one another with whatever gift each of you has received" (1 Pet. 4:8-10; see also v. 11). To use the apostle Paul's analogy in 1 Corinthians

12—we are members of the body of Christ, each carrying a specific and unique ability to serve within the community. Not one part of the body is or should be exalted over another as the resident expert. The unique contribution of each part is needed to keep the body healthy.

A few years ago, I asked a group of writers to make a list of their experiences and skills. Each member of the group created a profile of his or her areas of expertise. Next, I asked group members to list the experts they knew. Who could they interview if they needed to write an article on cooking for a large family or changing a tire? The participants had some difficulty identifying their own expertise. Most found it easier to recognize the expertise of other people.

When I did the exercise myself, I was surprised to discover that I both had expertise and knew a whole host of experts. I had something to teach other people. Nearly every person I knew had something to teach me. We are all experts. We are all seekers.

Try

1. Make a list of your areas of expertise—the experiences, training, and skills that you possess.
2. Make a list of all the people who are or might be experts for you. What have you learned from them? Who would you like to learn from?
3. What might be helpful or interesting for you to learn now? Choose one of the people from the list above. Invite them to teach you about their expertise. You might offer to exchange wisdom. For example, a friend could teach you how to change a tire and you could teach her how to bake bread.
4. As you approach conversations this week, think to yourself: "This person is an expert. I have something to learn from him or her." How does that thought change the way you approach the conversation?

Talk

1. Take time to recognize the expertise of each other. Say to each other, " (Name), I see you as an expert on _____."

2. How did your career training teach you that you were an expert? A seeker of expertise?

3. What biblical passages or theological teachings support the idea that we are all both experts and seekers?

4. Share a story about learning something from a person who you did not expect to be an expert.

8 ✸ The Power of Mutuality

Let us then pursue what makes for peace and for mutual upbuilding.

Romans 14:19

It happens every Sunday now. I plop into my row and like paper clips to a magnet, the children slip in beside me. Sometimes they get there first, saving seats for me. We giggle together, trading questions and stories until church starts.

"How is school?" I ask.

"Where's your daughter?" wonders Abby and her sister.

"What did you do on Saturday?" I ask them.

"Your hair is redder than usual," Jackson observes.

By the time we get to the sermon, I usually have one or two children tucked under my arm. Often there's a little one to hold during the hymn and a bigger one to hold the hymnal for us to share.

One Sunday someone said to me, "It's so kind of you to sit with the children."

"Oh no," I thought. "It's so kind of *them* to embrace me."

What I have with these children is not just about what I bring to them or what they give to me. It's about the connecting that happens between us, the relationship we are growing. Some might call it mutuality. The coaching relationship is no different. The power of coaching is never in the expertise and wisdom of the coach or the readiness and tenacity of the client. The power exists when client and coach come together in relationship. The power grows in the connecting that happens between them.

Episcopal priest and theologian Carter Heyward spoke about mutuality in her book *Saving Jesus from Those Who Are Right*. She said, "That God is our power in mutual relation and is not merely 'in' our power makes all the difference in the world. It shifts our attention away from the individual entities and 'selves' that we are, apart from one another, to the power that is constantly giving us our life together in this cosmos and, even through death, is holding us as one creation."[1] According to Heyward, then, sacred power does not come from Jesus or from us. Instead, sacred power exists "between and among us."[2] The sacred power is the relationship.

Coach Tim Pearson uses the Trinity as an image for talking about the nature of the coaching relationship. Tim said, "The three persons of the Trinity are in relationship to one another. They are in conversation with one another in the deepest and most profound way imaginable." Tim suggests that Andrei Rublev's icon of the Old Testament Trinity, depicting God's visit with Abraham and Sarah under the oaks of Mamre (Gen. 18:1-8), is a good representation of what coaching is all about. Says Pearson, "The icon represents the depth of the relationship among the Trinity and the communion of their conversation. Relationship and conversation for me are the wellsprings of coaching. Coaching occurs within relationship and through conversation." Tim encourages readers to look at the icon as an open circle, with a place left open for the viewer to come and participate in the conversation.[3]

Inside the coaching relationship, each person benefits. Each person will find value in the time they spend together, though the individual contributions and rewards will be unique to each person and each relationship. Both people will be enlarged by their connection together. As Carter Heyward has said, "This, in my judgment, ought to be the basis and aim of all pastoral care and psychotherapy—to enlarge our power in mutual relation. Both or all parties in the counseling or therapy situations should be 'enlarged' and changed through the relation."[4] To put this negatively, this means that neither party will be diminished by the coaching relationship.

As both coach and client, I have always found it difficult to define why the coaching relationship works. A friend once questioned me on this. "Is it the accountability?"

"Well yes, but that's not all."

"Okay—good questions then—does your coach ask good questions?"

"Yes, but that's not it either."

She went through a list of things that might make coaching effective: goal setting, permission giving, good resources, caring, prayer, presence, listening. All were good guesses, but not one of them defined for me why such power exists inside what looks like just a conversation between two people. Author G. K. Chesterton, best known for his Father Brown mystery stories, described the gift of relationship this way: "Through all this ordeal his root horror had been isolation, and there are no words to express the abyss between isolation and having one ally. It may be conceded to the mathematicians that four is twice two. But two is not twice one; two is two thousand times one."[5]

Perhaps add to this quote Jesus's words in Matthew 18, "For where two or three are gathered in my name, I am there among them" (v. 20).

What happens inside the coaching relationship—and inside many human relationships—is more than the sum of its parts. It has to do with connecting and mutuality and upbuilding one another. It's not always perfect. Sometimes relationships are downright messy. And our connecting does not always reflect the ideal of mutuality. There are the problems that exist in all human relationships—hurt, error, and misunderstanding. But in the end, the coaching relationship is at best an expression of intentional Christian community—with its blessings and some of its pains. As my daughter would say, "We are family together and with God."

Try

Some tasks take two people to complete. With your partner or a friend, engage in a task that you cannot do alone. When you are finished, reflect on how the task was an expression of mutual relationship.

Talk

1. Talk about your experience of sharing a task. Using this as an example, come up with a list of the characteristics of mutual relationship.
2. How do you imagine people can build mutual relationships? Share ideas.

3. How do you see sin or evil destroying the power of mutual relationships?
4. What are some ways to create healing in the midst of mutual relationships that have been damaged by sin?
5. What makes a pastoral relationship mutual when one person is in need?

9 ❋ Dual Roles and Relationships

Dear nice god,
I feel close to you. Like you and I are part of the same family.
Maybe we could get married and make it easier.
Your lover,
Tina [age 7]

When Pastor Maki's husband became ill, the leaders in her church came to the hospital and surrounded the Makis with prayers. When he died suddenly, the leaders continued to support her. They made meals, took over her church duties, and prayed with her daily. The comforter became the comforted—for as long as it was necessary.

Dual relationships happen. Our parishioners become our friends. Our friends invite us to coach them around an issue. We depend on our colleagues and parishioners for pastoral care in times of crisis. We offer words of wisdom and support to our family members in moments of crisis and joy. We preach at and perform the baptisms, weddings, and funerals of those we love. Each of these is an example of a dual relationship—a relationship that can be defined or labeled in more than one way.

At the very least, each of us will experience times when we shift roles with those we serve. A role reversal allows for the power in the relationship to shift from one person to another without necessarily changing the fundamental relational roles. So, in the opening illustration, the pastor and her parishioners shifted roles but did not necessarily begin a dual relationship.

Historically, therapeutic practice has cautioned therapists against dual relationships, fearing that any boundary crossing will lead to a boundary violation. In my training and practice as a spiritual leader, I have heard the same caution. Still, some therapeutic orientations see occasional role reversals as a sign of health. In family-systems theory, the kind of mutuality seen in role reversals is a key element in an authentic relationship. Edwin Friedman, a rabbi who is known for his work applying family-systems theory to church and synagogue, often said that healthy relationships allow for role flexibility. For example, a healthy family system would allow the over-functioning mother also to under function, giving her children the space to develop the ability to care for themselves and others.

Carter Heyward spoke about mutuality in her book *Touching Our Strength: The Erotic as Power and the Love of God*. Heyward talked about helping relationships as being—at least for a time—unequal, providing a structure that gives one person the role of supporting or caring for another person. These relationships might include therapist-client, physician-patient, pastor-parishioner, or coach-client. Heyward stated, "In any unequal power relationship, if the structure of unequality is assumed to be static (as in all racist or sexist relations, as well as in traditional modes of church leadership and psychotherapy), the relationship cannot enable authentic empowerment."[1] She went on to say that healthy relationships need to contain "the seeds both of transformation into a fully mutual relationship and of mutual openness to equality."[2] In other words, mutuality exists when both people are free to change and grow in the ways that they relate to one another. They need to be, "mutually empowered to become more fully themselves with one another."[3]

Knowing that dual relationships happen, spiritual leaders need to consider how to handle them. Although dual relationships or even role reversals may seem to emerge—to evolve organically out of a relationship's natural growth—they need to emerge with mutual consent. It is always necessary to discuss the various roles we play with one another. Conversations about our relationships and roles give all parties the opportunity to set rules and boundaries. In addition, these conversations about our relationships prevent us from entering into dangerous dual relationships—relationships that are unethical because they exploit or victimize another person. For example, a client of mine joined a congregation that was pastored by one of his friends. Before joining, he asked his friend, "Is it okay for me to join? Are you comfortable with having me be colleague, friend, and parishioner?" The two colleagues discussed how they would handle the multiple relationships they would have with one another. This discussion included conversation about what they would call each other in public, how they might limit discussing parish business when they were together as friends, and how they wanted to handle any life crises that emerged.

My coaching instructors at Coach U modeled this role shifting for me. When someone brought a personal situation to class, the instructor would query the student, "May I coach you?" The instructor's words served two purposes. First, they signified that she would be shifting her role from teacher to coach. Second, the words invited the student give her permission for the instructor to make that shift. The instructors cautioned us to use similar words before blazing ahead and coaching friends or family members.

Defining our dual relationships may seem cumbersome. Isn't relating to one another hard enough without having to have these talks about *how* we relate? At first, we may feel awkward about engaging with people about our dual roles. But these conversations are absolutely necessary for maintaining healthy boundaries. When we define our relationships, we offer our respect and care for one another. We make the relationship safe for everyone inside it. No one has to worry about hidden agendas or rules. In time and with practice, these conversations become natural and allow us to relate with more ease.

In a difficult time in my life, I experienced the gentle grace of this type of conversation. When my young daughter was rushed to the hospital, I called a friend for support. My friend happens to be my colleague and the pastor of the church I attend. At the end of our conversation, she politely asked, "I don't want to impose—but may I offer a prayer for you?" At that moment, I was fearful about my daughter's health. I couldn't think through the steps to a complicated social dance. My friend's words, like the gentle leading of a good dance partner, invited me to shift our roles from friends to pastor-parishioner. I followed, and the dance continued.

The mutuality we experience in healthy relationships is well defined in the Bible's "one another" passages. Jesus encouraged his hearers to "love one another" (John 13:34, 35; 15:12, 17). Paul asked the readers of his letter to the Romans to "welcome one another" (Rom.

15:7). Paul invited the Galatians to "bear one another's burdens" (Gal. 6:2). He asked the people of Ephesus to bear with "one another in love" (Eph. 4:2), to "be kind to one another, tenderhearted, forgiving one another" (Eph. 4:32), and to "be subject to one another out of reverence for Christ" (Eph. 5:21). In the book of Colossians, Paul invited readers to "teach and admonish one another in all wisdom" (Col. 3:16). In 1 Thessalonians, Paul asked readers to "encourage one another" (4:18; 5:11) and "do good to one another" (5:15). Each of these passages (and the many other "one another" verses) encourages mutuality, a communal or reciprocal flow of help and support within the community of faith.

Try

Make a list of your current primary relationships. Note for each relationship the various ways in which you connect: parishioner, pastor, friend, sibling, daughter, counselor, coach, educator, editor, mentor, and so forth. Review the list. Ask yourself:

- In what ways are your dual relationships healthy? In what ways might they be seen as unhealthy?

A relationship may be unhealthy for many reasons. In this context, think about relationships that are static, dual relationships that are exploitive, or even dual relationships that are undefined and thus confusing to you.

- What conversations do you need to have with the people you connect with about the nature of your relationships?

Mark these relationships with an asterisk and set up a time to have those conversations.

Talk

1. What boundaries have you traditionally set around personal and professional relationships? Make a list.
2. In what ways have these boundaries been helpful or unhelpful?

3. Discuss the values and dangers of dual relationships.
4. Case study. Is there a relationship that you find difficult or confusing? Present it to your partner or group. Gather the wisdom of each other around this relationship.

10 ❀ Defined Boundaries

> In those thirteen years [since my ordination] I managed to get married, father two children, complete my doctorate, write one book, start another, and become the senior pastor of one of the largest churches in the state. I also managed to work myself into a textbook case of burnout and a rather sleazy affair with the lady who taught the third grade Sunday school class.
>
> Rev. Daniel Thompson in *Viper Quarry*

Tina sat with her friend Gerry at the local coffee shop. She didn't bother to brush away the tears that slid down her cheek. "Gerry, I don't know what to do. I'm having feelings for Pastor John."

"What do you mean?" asked Gerry.

"I think I love him. John asks me these deep questions about my feelings. He is interested in what I have to say. I know he's my pastor—but it seems like it is personal, too. Like he cares for me in a special way."

The kinds of intimate conversations and situations that occur within our relationships as spiritual leaders can lead to feelings of intimacy that cross the boundary from a professional relationship to an intimate one. For people to mistake the kindness, enthusiasm, and care of a spiritual leader as romantic or sexual interest is not unusual. For a spiritual leader to engage in a romantic or sexual relationship with someone in his or her care is never okay.[1]

Issues to Consider

As a spiritual leader, it is important for you to think through how you will set boundaries, especially in terms of sexual and romantic feelings and conduct. Here are some of the issues that you need to consider.

STATE AND FEDERAL LAWS

These issues go beyond one's personal boundaries. Know your legal responsibilities. Make sure that leaders in your organization are aware of their responsibilities to and for the people they work with. Require criminal background checks for employees and volunteers who work with children and other vulnerable individuals in your organization.

WHERE YOU MEET

It is better to meet those you work with in a public place as opposed to your home. When you meet people in your office, have other people in the building. Ideally, offices have a window in the door, and the room is arranged so the staff person can be seen by anyone walking past the room.

PHYSICAL CONTACT

Consider what kinds of physical contact—if any—are appropriate to the relationship. When is it appropriate to engage in a nonsexual hug? Is it okay to hold hands while praying? Note that these boundaries may shift depending on the culture of the community you are in.

YOUR INTIMACY NEEDS

Often, our boundaries get confused when our own needs for emotional and physical intimacy are not being met. Think about your personal needs for emotional and physical intimacy. How do you fill these needs outside of your work relationships?

Warning signs. Think about what clues might cue you that someone is experiencing feelings for you that are outside the boundaries of your professional relationship. Know that in some cases there will not be clear warning signs. Also consider your own feelings—what are clues that you are experiencing romantic or sexual feelings for someone else?

EMERGENCY PLAN

Think about how you will handle the romantic advances of a client or parishioner. It's important to be able to define and express your boundaries while staying connected to the person you are in relationship with. It is not helpful to shame the person who approaches you with romantic interest.

You will also need to consider how you will handle your own sexual or romantic feelings toward those in your care. What do you need to do to protect the people you serve? Who can you talk with about your feelings?

A Final Word

When I was a child, the rule on the block was that we played by the rules of the host parent. If the parents said, "No screaming in this house" (even though other parents thought screaming was fine), then that's the rule we followed. As spiritual leaders, we function as the host. In our role, it is up to us to set and keep good boundaries. We cannot and should not look to the people we serve to set the boundaries for us. When we set good boundaries, we make the place we serve and our own presence a safe space for the people we minister to and with.

Try

1. Review the above list of suggestions. What do you need to do differently? What changes need to be made in the organization you work for?
2. Write a covenant with yourself on the issue of sexual and romantic boundaries. Do not forget to include ways that you will take care of yourself sexually.

Talk

1. Review the above list of suggestions. What would you add to the list?
2. Case study. Describe a situation that you found to be difficult or challenging. How might you handle it today? What could you have done to avoid the difficult situation?

11 ❀ Yours, Mine, and Ours

> I can find only three kinds of business in the universe: mine, yours, and God's. . . . Anything that's out of my control, your control, and everyone else's control—I call that God's business.
>
> Byron Katie, *Loving What Is*

It's tempting—oh so tempting—to make our relationships about discussing other people's business. You know what I mean. At the dinner table you say to your spouse, "Did you hear about Jerry and Mary? They're getting divorced." At a colleague meeting, the conversation picks up when the topic turns to the unexpected resignation of a local youth worker. "What happened?" you ask each other. You go to therapy and spend the entire hour complaining about your coworker. You say, "If only she'd stop criticizing me, then I could really do my job."

Gossiping. Informing. Complaining. Whatever we call it, we're talking about somebody else's business. In addition, we may be tempted to mess around in the business of our friends and neighbors. Advising. Fixing. Removing the specks from their eyes. And why not gossip, why not try to solve someone else's problems? It's less painful—and more interesting—than looking at our own lives. Perseverating over their business makes us feel better about ourselves. We'd never get ourselves into such a mess. And if we did, we wouldn't fail so miserably. We'd make it work. When we obsess about the mistakes (or even the successes) of others, we can avoid looking inward. Yes, we have logs in our eyes, but we're too busy futzing with the specks in other people's lives to get to our own logectomy.

In a difficult time in my own life, I turned to a colleague and friend for support. After I spent an hour complaining about the behavior of other people, my friend scribbled some words on a sheet of scrap paper and handed it to me. It read, "RX: Cultivate your own garden." I've kept that prescription for nearly twenty years. It reminds me to put my efforts where they belong—in my own life. It cautions me about how easy—and toxic—it is for me to think that I am responsible for worrying over and tending the gardens of other people. I've begun to use the same metaphor in my work with clients. When they talk about the behavior of other people, I will ask, "Who's garden are you working in?"

In her book *Loving What Is*, life coach Byron Katie speaks about three kinds of business: mine, yours, and God's. She adds, "If you understand the three kinds of business enough to stay in your own business, it could free your life in a way that you can't even imagine."[1] Gardens, business—they are both metaphors for knowing and understanding something about boundaries. In an authentic relationship, we focus on the people in the room. In our own lives, we work inside our own gardens. In many ways, this practice echoes the words of the Serenity Prayer, a staple for people in recovery, "God, grant me the serenity to accept the things I cannot change; courage to change the things I can; and wisdom to know the difference." We work on behaviors within our control and let go of the rest.

This practice can be especially difficult for spiritual leaders. As part of our work, we are often invited into the business of the people we serve. We stand with people at the most critical and challenging times of their lives. We are present at the bedsides of those who are sick and dying. We walk with people as they make commitments to be linked as life partners. We hear the intimate details of other people's lives. We pray with and for them. We hold their hands when their spouses and parents and children die. We are there for the baptisms, weddings, funerals. We are also present when they struggle with addiction, when they go to jail, when their lives fall apart. We get invited into the gardens of those we serve. It can be tempting to make our lives too much about their gardens, to forget that we have our own gardens to tend to.

Ask Yourself

Both as a spiritual leader and as a coach, I have found it helpful to use the following questions as I reflect on my life and work.

WHOSE GARDEN AM I IN?
If we have lived our lives messing about in the gardens of other people, seeing the boundaries of our own gardens can be difficult. It is helpful to ask ourselves whose garden we are playing in. We belong in our

own gardens. As spiritual leaders, we may work from time to time in the gardens of other people, but we should not be setting up tents in their gardens.

AM I WORKING IN THE GARDEN OF SOMEONE IN THE ROOM?

At times people will come to me for advice on behalf of a friend or spouse. Parishioners will approach with a complaint from an anonymous third party. Leaders will want to know about the work I am doing with this client or that family. For the most part, the people approaching us do so with kindness in their hearts. They want to be helpful. Or, they may fear going to the person they really need to confront and hope that the spiritual leader can do it for them. As a spiritual leader and coach, I work in the gardens of other people only by invitation of the owner. I tell those who come to me that I'd be happy to talk to the person concerned—if they approach me on their own.

WHAT DOES THIS WORK TEACH ME?

Despite keeping careful boundaries, we will have times when we become over focused on another person's garden. We will worry over them and talk about and to them. We may even neglect our own garden while tending theirs. When we are drawn so powerfully into the life story of another person, it is often a clue to our own lives. Perhaps something in our own life needs to be adjusted. Maybe there is something missing from our garden. Our obsession with another person becomes our teacher. We learn what needs to be taken care of in our own lives when we observe what we care too much about in the lives of other people.

IN GOD'S HANDS

We do not set up tents in the gardens of other people, but God has certainly pitched a tent in our gardens. This is the literal meaning of the word translated as "lived" or sometimes "dwelt" in John 1:14, "And the Word became flesh and *lived* among us." God's presence in our gardens reminds us that God is the true owner of our land. Whether we are working in our own garden or have been invited to do chores in someone else's, we have our hands in God's garden. We need to learn how to put the work of our own garden—and the work of the other people's gardens—back into God's hands. As people of faith, we do this through prayer. The pastor of my church preached, "We pray because the light is not overcome by darkness. We pray because God chooses to have us care for others and the world through prayer. We pray because God prefers that we pray for these people than make them a topic of gossip or forget them."[2]

The summer after my college graduation, I took a group of young people camping in the mountains. At the top of a very high mountain, we pitched our tents during a heavy rainstorm. I'm not an experienced camper, so our tent wasn't the sturdiest. Sitting inside, we could hear the winds whip around us. Before the storm was over, at least one corner of the tent had come loose. One of the young people asked, "Are we going to die?" Another said, "What can we do?" The answers: "I don't know" and "Nothing." For maybe the first time in my life, I understood what it meant to put it all in God's hands. Praying to God would not insure our physical safety. It would—and did—assure us that God would be present with us no matter what damage the storms wrought. Before sleeping, we did the only thing we knew to do: we prayed, asking God to dwell with us in the storm. The next morning we were damp but not dead. Again, we did the only thing we could do: we prayed our thanks to God for comforting us through the night.

Try

1. Observe your conversations and thought patterns this week. Ask yourself:

   - Whose garden am I in?
   - Am I working in the garden of someone in the room?
   - What does this work teach me about my own garden?

2. What do you need to do to cultivate your own garden? Make a list of things you want to accomplish in your own garden.

Talk

1. Discuss times you have been or are tempted to work in the gardens of another person. What is tempting about being in someone else's business? What techniques have you found helpful in disengaging yourself from the business of other people?

2. Share with each other your plans to work in your own garden.
How can you support one another in staying in your own gardens?

---

12   ❀   The Power of Now

Realize deeply that the present moment is all you ever have. Make
the Now the primary focus of your life.

Eckhart Tolle, *The Power of Now*

Much human suffering comes from rehashing the past or agonizing
over what the future will bring. Keeping our mind and body focused
on the present moment alleviates this pain. Jesus advised his followers to let go of their preoccupation with the past and their worry over
the future. In Luke's Gospel, Jesus invited a man to follow him. The
man replied, "Lord, first let me go and bury my father" (Luke 9:59).
The request sounds reasonable enough. We commend those who take
care of family business, especially the solemn task of burying the dead.
Jesus answered the man, "Let the dead bury their own dead; but as
for you, go and proclaim the kingdom of God" (Luke 9:60). Another
would-be follower said, "I will follow you, Lord; but let me first say
farewell to those at my home" (Luke 9:61). Again, we might praise the
man for practicing good closure. Jesus did not. He said, "No one who
puts a hand to the plow and looks back is fit for the kingdom of God"
(Luke 9:62). Jesus encouraged his followers to let go of the past, attending instead to the immediate tasks of the day.

In the same way, Jesus wanted his followers to let go of their worries about the future. At the end of Jesus's discourse about worrying
in Matthew's Gospel (Matt. 6:25-34), he said, "So do not worry about
tomorrow, for tomorrow will bring worries of its own. Today's trouble
is enough for today." Later in Matthew's Gospel, when Jesus spoke
about the coming time of trial, he again proclaimed the value of living
in the moment saying, "When they hand you over, do not worry about
how you are to speak or what you are to say; for what you are to say
will be given to you at that time" (Matt. 10:19).

Jesus's advice to his first followers can inform the way we live our lives. My congregation threw a seventh birthday party for Maryanne. This little girl was born with many health struggles. The doctors predicted that she would never walk. At seven, she walks well enough to wander around the sanctuary during worship. Maryanne still faces many health issues, but her quality of life is better than anyone could have imagined. As I watched Maryanne smile and wiggle, twirling her favorite dishtowel, it occurred to me that the only way she and her family have survived is by living in the present. Maryanne and her parents, Douglas and Natalie, live lives that witness to the promise Jesus made to his first disciples about the time of trial—that he would give them whatever they needed to face the present moment. Because of her multiple health struggles, caring for Maryanne requires more-than-average patience, strength, and courage. Because both Maryanne and my daughter, Elly, have seizure disorders, Maryanne's parents and I often take time to talk on Sunday mornings. Natalie has told me that the only way to get through this trial is one day at a time. Often she will end our conversation promising to pray for me and offering to help me navigate the health and school system. In doing this, she helps me face my present moment. Natalie and her family are gifted with the ability to live their lives in the now, fully relying on Jesus.

Eckhart Tolle, author and spirituality teacher, calls *now* "the most precious thing" because it is all that we have.[1] We can review our pasts or imagine a fictional future time, but we live our lives in the present. The work of the coaching relationship tends to focus on bettering the present moment. In order to do that, clients need to consider what "better" looks like for them. I often ask clients, "What do you want to be different in your life because of coaching?" Once someone articulates the vision, work can begin on bringing vision into practice in the present. For example, one of my clients wanted to transition from working as an administrator to writing full time. As we began our work together, we talked about how she could incorporate daily writing into her life right now rather than waiting for the time when she could do it full time. She did—beginning by writing five pages a day. As these daily pages became habit, my client expressed to me how satisfying it was to be living her vision now instead of waiting for it to happen.

I am tempted professionally and personally to live outside the present moment. Like a mystery reader, I want to know "who done it" and why. I perseverate over past mistakes. I worry about future failure and crises. In these moments of despair over past or future, I think about my friends from church, Maryanne and her parents. They inspire me. I know that Maryanne reached her seventh birthday one step at a time. I close my eyes and see her walking to communion, one wobbly step after another. I know that this is all God asks of any of us.

Try

Often our senses are what keep us focused on the present moment. Spend one day this week paying attention to what you experience through your senses in the present moment. You may want to plan activities that are especially sense centered—such as baking (and eating), creating art or crafts, engaging in outdoor activity, or taking a bubble bath. Afterwards reflect on what the experience was like for you. Use whatever means is meaningful to you—journaling, painting, dancing, praying, dreaming, or discussing.

Talk

1. Share what you did for your sensory experience. Consider:

    - In what ways did engaging in a sensory experience help you stay connected to the present?
    - What effect did focusing on the present moment have on your mood or experience of the day? For example, did you feel less or more stressed? Did time pass more or less quickly?
    - In what ways might this experience teach you how to stay connected to the present?

2. Talk about the benefits and challenges of focusing on the now.
3. Discuss times when you have found it valuable to look at your history and your future.

13 ❀ An Action Focus

Am I a part of the cure or am I a part of the disease?

Coldplay, *A Rush of Blood to the Head*

"Life sucks and then you die."

"Nobody likes me, everybody hates me; think I'll go eat worms. Big fat juicy ones, eensy weensy squeensy ones—see how they wiggle and squirm."

We all complain. Sometimes it feels great to moan and groan about everything from what's wrong with the world to what's wrong with the people who live inside our house. Look at the three bears. Papa's bowl of porridge was too hot; Mama's was too cold. Neither much cared that Baby Bear's porridge was just right. We're not the first group of people to complain and we won't be the last. Remember the people of Israel. Wandering in the wilderness for 40 years, stuck with a diet of manna and water, I'll bet they wondered if the land promised to them was just Moses's idea of a joke. They complained—quite a bit actually—and who could blame them? Naomi complained about the raw deal life handed her—both sons and a husband dead before their time. She said to her kinspeople, "Call me no longer Naomi, call me Mara, for the Almighty has dealt bitterly with me" (Ruth 1:20). In the midst of a terrifying storm, the disciples woke Jesus and complained, "Teacher, do you not care that we are perishing" (Mark 4:38)?

At times in my life complaining has seemed helpful. At one point, when the churches I was serving were troubled and my health was failing, my words of complaint were my way of stating what wasn't working and how I wanted it to be better. When I complained, I was both making a lament to God and seeking support of God's people for the stuff that pained me. Complaining can be a form of prayer. It does connect us with what does not work. It can also get us stuck. We get wedged in the rhythm of bitch and brag, enjoying how it feels to simply let off steam, and fail to address the issues that drive our dis-ease. We need to ask ourselves, "Am I a part of the cure or am I a part of the disease?" When we get stuck complaining, we may be adding to the toxicity of the systems we are in. We risk becoming like Lot's wife, who in her sorrow looked back and could no longer move forward.

She ceased living. She got stuck, becoming an inanimate object—a pillar of salt. When we get stuck inside our griefs and grievances, we cease moving forward, too. We may give up on the life that surrounds us. We can become blind to God's blessings. When we work on solving whatever problem our complaints have surfaced, however, we become part of the cure.

In the midst of a time when complaining seemed to be my only prayer, I saw a headline in the Oprah magazine that struck me: "Stop complaining and start asking for what you want." These words reminded me of Jesus's advice, "Ask, and it will be given you; search, and you will find; knock, and the door will be opened for you" (Matt. 7:7). I cut out the headline, put it on my bulletin board, and made it my New Year's resolution.

That same year, one of my coaching instructors addressed the challenge of complaining. She said, "I allow every client a five-minute ride on my BMW."

"And that means?" queried a student.

"It means that the client can bitch, moan, and whine for five minutes. Then they need to stop complaining and start solving."

Coaching creates a safe place for our whining. The client can tell the truth about what hurts and frustrates. The coach listens without judgment—accepting the client in the midst of her or his feelings. But whining time is limited time because coaching is ultimately a process that asks for action. With love and respect, the coach asks the client to address the issue in a way that moves toward a healthy solution.

Our complaints are often clues to what we need or desire in our lives. The leader who complains about being lonely may feel a need for a more collaborative work environment. The woman who complains about a friend who uses her as a counselor may need a more reciprocal relationship in her life. A leader who complains about not having enough time to do his work may be expressing a need to feel more prepared at work. Once needs are identified, clients can envision what might fill that need. In the cases above, the solution might be a new job, reorganizing an existing relationship, an extra day off. Finally, clients strategize about how they can move toward this new goal.

On a snowy winter night, I sat with a friend at the dining room table drinking wine and eating chips. We were sharing the stories of our days. My friend said, "You don't want to hear this. You must listen to people complain all day."

Actually I don't. Oh, sometimes we begin with a short BMW session, a lament about the church and how they long for this or that to be different. For the most part, however, people of faith know that Jesus brought a message of transformation. As God transformed Jesus on the mountain, God transforms us. We are not Good Friday people, abandoned to a dark and dismal grave. We have been touched by Jesus's light, transformed by his rising. We have been changed by God so that we can be the people God has called us to be. Yes, we get it wrong. Yes, we complain. And yes, by God's grace, God transforms our complaining to acting.

Try

Spend one day not complaining. How does this change the ways you experience life?

Talk

1. Discuss the effect that complaining has on the ministry you work in, on your family, and on other primary relationships.
2. Share examples of the ways God transforms people and organizations.
3. Take turns sharing a regular complaint—something you tend to whine about regularly. Together, look inside this complaint.

   • What does it tell you about what you need?
   • What does it tell you about your strengths and assets?
   • How might you transform the situation?
   • What might you ask for or do to move forward?

14 ❀ Self-Care

My friend Bonnie's kids went to a kindergarten with a sign over the front door that said, "Start out slow and taper off." It's so easy and natural to race around too much, letting days pass in a whirl of being busy and mildly irritated, getting fixed on solutions to things that turn out to have been just farts in the windstorm.

Anne Lamott, *Operating Instructions:*
A Journal of My Son's First Year

Tip me over and pour me out.

"I'm a Little Teapot," traditional children's song

I had invited a friend and her daughter over to play and do Valentine's crafts. My daughter was being monitored for seizures, so I knew we would be home. When I had extended the invitation, I thought we'd be bored and need the company. I didn't expect to be weary. I was. Days spent watching my daughter's every move on top of my usual load of writing, seeing clients, and caring for family and friends had left me feeling like someone had "tipped me over and poured me out." As the girls played in my daughter's bedroom, my friend and I sat on the bed. "Do you want me to get you a glass of wine?" she asked. "Absolutely." I responded. Later, as I sipped the wine, I thanked her. She said, "I knew you wouldn't get it for yourself."

She was right. I wouldn't have. Like other caretakers I have known, it's easier for me to recognize the needs of other people and extend care to them than to nurture myself. Like so many people of faith, I heard the "love your neighbor" part but ignored the "as yourself." Perhaps you're one of those, too. We heard what Jesus said: "No one has greater love than this, to lay down one's life for one's friends" (John 15:13). Preachers sometimes use Jesus's words to illustrate discipleship. We may also use them to justify giving until it hurts. However we defend it, we do it. We care and love and give until we lose all of our strength. Little remains inside of us. Perhaps we even lose track of the passions that might nourish us and replenish our starved soul.

When we get to this point of total exhaustion, we often take comfort in things that harm us. We may take our despairing feelings and use them to lash out at others or ourselves. We might sink into bad habits—like drugs, alcohol, or promiscuity—as a way to fill the hunger inside us. And many of us will figure that the only way to feel more filled up is to caretake even more, so we continue to overextend ourselves. These actions cannot really fill us up. They will not nourish or comfort our tired bodies. And they cannot replace the passions and expressions that fed our souls.

Perhaps the apostle Paul could be "all things to all people," but we cannot (1 Cor. 9:22). If the bulk of our working lives are spent practicing a helping profession—for example, as coaches, spiritual leaders, educators, physicians, and therapists—we will need to create a life that is supported by more than the care we extend to other people. Getting healthy requires that we look at our lives and tell the truth. We need to see that we, too, need love and care. We need to understand our limitations. We cannot, and should not, do everything—no matter how kindhearted or dutiful these gestures are. Colleague and client Nicole Reilley, pastor at Santa Margarita United Methodist Church in Rancho Santa Margarita, California, put it this way: "Sorry, Super Pastor is dead. God is fed up with my being overly responsible." Amen! When we work so hard at loving and caring for other people, we are overfunctioning. Our overwork leaves no room for God (or other people) to take responsibility for the work of caring. When we take the scary step of letting go of our need to be in charge of the whole world, we can begin to trust in God. As songwriter Dar Williams puts it, "The world's not falling apart because of me."[1] When we let go of being superpastor, superparent, superspouse, or supercoach, we can rest in the loving and caring arms of God.

And this rest—this letting go of being in charge and really resting can fill us up again. A friend pointed to the words of runner John Bingham to support her claim that when we rest we heal. Bingham writes:

> Resting is not doing nothing. Resting is giving the body a chance to recoup, to renew itself, and ultimately to rebuild itself into a body that will move faster or farther. The rest phase is the only time that the body has to bring itself up to your expectations. The training effect that we all want, the changes in our body's ability to handle the stress of running occurs during the rest phase not the activity phase. The adaptation process takes place while you are resting. The days when you don't run are the days when your body incorporates the new strength needed for the next run.[2]

Bingham's words apply to running but they might easily apply to anything we do: leading, coaching, counseling, parenting, writing. Our mind, body, and spirit also need time off to strengthen for the next shift of working. Runners who do not take time out for their body to adapt run the risk of physical injury. Those of us helping professionals who do not let our mind and spirits rest risk the injury of our souls. Truly, rest is healing.

On that difficult Valentine's weekend described above, my daughter and I went card shopping. My daughter has a huge heart, so she had a long list of people she needed to buy cards for. And her ideas were good, too. For a friend who likes to fish, she bought a card covered in glittery, colorful fish from the movie *Finding Nemo*. After gathering several cards to purchase, she found one covered in princesses. "This one is for me!" she said. This is the girl who prays, "I pray for my wonderful family—Mom and Dad and Sam. I love them and am very proud of them. I pray for me—I love me and I am very proud of me." How could I refuse? Later, I watched her gazing at her sparkling card with a wide grin on her face. I wanted to take a picture and frame it as a reminder to practice good self-care. Practicing good self-care—loving ourselves through our thoughts and actions—is a reminder of God's abundant love and care for us. And it's probably the best way to get out of the cycle of loving until it hurts.

Oddly enough, that same Valentine's weekend, the pastor chose self-care as the topic for her children's sermon. She asked the children, "How do you take care of yourself?" Hands popped up and children shouted answers: eat well, exercise, sleep. "Take the medicine the doctor gives you," added the pastor. More hands went up: go to school, pray, attend church. Then the conversation moved to the don'ts—don't smoke, don't drink alcohol, and don't take drugs. As the children's time came to an end, the pastor spoke with the congregation about the children's need for good role models—adults who took care of themselves. She said, "The children look to you as their example."

Perhaps if we cannot take care of ourselves because it's good for us or even because it reminds us of God's care of us, maybe we will do it because it helps the ones we serve. During my coach-training program, my instructors frequently reminded us that our lives were a marketing tool. Though the sentiment seemed crass at the time, I have come to understand what they meant. As I have sought out my own mentors and coaches and even as I have worked to form new friendships, I have looked for people whose lives are healthy and whole. Their good self-care encourages and inspires me. I watch their lives and learn how to better take care of myself: how to set aside time for personal reflection or begin an exercise program. I see these mentors taking classes or reading books that nourish their passions, and their behavior encourages me to feed my own passions. In turn, I have noticed that my clients want to know how I juggle self, career, and family. They often look to me for wisdom I do not believe I have. But I know that what they really are seeking is what we all seek: a role model, an example of how the juggling might be done.

In the end, of course, self-care depends on us. Like my daughter who did not wait for someone to surprise her with that much-desired princess valentine, we need to give ourselves what we need. Not many will pat us on the back for caring for ourselves. Some people—even other leaders—may criticize our attention to self, labeling it as selfish. In those moments—and they will come—it's helpful to have coaches, colleagues, and friends who will remind us to *take care*. A friend of mine will often close her e-mails with the words, "Take care of yourself." Another friend will frequently give me verbal permission slips to set aside time to exercise and to feed my spirit. My coach continually asks me to voice what I need to do—not what I think I should do. These voices remind me to care for self. But they are not enough.

I cannot depend on other people to remind me to fill my well. I need to "set up road markers" for myself (Jer. 31:21a). A friend of mine did this in a unique way. During a time when her life was changing rapidly, she began training for a bicycle trip. This training—and the five-hundred-mile bicycle trip—nourished her. After her solo journey, she began a new position. She bought an artist's rendering of jars in colors that she loved as a reminder to be intentional about filling her spirit place. She knew how important it was to do her work from a full jar as opposed to an empty one. Several years and another job change later, my friend has hung the picture in the hall that leads to the room she has set aside for self care. She can see the print from her living room and kitchen. It reminds her to go to that place where she can be filled up. I loved her idea so much that I've shared it with several clients and now am looking for my own symbol. Until I find one, I have placed the cards and gifts of caring friends around my office. When I look at them I hear their reminder to do the work God has called me to: to take care of myself so that I can care for other people.

Try

Find a soul symbol—an image that you can use as a reminder to take care of yourself.

Talk

1. Define self-care.
2. Name biblical passages that encourage self-care. Then, look for biblical passages that seem to encourage self-sacrifice. How do you balance the two messages?
3. In what ways do you believe self-care to be essential for spiritual leaders? In what ways do you think self-care is "overrated"?
4. What tools have helped you to practice good self-care?

15   ✸   An Imperfect Beauty

> So fearful are we of bad moods or misunderstood statements that we keep ourselves tight and polite, which chafes at me.
>
> Joan Anderson, *An Unfinished Marriage*

Wabi-sabi is a Japanese aesthetic that recognizes that beauty exists in broken and imperfect things. As I understand it, *wabi* means "beauty" or "perfection." *Sabi* refers to the kind of beauty that comes with age and imperfection. For practitioners of wabi-sabi, beauty is present in that which is humble, modest, unconventional, incomplete, and irregular! In an era that links beauty with such things as perfectly white teeth or immaculately decorated homes, wabi-sabi graces our lives. There's hope for our broken-in, broken-down bodies and homes. Beauty can be found in a flawed piece of pottery, our rounder-than-average bodies, or a wildly overgrown garden.

As an idealist, I want my conversations with people to be perfect—meaningful, rich, and without miscommunication. I am inclined to equate *beautiful* conversations with those magical moments when two people connect deeply and time falls away as the conversation moves and builds and grows. When the conversation fails to live up to my high expectations, I worry over what I could have done better. I'm not alone. I've spent countless hours with friends, clients, and parishioners rehashing old conversations, listening to them struggle with what they "would have, could have, should have" said or done.

Applying the Japanese aesthetic of wabi-sabi to our relationships, we can see the beauty in each imperfect and incomplete human encounter. Each conversation, each moment spent with another is part of a complex whole—imperfect yet beautiful. Every conversation—even with the same person—will be unique. Some of our encounters will be peppered with the excitement of discovery. Other conversations will be messy—marked by misunderstanding, complaints, or even anger. Still others will be graced with forgiveness and mutual understanding. None of these encounters needs to define the whole relationship. Instead, each encounter becomes part of a whole, rich relationship. And as such, each encounter is both beautiful and blessed.

In Stephanie Kallos's novel *Broken for You*, she tells the stories of people who have been broken by life's tragedies and disappointments: the untimely deaths of loved ones, loss of love, loss of health, and the sins of previous generations. As the story unfolds, the various characters—each hurting—find healing in coming together and using the broken pieces of their lives to help each other. At one point in the novel, a character says, "Every relationship worth keeping sustains, at the very least, splintered glazes, hairline fractures, cracks. And aren't these flaws the prerequisites of intimacy?"[1] In the community of faith we recognize our brokenness as sin. But we are more than our sin. As one of my colleagues is fond of saying: "We are not just broken. We are broken and blessed." God blesses and loves us as we are—broken and imperfect.

As we approach our relationships, we know that we are both broken and blessed. Wabi-sabi changes the way we approach each encounter and therefore changes the encounter. We are able to let go of the need for this meeting to be perfect. We no longer expect this person or this conversation to fulfill all of our needs. We relax. We know that God blesses and mends broken pieces, creating beauty from our messes. We look for the grace and beauty in what happens. Each moment with this person is a gift.

Try

Approach your conversations this week with the aesthetic of wabi-sabi. How does this change the way you function—before, after, or during the encounter?

Talk

1. In what ways does the Japanese aesthetic of wabi-sabi reflect your theology?
2. Tell a story about one of your relationships. Talk about how the principle of wabi-sabi applies to this relationship.
3. What would it look like to use the philosophy of wabi-sabi in relationships?

16   ❀   A Spiritual Journey

I am collecting words for this journey we take: trip, drive, expedition, adventure, crossing, passage, procession, peregrination, trek, excursion, jaunt, junket, sally, tour, cruise, voyage, pilgrimage, progress, safari, passing, travel, wend, meander, proceed, push on, journey, roam, explore, track, and traverse.

Author's personal journal

One Saturday my husband called in the middle of the afternoon and said, "Honey, you probably won't like this but . . ." When your husband begins his sentence with, "You probably won't like this but," chances are pretty good you won't. My hackles went up. I braced myself. What now? A Sunday afternoon tea with the Ladies' Bible Society? An outing with the youth that would involve sleeping on bug-infested ground and walking miles to use an outhouse? An exclusively all-sports cable package? "What? Tell me?" I asked. "I signed us up to go to a seminar on vacations. *But*, if we go we can get a free dinner at Applebee's and two nights at a hotel." "When?" I inquired. "Today." Today. The today I had planned to spend writing. The today I had planned to do a thousand things, not including listening to sales-minded men and women pushing pricey hotels.

We went, me dragging my feet. We sat through a 50-minute presentation accompanied by a slideshow of beaches. We said no ten times before they put a package in front of us that we could afford. I'm now a proud member of this club—enjoying discount vacation packages. Had I been rich, they would have had my business earlier—because they were selling journeys and experiences—not hotel rooms. I spend most days stuck in the rut of a comfortable routine; this journey offered the promise of adventure. The line that got me was this: "Do you remember what you got for Christmas when you were 10? Do you remember the trips you took?" I remembered the trip.

When John Steinbeck was in his late fifties, he took his dog Charley across America and wrote about it in the book *Travels with Charley*. It was the first book I read after becoming a pastor. I remember sitting at my tiny kitchen table, eating a frozen dinner for lunch, and reading about Steinbeck's journey across the country. Many pages in my copy are marked up or dog-eared. At the beginning of the book, Steinbeck says this about the nature of journeys:

> Once a journey is designed, equipped, and put in process, a new factor enters and takes over. A trip, a safari, an exploration, is an entity, different from all other journeys. It has personality, temperament, individuality, uniqueness. A journey is a person in itself, no two are alike. And all plans, safeguards, policing, and coercion are fruitless. We find after years of struggle that we do not take a trip; a trip takes us. Tour masters, schedules, reservations, brass-bound and inevitable, dash themselves to wreckage on the personality of the trip. Only when this is recognized can the blown-in-the-glass bum relax and go along with it. Only then do the frustrations fall away. In this a journey is like marriage. The certain way to be wrong is to think you control it.[1]

The journey of life cannot be fully managed or controlled—no matter how hard we try. Life happens. We do not take life and mold it—life takes us. Or maybe, more accurately, God does. Maybe God nudges us or perhaps, like a mother cat, God picks us up by the back of our necks and points us in the right direction. The joys of journeying cannot be planned or orchestrated but happen between the events on our careful itinerary.

My husband and I travel to Montreal a good bit, as his mom lives in northern Vermont. On one of our first trips after we were married, we bought frankincense and myrrh at one of the street markets. It seemed like a good idea, a great little object lesson for the children's sermon—until we forgot to declare it at customs and spent two hours explaining why we needed it.

"Are you planning to smoke it? Sniff it?"

"Well, what do you do with it?" yelled one of the guards.

Ummm . . . preach about it? Show it to the kids?

We got a lecture on the invasion of the fruit fly (due to careless, evil people like ourselves) and about drugs. But, in the end, we got to keep our frankincense and myrrh—and we had a great story for our sermon. Serendipity. As Steinbeck said, "The trip takes you." Or God does.

I've been corresponding with an old friend who is going through a particularly tough time in her life. In a recent e-mail, she said something like, "I trust that this is God's gig—not mine." Her words were a good reminder. I like to think that I'm in the driver's seat of this journey through life. As a coach, it's tempting to consider myself a travel agent for my clients' journeys through life—consulting and advising on the best kinds of trips. Some people who define themselves as coaches do little more than play god—directing clients around specific theories of personal or church growth. In my training and work as a coach, I have learned that this truly is God's gig. The spiritual journey is the whole of it. We cannot separate out our career or our money or our time or our family or our prayers. It is all about God. Every inch of our lives, every moment we are here is about doing what God has called us to do. Every moment matters. God is present in all that we say and do, in everyone we meet, in every experience of life, good and bad. As a coach, I'm simply a spiritual companion, a soul friend (*anamcara*), walking with other people on their spiritual journeys.

As I do this work, the journey passages in the Bible have become helpful to me both in understanding the nature of journeys and in defining what I do as a coach. First, journeys occur in steps not leaps. Abraham and Sarah were called by God to live in a new land. When they traveled, the Bible says: "Abraham journeyed on in stages" (Gen. 13:3). When I feel impatient for my clients, wanting them to leap when they feel more comfortable crawling, I remember that Abraham and Sarah did not get to their destination all at once but in short spurts.

Second, journeys take time. Moses and Aaron were called by God to lead the people out of Israel and into the promised land. Then, the people of Israel journeyed on for another 40 years in the wilderness. No doubt, for some of the people on that trip, the wandering became their destination—not the promised land. No client or coach wants to hear that a journey might take 40 years. But some journeys do. As a coach, I need to remember that the work happens on God's time—not according to the client's yearnings or my professional schedule. And, as the old saying goes, "Not all who wander are lost."

Third, God provides for those who journey. It's tempting to think that I'm the expert, that what I provide as coach and companion actually supports and strengthens the client. It may. Still, in the end, I know that the client is most blessed by the provisions only God can provide. As the people of Israel journeyed, God protected them and provided for their needs. God provided manna to eat, water to drink, and God's own presence as a guide for them. "The LORD went in front of them in a pillar of cloud by day, to lead them along the way, and in a pillar of fire by night, to give them light, so that they might travel by day and by night. Neither the pillar of cloud by day nor the pillar of fire by night left its place in front of the people" (Exod. 13:21-22).

Fourth, God has a plan. Most coaches have plans as well. So do clients. Part of the challenge of coaching is to remember that this is God's gig—and it's God's plan that counts. When the people of Israel were in exile, God asked them to remain for 70 more years. God reassured them with these words, "For surely I know the plans I have for you, says the LORD, plans for your welfare and not for harm, to give you a future with hope" (Jer. 29:11). One of my first editors told me that she approached her work with the intent to "first, do no harm." It's a good intention for coaches and spiritual leaders, too. It reminds me to tread lightly—for God is making the way here, not me.

Finally, God uses journeys to change us. The Bible is full of stories of people who get changed on journeys. When God called Moses, he was fearful (Exod. 3:6) and filled with self-doubt (Exod. 4:1-17). But, as he stood up to Pharaoh and led the people out of Egypt, God strengthened Moses. He became a good leader and judge to his people. After Jesus called the disciples to journey with him, their lives were forever changed. They no longer lived the simple village life. These men and women traveled with Jesus, listening to him teach, and finally went out on their own to preach and heal. Even Paul's conversion came in the midst of a trip to Damascus. When coach and client agree to work together, they begin to journey together. Knowing that God uses journeys to change people, I never doubt that God is working within the journeys I make with my clients to change both of us for the better.

On the way home from church one evening, we passed one of our favorite restaurants. My daughter said, "I want to have dinner there with all the people I love: the pastor; the piano teacher; God; you, mommy; the pastor's aunt; and the pastor's mom." Her words brought an image to my mind: the six of us sitting at a table with one empty chair, similar to the empty chair my Jewish friends leave for Elijah at Passover. Since then, each time I meet with a client I think about pulling up an empty chair for God. It might remind us of what we already know to be true: in coaching and in life, this is God's gig, not ours.

Try

Plan a special meal with those you love. Leave an empty chair for God. At the beginning of the meal, ask someone to open the front door and invite God to dine with you. Create a special prayer to say, welcoming God to your table. In what ways does this ritual change your mealtime?

Talk

1. What journey passages in the Bible do you connect with? For what reasons?
2. Share a story about how you believe God has guided you on your life's journey.
3. What techniques do you use to remember that this is God's gig?

 # PART 2

THE COACHING TOOLBOX
Practical Skills for Spiritual Tasks

❀ Introduction

> A tool that is carefully chosen, prepared, and maintained can last a lifetime.
>
> *Reader's Digest New Complete Do-It-Yourself Manual*

When my husband and I bought our first house, my dad gave me a fully equipped bright red toolbox and a power drill. I felt like I'd won the jackpot. Building and assembling things has been one of my secret passions since working in the theater during college. Figuring out how things get put together and then doing it gives me great joy. I loved measuring, sawing, assembling, and painting. For years I had struggled to build and assemble with a motley collection of borrowed and hand-me-down tools. Shortly after we moved into the house, we bought a whole slew of Scandinavian-design furniture. I spent an entire day putting together those chairs and stools, bookshelves and coffee tables. With my new tools, this task was fun and satisfying.

A friend of mine has recently started attending seminary. Over coffee, she complained about her pastoral care class. "It's just not practical. The class doesn't tell you *how* to do it." I wished I could have handed my friend a big red toolbox of ministry skills that would teach her the how. But my toolbox held hammers and screwdrivers not skills.

This section is designed to be a sort of "toolbox of skills" for spiritual leaders to use in connecting with individuals and groups. As you read, discuss, and practice these skills, keep in mind the following:

NO TOOL CAN DO EVERY JOB WELL
This toolbox contains a bunch of tools. You will have to look at the task at hand and discern what tool to use.

IT TAKES PRACTICE TO USE A TOOL WELL

I can remember a friend telling me about trying to screw down concrete board with her power screwdriver—only she had the screwdriver set to unscrew the screws. Oops—it was moving left (left-loosey) instead of right (righty-tighty). It takes practice to use power tools and relationship tools. Take your time learning these skills and be patient with yourself and your partners!

NO TOOLBOX IS BIG ENOUGH TO HOLD A COMPLETE SET OF TOOLS

This toolbox is a good start—but it won't provide you with all that you need for every situation. The resource list in the back of the book will point you to additional tools. This is just enough to get you started—kind of like the starter tool set my dad gave me.

17 ✸ Be a Fierce Presence

> It has been my experience that presence is a more powerful catalyst
> for change than analysis.
>
> Rachel Naomi Remen, *My Grandfather's Blessings*

> Perhaps what is needed is not only to learn good medicine but to
> become good medicine. As a parent. A friend or a doctor. Sometimes
> just being in someone's presence is good medicine.
>
> Rachel Naomi Remen, *My Grandfather's Blessings*

In the first week of my first call, I received a letter from a beloved
seminary professor and friend. He wrote, "You will be good news
to the people in those two churches." It was the first time that I
considered that ministry might include *me being me* and not just *me
doing church*. In the course of my 10 years in parish ministry, I practiced the ministry of presence. I stood watch with families at the bedsides of loved ones who were dying. I spent the night holding the hand
of a single mother who was giving birth alone. I sat with families at
funeral homes and wedding receptions. Still, I never felt really useful.
People would say thank you. They told me that my presence meant
something. I didn't see how.

Then I got to be on the receiving end of the ministry of presence.
Out of the blue, my daughter Elly suffered two grand mal seizures. As
we waited for her to wake up in the hospital, a friend sat with us. She
held our hands and prayed with us. She came again the next day, bringing her mother and treats. They sat with me while my daughter had
tests. When Elly got out of the hospital, we needed to watch her constantly for more seizures. A friend brought me dinner and shared it
with me. Another came for a morning—and stayed on through lunch.
The friend from the hospital brought her mother—and ice cream—

over to the house. I cannot remember much of what these women said. The words didn't matter. I cannot remember their prayers—though we prayed together. What I do remember is *the women's presence*. I held tightly to them and to those moments together. The new situation was scary—and left me feeling lonely and alienated from normalcy. I looked forward to the presence of friends and family. Their presence was good medicine—good news—for me.

Our presence matters. We are good news to one another when we hang out through the messy stuff—the tears and bad words and unfixable situations. We are good news when we have nothing to offer but our availability. We are quiet support—like the foundation of a house, present but not often noticed.

Paying Attention

At a recent workshop, the leader asked each of us to answer the question, "Who pays attention to you and why?" One of the participants spoke about a friend who was a gifted listener. "The first time I met her was at a busy conference. She stood right next to me and treated me like the most important person in the room. She gave me her full attention. I felt like royalty."

In the coaching relationship, fierce presence is the practice of giving the client one's full attention. In all of our relationships, one of the gifts we offer and receive is presence: being fully engaged in the moment. Like children at play, we become so occupied with the present that we lose track of time. When we experience fierce presence, we know that we have been seen, heard, and understood. Someone "gets" us. We feel valued.

Many of our encounters, however, lack this quality of presence. We are distracted or distant. Most of us are pretty good at faking presence. We say "uh-huh" into the phone as a friend recounts her day, all the while checking e-mail. At a conference, a colleague moves his head up and down while scanning the room for someone more important to talk to. At meetings we stare intently at each speaker, thinking about a problem at home or formulating our next comment. As a result, we move through our lives in a fog, only half aware of what has transpired over the course of each day's conversations.

Practicing Fierce Presence

Learning to be fiercely present takes practice. My children have been the best teachers of this art. Even with them on my lap, my attention wanders to the book I'm writing or a client's situation. Gently but firmly, my daughter touches my cheek with her hand and turns it toward her. "Mommy, look at me." She lassoes my attention again and again until I finally let the meandering thoughts go and focus solely on her.

The same techniques of meditation, focusing on the breath, can be used to learn to be fiercely present.

TRY THIS

Here are some actions that support the practice of being present:

Put other work aside. Close folders, books, the Internet connection, and anything else that might pull your attention.

Minimize potential distractions. In the office, shut the door, turn off the phone's ringer, and shut down the computer. At a public venue, take the nonpower seat—so that all concentration can be on the person you are talking with. Avoid looking at your watch.

Pray. On many days it seems that it is only by God's grace that I can focus on anything. Between the children; my writing; the needs of my editing clients; the stuff in the house that screams, "fix me, clean me, straighten me"; and my own personal worries—it's amazing that I have even one brain cell left to use with a client. For that reason, I always ask God to center me, to calm my worried mind, and to create a space where I can pay attention to the needs of the one before me at the moment.

Focus your body. Both my piano and clarinet instructors believed that the proper posture laid the foundation for playing good music. Good posture doesn't hurt in our interpersonal relationships either. Turn your body toward the person you are speaking to. Lean forward. Keep your hands and arms in an open position.

Open your mind. In a conversation, we open our mind to the other person. Our personal thoughts and distractions are quieted so that we can be open to receive the gift of the other—his or her thoughts, emotions, and needs. Our agenda is put aside. This time is not about us but about them.

Stay present. Inside the conversation, the only time that matters is now. Each time our mind wanders, we feel the imaginary hand on our face, turning us back toward the present. Intrusive thoughts are shooed away, like flies. Important inklings—persistent insights we want to share with the other—are jotted down for a later time.

Who Pays Attention to You and Why?

When the leader asked me, "Who pays attention to you and why?" I could not think of a single soul. All week I had been chasing my then three-year-old daughter around the beach, often stopping her to lecture about the importance of paying attention to one's parents. Then I remembered the bag of treats in my room. Just before I had left for vacation, a friend had packed up a bag of snacks, some homemade, all within the confines of my narrow dietary needs. She had certainly been paying attention to me. I recalled the six-year-old girl who sits with me and my daughter in church. Each time I take out my journal to jot down a note, she asks about it. She watches my every move and imitates many of them. I remembered the patience of the women who came to sit with us, to *attend* to us, in the days following my daughter's first seizures. As the faces of people who have paid attention flashed in my mind's eye, it occurred to me that these are the people who have taught me how to attend to others. If I am able to be fiercely present to another it is because I have experienced that same gift from other people—strangers and friends. And I would boldly say that it is here—in those moments of fierce presence—that I have seen Jesus. Yes, I know Jesus to be present in communion, in baptism, in the reading and preaching of the word. But those experiences are given depth and richness by the Jesus I meet in those who attend to me—who pray with me, who bring me bread, who hug me and welcome me to sit and eat with them. When we attend to others, giving them the gift of our fierce presence, Jesus becomes present to other people as well.

Try

Practice presence. Find ways to simply be present to others this week. Here are some hints:

- Find people who you feel you have nothing to offer—either because their problems are too big or their resources are too vast.
- Choose people who are not on your networking list—people who don't hold social capital for you to get where you are going.
- Clear enough time so that you can be truly present—and not looking toward your next engagement.

Afterwards, reflect on how the experience affected you.

- Does "being present" time pass quickly or slowly? In what ways?
- In what ways are you different because you have been present to another?
- In what ways did their presence affect you?

Talk

1. Share an experience of how someone was good news or good medicine to you. How might these stories change the way you minister to people?
2. Talk about the practice of being present to another person.

   - What kept you focused?
   - What changed as a result of being fiercely present?

3. List practices that you use or have experienced as ways of avoiding being present. What can you do to change your behavior?
4. What does a ministry of presence look like (and not look like)?

18   ⊛   Welcome

Welcome one another, therefore, just as Christ has welcomed you,
for the glory of God.

Romans 15:7

I once heard Maya Angelou say in a television interview that children
need to see our eyes light up when they walk into a room. We need to
know that we matter to someone. My grandmother did this for me—
and for every person who walked through her doors. With barely a
word, she'd find you a place at her kitchen table, wrapping you up in
love and cookies. Grandma's welcome was so delicious I wanted to
share it with all my friends.

In looking for a church home, we wanted a place where eyes light
up at the sight of children and strangers. After more than a year of
visiting churches, we found a congregation that offered that delicious
welcome. In this place, we experience the sense that we matter to
someone every single Sunday. I see it most clearly with my young
daughter. She has found a loving welcome in more than one corner of
the church. Early in the service, she runs up to the pastor to give her
a hug. At the children's sermon time, she crawls on the lap of an older
child. During the sermon, she wanders over to sit with the church
pianist and her family. In the middle of the offering, she heads back to
sit with a friend's mom or aunt. My daughter believes she belongs in
each of these arms just as much as she belongs with me.

Welcoming Messages

Coaching provides this sort of "kitchen-table welcome." Like my grandmother and the people at my church, the coach creates the safe space
spoken about in part 1. Without this safe space, the coaching relationship cannot flourish. This welcome does not just happen. The coach
works to create it by giving the client specific messages that communicate hospitality. Here are some of the messages.

I AM GLAD TO SEE YOU
The coach might communicate this welcome by warmly greeting the
client. When a client needs to communicate with the coach between

sessions, the coach welcomes the client's call or e-mail. The client is not a bother or interruption.

YOU MATTER, YOU ARE WORTHY OF MY TIME

The time spent with the client is not the opening act—something to pass the time until the really important people show up. The coach treats the client as the main event. The coach can communicate this by devoting his or her full attention to the client and the conversation. The coach does not answer the phone or the door or pay attention to the other people in the room. If the conversation happens on the phone, the coach does not multitask—sorting mail or doing other household chores while having a coaching conversation. The coaching hour is holy time—moments set apart for the purpose of conversation.

I AM INTERESTED IN WHO YOU ARE AND WHAT YOU DO

Many stories surface in the course of the conversation. In a different sort of relationship, pursuing a tangent such as favorite musical groups or great vacation getaways might be okay. In this relationship, the conversation centers around the client and what the client thinks, feels, and does. The coach keeps the focus of the conversation on the client. Stories about other people and events might be interesting but they are always followed by questions like, "So what does this mean for you?" or "What did this experience teach you about yourself?"

YOUR WORDS ARE PRECIOUS AND WILL NOT BE SHARED

Most of us have had the horrible experience of discovering that a trusted confidante shared our secrets with someone else—without our permission. It's a crushing blow to lose both our secret and our trust in someone we cared for. The coach must provide confidentiality, not sharing with others the content of the conversation or the existence of the relationship itself.

I have noticed one exception to the confidentiality rule. My coach will sometimes tell me about the struggle or success of another client. When I was working on developing a networking strategy, my coach shared how another client had found success. She spoke about this client's strategies—developing a 30-second speech about her work, then attending a networking group and topical conferences. None of these strategies revealed the identity of her other client. I have adopted the practice of sharing client successes with other clients. You have heard some of the stories—with identifying details changed—in this book.

YOU CANNOT SHOCK ME

When our high school days were long past, my brother and I told our mother about some of our exploits. She is utterly and delightfully shockable—gasping at every revelation: "You didn't! Oh my!" While this might be an expected and even fun reaction from one's mother, it doesn't work so well in the coaching relationship. The client needs to be able to speak his or her truth in a place where it will not be judged. When a coach expresses shock, disappointment, condemnation, or any other extreme reaction, the safety net disappears. The client gets pushed against a measuring stick that he or she may not have expected—and certainly does not need. The client ends up having to defend, deny, excuse, or apologize for his or her actions or beliefs. This time would be better spent asking the question, "What now?" In my experience as pastor, coach, and friend, people often judge themselves much more harshly than I might. They do not need my judgment, too. What they need is a place where they can discover how to proceed in the midst of a new and maybe difficult reality.

I RESPECT YOU

The word *respect* comes from the Latin word *respectus*, which means the act of looking back at someone or taking a second look. The coach communicates to the client that he or she is worth this second look. Beyond that, the coach expresses his or her trust in the client's choices. The coach does not dismiss or diminish the thoughts, feelings, and actions of the client.

I APPRECIATE YOU

By its nature, the coaching relationship is an unequal one. The relationship is designed to focus almost exclusively on one person. Still, the coach and client are equals and the relationship does contain some element of mutuality. One way the coach welcomes the client and expresses this mutuality is by appreciating the contribution of the client to his or her own growth. For me this has meant telling clients when something they have said or done has affected my thoughts or actions. For example, one of my clients spoke about a question that has helped her to make better choices in her life. In the month that followed, I used that question in my own life and with many other clients. When I saw the client again, I thanked her for the question and told her how it had an impact on me.

WELCOMING ONE ANOTHER

In our work as spiritual leaders, the practice of hospitality is foundational. It's what Christian community is all about. The Christian concept of community is based on Jesus's radical inclusion of outsiders. He loved and embraced people who the rest of society shunned. In Romans, Paul wrote to a community divided by faith practices. He advised, "Welcome one another, therefore, just as Christ has welcomed you, for the glory of God" (Rom. 15:7). In other words, as Christ welcomed *you*, welcome each other. We are called to welcome one another *just as* Christ has welcomed us—as the complex, rich human beings we are. We welcome each other despite our brokenness, despite our differences.

I remember my pastor talking one Sunday about the "scare" evangelism technique: "Do you know where you are going when you die?" She suggested that telling people, "God loves you," might be more effective. When we welcome other people, we do just that—we extend Jesus's love to them. We gift them with something they may not get anywhere else—we embrace all of who they are and who God is calling them to be.

Try

For the next week, use the techniques above to practice communicating welcome to the people you interact with. At the end of each day, reflect on the following questions.

- How did the practice of communicating welcome change the nature of the relationship?
- Were there moments when you had to struggle to extend welcome to someone? What happened? What made it difficult to welcome the person?
- Who did you find it easy to welcome? What made it easy to welcome that person?
- Were there moments when you felt the practice of welcoming another person to be unhelpful? What happened? In what ways do you think it was unhelpful?

Talk

1. Share your experiences of communicating welcome. Use the above questions to reflect on when this practice is helpful and when it is less than helpful in your work as a spiritual leader.
2. Share an experience of feeling welcomed by another person in a relationship. How did that change your experience of the relationship? How did it change you?
3. Discuss the additional ways of extending welcome to other people within a relationship.

---

19 ◉ Affirm

I looked over during the race and saw that this man had tears streaming down his face. . . . "What's wrong?" I asked. "Are you hurt?" "No," he replied softly, "I'm not hurt." "Then why the tears?" I asked. "Because . . . I just realized that in my entire life, no one has ever cheered for me before."

John Bingham, *The Courage to Start:*
A Guide to Running for Your Life

I once read that children in the worst possible circumstances will survive—even thrive—if they have one person in their lives that loves them unconditionally and cheers them on. How true! A child—or an adult, for that matter—will live up to your expectations of them. If you expect them to be horrid, they will not disappoint you. If you expect success and provide some kind words and real encouragement—they will likely meet those expectations as well.

You probably know this from your own life. You understand how rare and wonderful it is to have someone love you for being you. You understand how precious it is to have someone cheer for you to make it! You also know how frustrating (and sad) it is to experience the opposite—the advice giving, the silence, the criticism, and the judgment that you get when you do not meet the expectations of others. Their words can be well meaning and given out of concern. Still, they do not help, and the judgments of others often can limit us and steer us in the wrong direction.

One of my clients struggled with the lack of appreciation and affirmation she got in the parish. "No matter what good I do, I don't get any compliments." Her parishioners encouraged her to find affirmation in other places—from her spouse and friends. "Don't expect the people in this or any church to praise you. It won't happen." On the phone, she asked me, "So is that true? Should I just give up on getting praised? And is it the same everywhere—at every church and also in business?"

I couldn't answer her question. I still can't. I believe that affirmation exists. Sometimes it happens in the church; often it doesn't. Expecting anything—good or bad—can lead to disappointment. We can never be certain that reality will meet our expectations. A far better tactic would be to create an atmosphere of affirmation in our relationships with others.

When one of my son's teachers told me that children respond much better to positive rather than negative reinforcement, I began noticing the many small and large things my son does right in a day. Wanting to create an atmosphere of appreciation in our home, I began to point out these successes. In addition, we began to take time each night before bed to talk about three things that he believed he did well during the day. Not only does he beam with pride in himself, he's far easier to parent. Believing he can seems to empower him to accomplish great things. In addition, he has started to notice and call attention to the good in those around him, including his younger sister.

I have tried the same techniques with my clients. I point out their successes—not just the big things, such as a promotion, but also the smaller achievements such as staying committed to an exercise program for a few weeks. I encourage my clients to turn around their self-talk and affirm their own behavior. Like my son, I see my clients standing taller—more aware of their strengths. The criticism that comes with just being alive doesn't see to irk or gnaw at them as much. It's as if affirmation creates a natural buoy against the challenges of the world. The clients who get affirmation—both in the coaching relationship and from themselves—seem to need it less and less over time. Their confidence increases—as does their ability to support and encourage other people.

Affirmation Tips

Here are some tips for offering affirmation:

CULTIVATE LONG MEMORIES

When the people of Israel wandered in the wilderness, complaining about the miserable food, they forgot how God had provided for them, how God had freed them from slavery and kept them safe from harm. (They also couldn't see God's goodness in the present moment, but that's another story!) We have the same problem. We may see our struggle and forget that God has brought us safe thus far. We may look at our current failures and forget our past achievements. To support clients in developing better memories, I ask them to write down all of their life achievements. Sometimes we review this list together, affirming their many strengths and successes.

DIRECT AFFIRMATION

Ask, "What do you need support and affirmation for?" Like a massage, being affirmed feels good. But a great massage targets the areas of special concern—the knot in the neck or the nagging pain in the lower back. Affirmation works best if it is targeted to areas of special need.

BE CONCRETE

Use concrete evidence or examples in your affirmation. When I noted to a client what a good spiritual leader she was, I pointed to some of the qualities that I saw: she prayed for her congregational members daily and she continuously communicated her vision for the purpose of the congregation. It can also be helpful to point to external evidence—concrete results or anecdotal evidence. If you do not have access to this information, you might say something like, "I have a gut feeling that you're a great parent. What kind of evidence do you see that points to that?"

LOOK ON THE BRIGHT SIDE

When someone shares a story of perceived failure, shine light on the other side of the tale. How does the story also demonstrate their good qualities and achievements? One client struggled to finish his book. He listed for me his failures as a writer. I asked, "What do you do well?"

I nudged him to see the other side of these perceived failures—for hidden in our weaknesses are often nuggets of strength. I wondered if his dogged attention to detail might be seen as the gift of thoroughness and a sign that he could notice and reveal for readers the complexity of an issue. Together we came up with a list of four strengths.

TEACH THEM HOW TO AFFIRM

You know the adage, "If you give a family some fish, you feed them for today. If you teach a family to fish, you feed them for a lifetime!" It's the same with affirmation—if you offer affirmation, you give hope for today. If you teach someone how to affirm, you give them hope forever. People need to learn how to love and affirm themselves. As the examples above illustrate, involve people in seeking out and affirming their own goodness. I often give clients the assignment of noticing what they did right in a day, then writing down these discoveries along with affirmations for themselves.

WHEN IN DOUBT, AFFIRM

When my daughter was given a new medicine, the doctor warned us that it could cause a life-threatening rash. "What do I do?" I asked. They told us to bring her in. Knowing that the rash was an allergic reaction, I asked if I could give her Benadryl. They told me it wouldn't totally fix the problem, but it would help a bit—and, above all, "Go ahead and give it. It can't hurt her." Affirming another person will not fix everything. But it does help. And, above all, it cannot hurt. So when in doubt about what to do: affirm.

BE GENEROUS

When a friend of mine was growing up, his parents held back on their praise because they didn't want him to get a "big head." I rarely meet people who have been over-affirmed. Most of us tend to ignore the good stuff and cling to the criticism. When I was serving a parish, I would undoubtedly carry with me the one person who said, "Your sermon stunk," and toss aside the long list of comments that praised the message. Most of us are the walking wounded, nursing our failures. For this reason, I try to be generous with my praise. I figure that I need to be, if people are only going to remember a small percentage of it!

A Final Word

The first point in every one of my pastor's children's sermons is this: "Affirm." She always begins with these words: "We thank God for the gift of these beautiful young people, don't we church?" The congregation responds with a resounding, "Yes!" The affirmation goes on: "We are so glad you are here today, aren't we church?" Again, "Yes!" She tells the young people that we love them and want them to succeed; we want them to go to school, to grow up to be fine adults. Whenever possible, she calls attention to the young people who do well—who achieve perfect attendance, who make good grades, who get into college. These achievements are rewarded with affirmation, applause, and sometimes flowers. In these moments, the children beam with pride. For this moment, at least, someone is looking at them and saying, "Yes, you are good. Yes, you are loved."

These children's times remind me of Paul's words to the church in Corinth: "For the Son of God, Jesus Christ, whom we proclaimed among you, Silvanus and Timothy and I, was not 'Yes and No'; but in him it is always 'Yes.' For in [Christ] every one of God's promises is a 'Yes.' For this reason it is through him that we say the 'Amen,' to the glory of God" (2 Cor. 1:19-20). Too many times what we hear, however, is that "Yes and No" Paul talked about, often phrased as, "Yes, but":

Yes, but I don't love you.
Yes, but I don't like the way you look.
Yes, but I don't think you're smart enough.
Yes, but I don't think you have enough talent.
Yes, but I don't want you.

In a world where we too often hear words that hurt and demean us, we need to hear the yeses. When those yeses do not come from the people in our lives, we can count on Jesus. Jesus's promise to us is always a resounding yes: Yes, I love you. Yes, you're beautiful. Yes, you're a gifted, smart, and perfect child of God. Yes, I welcome you. In Jesus's love and care for us, we find the ultimate affirmation.

Try

Be a cheerleader in your relationships with others. Using the techniques above, look for opportunities to affirm the people you connect with.

Talk

1. Talk about the biblical or theological reasons for affirming other people.
2. In what ways did the practice of affirming others change the atmosphere of the conversations or the relationship?
3. What would it take to create an atmosphere of affirmation at the place you work?

---

20 ❀ Practice Generosity

What have you done for me lately?

Janet Jackson, *Design of a Decade*

As humans, we like parity in our relationships with others. A tit for a tat. An eye for an eye. A kiss for a kiss. At its best, our desire for parity keeps relationships healthy. We enjoy flexibility in our roles. Both parties give and take love, time, gifts, and kindnesses. Like the ocean waves, the relationship ebbs and flows naturally. At its worst, parity leads to keeping accounts. We notice that at lunch, we asked all the questions while our colleague did all the talking. We take note of when gifts and cards are given and received. We pay attention to who does more of the calling, e-mailing, and inviting. We judge the people we connect with—and our relationships—against these accounts. We wonder, "What have you done for me lately?"

This isn't new, of course. Look at Peter. When Jesus taught the disciples about sin and forgiveness (Matt. 18:15-20), Peter asked him, "If another member of the church sins against me, how often should I

forgive? As many as seven times?" (v. 21). Peter was asking an account-
ing question. He wanted an equation, a number, a way to measure the
give and take of forgiving another. I'm sure that Peter thought he was
being generous when he suggested that he might forgive as many as
seven times. The number seven implies "fullness or completeness."[1]
Jesus answered Peter, "Not seven times, but, I tell you, seventy-seven
times" (v. 22). The number Jesus offered is not to be taken literally.
Jesus meant forgive as many times as necessary. In other words—
don't keep accounts of your forgiveness. Forgive generously.

Jesus echoed this call to generosity at other points in the Gos-
pels. In a conversation about hospitality, Jesus encouraged his followers not to invite other people in hopes of being repaid (Luke 14:12-14).
Jesus said, "But when you give a banquet, invite the poor, the crippled,
the lame, and the blind. And you will be blessed, because they cannot
repay you." (vv. 13-14). When the woman with the "alabaster jar of
very costly ointment" anointed Jesus (Matt. 26:7), the disciples were
outraged at the expense. "For this ointment could have been sold for
a large sum, and the money given to the poor" (Matt. 26:9). Jesus did
not chastise the woman or her generous gift. Instead, he called it a
"good service" (literally a "beautiful deed"). When Jesus spoke about
retaliation (Matt. 5:38-42), he asked his followers to forget the rules
that had punishment fit the crime ("an eye for an eye"). Instead, he
advised a sort of reckless generosity: "Give to everyone who begs from
you, and do not refuse anyone who wants to borrow from you" (Matt.
5:42).

My daughter has become my role model in generosity. Each fall
the local schools have a food drive. When my daughter and I went
through our cupboards to find food to donate, I grabbed the food that
seemed the easiest to give away (the stuff I don't like): canned aspara-
gus, peas, and lima beans. My daughter chose the food she loved the
best—the alphabet-shaped spaghetti with meatballs and her favorite
boxes of macaroni and cheese. My generosity was a cheap sort—giving away what I perceived I would never need. My daughter was generous—she gave from her treasures.

In coaching school, the instructors taught us to be generous in
our relationships with other people, especially our clients. They repeatedly coached us to "make the client right." It means that when a
colleague, friend, or congregant has disappointed us, we need to be-

lieve the best about his or her actions. For example, when a colleague misses the fourth community ministry meeting in a row, we may be tempted to criticize ("She isn't committed to the work"), project our fears ("He doesn't care about us"), or predict disaster ("She'll never succeed if she can't remember something as important as this"). All of these approaches label the colleague as wrong. We make the colleague right when we offer praise ("He's so committed to his work in his parish, he has trouble leaving for meetings"), believe the best ("She must have another commitment"), or ask for more information ("Steve, we miss you at the meetings. Can you talk about what works and doesn't work about them for you?).

Some Tools

In working with the concept of practicing generosity, I am interested both in making the client right and supporting the client in making others right. I use several tools to work with clients on practicing generosity. Here are a few of them.

LET GO OF BEING RIGHT

In the context of the relationship, I let go of my need to be right. This includes letting go of my need to be smart, wise, helpful, or loved. This creates room for the client to be right—and to discover what is right for him or her. For example, if I share an inkling with a client, and the client thinks it's a load of garbage—I let them. The client needs to discover his or her own path.

LISTEN FOR STRENGTHS

I listen for signs of strength in my clients and point to them as frequently as possible. I invite my clients to list their strengths, to recall times when depending on their strengths worked, and to discover how these strengths can help them in their current situations.

INFORMATION, NOT JUDGMENT

I ask the clients to consider events, comments, and actions as information instead of judgment. One sure way to get stuck is to believe that there is only one right way to think or act. If a client presents a story that identifies him or another person as "wrong," I might say,

"What if this story wasn't about who is right or wrong? What if it is just information? What might it teach you?" I might also ask the client to look at the story again, considering that all parties might be "right."

STEP OUT OF ROLES AND DICHOTOMIES

I ask questions that invite the client to shift out of the hero or victim role in the stories they tell about themselves. These roles play into the "right-wrong" dichotomy. Shifting out of these roles helps the client to see the events as events and not as a judgment about who they are.

MAKING OTHERS RIGHT

For those of us used to keeping accounts in our relationships (and who isn't?), making others right can be difficult. Most of us cling to our right to be right. We live in a culture where winning matters—and every winner needs a loser. As spiritual leaders who preach about truth, we may see pointing out faults or confronting evil as part of our calling. We may believe that it is our job to mend, fix, or correct other people. And, if we do not believe this, many of the people we work with may want us to do this work. (Many of my clients may come into coaching believing that I hold the wisdom or truth that they need to survive!) We may get in the habit of approaching the people in our lives as projects to be worked on or as students needing instruction. When we do that, we imply that there is something wrong with these people. When we practice making other people right, people feel better about themselves and consequently do better. I have a friend who constantly tells me that I am a good parent. She always has an example or two to add to her praise ("I like the way you tell your daughter that you love her."). I've noticed that on the days she points out my successes, I *am* a better parent. Right begets right.

No doubt there are times when we need to sit down with a sister or brother and express our frustration, pain, or disappointment. We are human; we sin against one another. In times of great or repeated sin, the most loving thing we can do is to confront the sin in a graceful way. Jesus spoke eloquently about this in Matthew 18 when he laid out a plan for resolving disagreements in the community of faith (Matt. 18:15-20). Even here Jesus is generous, asking that the people of faith approach the offending member more than once.

I have always loved the beginning of Paul's first letter to the Corinthians. Paul often began his letters with thanksgiving for the re-

cipients. Here his words seem even more poignant because of the difficulties in the Corinthian church. The people of Corinth were divided,
quarreling over practices and status. Still Paul believed the best about
them, writing, "I give thanks to my God always for you because of the
grace of God that has been given you in Christ Jesus, for in every way
you have been enriched in him, in speech and knowledge of every
kind—just as the testimony of Christ has been strengthened among
you—so that you are not lacking in any spiritual gift" (1 Cor. 1:4-7).
Paul spoke of the grace present in this group of jealous, quarreling
people, of Christ *enriching* them with speech and knowledge. That's
generosity!

Try

1. In your encounters with people this week, pay attention to your
   natural inclinations. Are you inclined to make people wrong
   or right? What evidence do you have for this? If you see
   that you are inclined to make people wrong by giving them
   advice or correcting their speech, how might you modify your
   behavior?
2. Use one or more of the techniques described above as you
   relate with yourself and other people. How does this change
   your experience with yourself? With others?

Talk

1. When you think about loving generously, what other scripture
   passages come to mind?
2. Talk about the practice of making others right.

   - How do you "make other people right"? Give an example.
   - When do you think this is helpful?
   - When might it be difficult or dangerous?

3. What are other ways you practice generosity in your relationships with other people?

21 ⊛ Listen Well

> Courage is what it takes to stand up and speak; courage is also what
> it takes to sit down and listen.
>
> Winston Churchill

A client called to discuss a difficult parish situation. We spoke for 10 minutes. Or more accurately, she spoke for 10 minutes. I listened, gave some cues that I was involved in her story (mmm, yes, uh-huh), and asked maybe one question. At the end of the call she said, "Thank you. You've been so helpful!"

"I didn't say anything. Maybe you should call me the psychic coach!"

She laughed. Then she said, "It was the listening that helped. I needed someone to hear what I had to say."

Being listened to is a basic human need. The practice of supportive listening is so crucial to every relationship that this topic will be covered over four chapters. This chapter will define the qualities and effects of supportive listening. The next chapter, "Prepare to Listen," will explore techniques for setting aside one's preoccupations in order to focus on the conversation. "Use Listening Tools," chapter 23, will discuss tools for listening better within a conversation. Finally, chapter 24, "Practice Silence," will consider how healthy silence can be a part of listening well.

Defining Supportive Listening

Healthy relationships require reciprocal listening—each party gives and receives attention. Listening is more, though, than simply participating in a ping-pong-like exchange of speak-listen-speak-listen-speak. It may look that easy. After all, what can be difficult about taking turns practicing the passive act of hearing another speak? All we need to do is sit quietly and take in what the other person is saying, right?

But listening is anything but passive. It requires being actively present to the person we are with. When we listen well, we become present to our partner in a significant, deep way. Listening is a rich art that provides the recipient with much more than an open ear. Ideally, a supportive listener communicates the following:

- "I am present to you." The listener is fiercely attentive to us, focused on what we are saying and how we are saying it. The supportive listener has dismissed as many personal and environmental distractions as possible.
- "I care about you." The listener's fierce attention embraces and cares for us. Because the person is willing to set aside his or her time for us and enter into our story, we know that we matter to this person.
- "I accept you." The supportive listener does not judge. He or she accepts and welcomes us as we are.
- "I support you and your needs." The role of the listener is to bear witness to our lives in a way that supports what we need in the moment.
- "I am honored that you trust me with this information." The listener appreciates our choosing him or her to receive this particular story of our life.
- "I understand." The listener communicates that he or she comprehends our experience and asks for clarification when our words or meaning are confusing.
- "You are not alone." The act of speaking and being listened to connects us with another person. We are no longer alone in whatever suffering or success we are speaking about.
- "Is this what you are saying?" The listener reflects back our stories, like a mirror, helping us to more clearly understand what we are communicating.
- "This is what I think." We receive thoughtful responses to our stories, helping us to gain insight.
- "I remember . . ." Supportive listening stretches between conversations. Our listening partner remembers and holds before us stories, sorrows, and dreams we have shared in the past.

The Effects of Supportive Listening

Recently a client shared her life vision with me. She had already shared it with a family member who could not hear it. Instead, the family member took the confession as an opportunity to launch an attack on how my client was selfishly pursuing her own passions. Before my client read to me her vision story, I asked her what type of a response would be most helpful to her. I wanted to know both how to listen and how to guide our follow-up conversation. As she spoke about what she hoped her speaking this vision aloud might give her, it became clear that she most needed someone to bear witness to her story. After that, she wanted someone who could hold her vision for her—reminding her of what she hoped for her life when she lost her way. After our conversation ended, it occurred to me that a good listener's presence and response can support and encourage us toward growth. This growth includes the following:

WE BETTER UNDERSTAND OUR SITUATION
We might come to a conversation feeling confused or distraught. Simply talking about it to someone can help us to get clear about what we are thinking, what issues need to be addressed, and what steps we might take next.

WE ACCEPT OUR SITUATION
When people experience loss through death, they need to repeatedly tell the story of their loss. Talking about what happened to us makes it feel real. The listener's presence helps validate our experience and our feelings about it. By telling our story, we can accept its presence in our life.

WE MAKE MEANING FROM OUR EXPERIENCES
When we tell our story to a sympathetic listener, we begin to construct meaning around what happened. Our tragedies do not haunt us as the punishment of an unjust god. Instead, we look for ways in which we can find deeper meaning in the "changes and chances of life."[1]

WE EXPLORE THE CONTEXT OF OUR EXPERIENCES
Each of us understands our life within the context of our own narrative constructions. As Christians, we understand our stories at least partly from the context of Christianity and the stories and doctrines that define our particular belief system. We story our lives within many contexts—individual, familial, cultural, and so forth. Any life experience or situation can become another context from which we story our life experiences. When we share our stories with another person, they bring their own context as well as their curiosity about our contexts. Someone's ability to listen closely for context helps us explore and understand our story in new ways.

WE GAIN INSIGHT

In high school, I used to love those pictures that shifted from one image to another. The most famous of these is Edgar Rubin's vase-faces illusion, where a white vase becomes the shadows of two people. Speaking our stories to a supportive listener can have a similar effect on us. The way we understood our story when spinning it out in our head shifts when we speak it aloud and respond to the questions of the listener. Perhaps we gain clarity. Or we define the story differently—what we saw as crisis becomes a turning point. We gain insight into something that seemed to be just a pile of muck.

WE BEGIN TO INTEGRATE OUR EXPERIENCES INTO OUR LIFE STORY

Understanding our individual life experiences as an integral part of the whole is helpful. We need to know how an experience relates to who we are and what God is calling us to be and do in the world. The responses and reflection of a supportive listener can help us integrate single experiences into the stories of our lives.

WE SEE AND FACE THE TRUTH

When a supportive listener reflects back to us what we are saying—and how we are saying it—we have the opportunity to discover what is true. We all lie. Most of us tell the little lies that please other people or keep us stuck in unhealthy practices and relationships. We fear losing a friend, so we tell ourselves that we don't mind it that she always shows up late to our meetings. We do not want to face the truth about our eating habits, so we tell ourselves that one doughnut a day can't be all that bad. We want our marriage to work and so we tell ourselves that our spouse's controlling jealousy is a sign of deep love. The simple act of speaking this aloud to someone who listens well and asks probing questions can help us to define what we know to be true.

A Holy Gift

Jesus called attention to the value of listening. When he taught in parables, he would often say, "Let anyone with ears listen!" (Matt. 13:9). Jesus did not have much patience with people who did not listen to him or his disciples. He was hard on those who could not hear his teachings, saying, "Then pay attention to how you listen; for to those who have, more will be given; and from those who do not have, even what they seem to have will be taken away" (Luke 8:18). When Jesus sent the disciples out to preach and heal, he instructed them, "If anyone will not welcome you or listen to your words, shake off the dust from your feet as you leave that house or town" (Matt. 10:14). Maybe one of the best examples of Jesus's call to listen comes from the story of Mary and Martha. When Jesus visited them, Martha became distracted by the tasks necessary for good hosting. Mary "sat at the Lord's feet and listened to what he was saying" (Luke 10:39). The form of the Greek verb should really be translated as "kept listening," suggesting a persistent listening. When Martha called attention to Mary's idleness, Jesus said, "Martha, Martha, you are worried and distracted by many things; there is need of only one thing. Mary has chosen the better part, which will not be taken away from her" (Luke 10:41-42). Jesus praised Mary's attentiveness, her willingness to set aside the distractions and worries of the day and listen to her guest.

At the end of Matthew's Gospel, Jesus taught that when we welcome another person we welcome him (Matt. 25:31-40). When we practice supportive listening, we welcome the Jesus that we meet in one another. This is holy work. We set aside our worries and distractions to attend to the needs of the person before us. In the midst of all that presses upon us, we "keep listening," persistently paying attention to the God in our midst.

Try

For the next week, just listen to people. If possible, try not to share your opinions, judgments, reactions, thoughts, stories, advice, or ideas. Try not to ask questions. Allow for the presence of silence. Pay attention to the people who are speaking. Make it clear that you are paying attention. Look at people, nod your head, and make listening noises. This experiment is easiest to use with groups— at committee meetings, study groups, and other places where you are not depended upon to make a contribution. In your one-on-one conversations, make an effort to listen more and speak less. Give up any need to respond. At the end of the week, reflect on the following questions:

- What did you notice about your internal noise during the week? What threatens to get in the way of your ability to listen?
- What effect did the practice of intense listening have on you? On your relationships?
- How do you think this practice could affect the way you listen to other people?
- How did other people react to this experiment?

Talk

1. What biblical examples of listening guide your ministry?
2. In what way is listening a holy act?
3. Share a time when someone practiced supportive listening with you. What did it look like? How did it affect you?

---

22 ✸ Prepare to Listen

His extraordinary eyes were brilliant with an unmistakably genuine interest, and it was then that I realized he possessed that rare and fabled gift for making a stranger feel special, cared for, even cherished—and all within the space of a few minutes.

Susan Howatch, *Ultimate Prizes*

"So what do you think about that?" my spouse asked.

"Ummm. Ummm. What do I think?" I stuttered.

"You weren't listening."

Caught. My attention had wandered for a moment. But in that moment my spouse told me something important to him.

I apologized. We started over. I focused on him and what he had to say to me.

We all do it. In the middle of hearing Mildred discuss her painful arthritis for the third time in as many visits, we wonder if that pain in our side could possibly be appendicitis. Instead of listening to our child quote the entire script of the latest SpongeBob episode, we nod our heads and silently plan the adult study class. While our colleague tells us his views on the most recent church controversy, we formulate our rebuttal. It's tough to pay attention.

You have been on the other end, too. You are telling a story about your life. It's juicy stuff—sad or funny or life shattering. You are getting to the good part when you realize that you have lost your audience. If you're in a gracious mood, you might roll your eyes and think, "Well, that's just how so-and-so is." If you're feeling upset, your conversation partner's behavior might irritate you. But if you're feeling bad about life and yourself, this behavior might crush your spirit—leaving you feeling isolated, unloved, or marginal.

Steps toward Listening

The first step toward listening more effectively is preparing to listen. This involves setting aside personal preoccupations, admitting preoccupations, and focusing.

SET ASIDE PERSONAL PREOCCUPATIONS

Our persistent worries or fleeting distractions can get in the way of fully attending to another person. In graduate school, I had a mentor who could not sit still. When we met at his home for supervision, he would often be sweeping or dusting as we talked. A colleague of mine is obsessed with her cell phone. Once she answered it six times during a 60-minute meeting. Each time she hung up, she had to reorient herself to the group's agenda. E-mail, pressing tasks, challenging life situations, worries about loved ones, or concerns about our own personal health issues can all get in the way of our being able to listen.

I meet with most of my clients on the telephone. It's become important for me to create a ritual that enables me to set aside the demands and priorities of my home office. I turn off the computer, close my project notebooks, shut off the ringer on my other telephone, and close my office door. I move from my desk to a coaching chair, taking the phone and my client's folder with me. I spend some moments in silence—asking God to care for my personal concerns so that I can be free to listen to and connect with my client. When I meet with clients in person at a local coffee shop, the drive to the meeting place provides a great transition. Once at the coffee shop, I try to choose a chair that faces the wall, so that all of my attention can be placed on my client.

Setting aside one's preoccupations can take many forms. A spiritual leader I know has set up a separate conversation area in her office. When people come to talk to her, she moves from her busy desk to the empty table, signifying that the focus has shifted from paper to people. Another leader I know uses her time in the car between visits to "decompress" from her pressing concerns so that she can focus more effectively on the people she meets with. Some leaders use visual or auditory cues. One hits a Tibetan prayer bowl. Another lights a candle. A third turns on soothing music to drown out the noise of the busy office beyond the door.

ADMIT PREOCCUPATIONS

There will be times when it is impossible to set aside your preoccupations and focus on the conversation. Your three-year-old has just spilled a gargantuan-sized box of Cheerios when your council president calls to tell you about her impending divorce. You have a fight with your spouse moments before a young couple comes in to discuss their upcoming marriage. Ed McMahon shows up at your door carrying balloons and a check for a hundred thousand dollars as you were sitting down to talk with your best friend. Who could concentrate? At those particular moments, admitting you are not able to listen well is helpful and appropriate. You might choose to ask for a short break to deal with the immediate crisis, then center yourself and focus your attention on the person in need. Rescheduling the conversation for a better time might be necessary.

In a recent conversation with a colleague, she admitted her total exhaustion and inability to listen. I appreciated that. Though I needed to talk, I also needed to speak to someone who could listen to me. My colleague's ability to know and confess her current state freed us from what could have been a frustrating experience.

FOCUS

In the beginning of every conversation, on the phone or in person, there is a moment of turning away from distractions and turning toward one another. We become like a camera, bringing the object of our conversation into focus, causing everything else to become a bit blurry. We use verbal and nonverbal cues to focus and show that we are paying attention. We put down or turn away from our other work. That might mean putting the computer on sleep mode and closing files and books. We lean forward and make eye contact with the speaker. We nod our head "yes" or provide short verbal cues such as, "Say more."

For those of us who are easily distracted, the practice of focusing on the conversation at hand might have to happen repeatedly. In nearly every meditation program, participants are encouraged to focus on their breaths. This practice is often coupled with dismissing distracting thoughts like one might swat away a fly. These practices from meditation can be helpful when distracting thoughts or events threaten our ability to focus on the conversation at hand.

A Final Word

I love to watch cooking shows on public television. I am always impressed by the work that goes into *preparing* to cook on television. The appropriate ingredients are laid out in various sized bowls and organized on the counter. The cook doesn't have to root through the cupboards to find the cardamom. Because it is a cooking show—and on camera—distractions have been eliminated. No children wander through the kitchen asking for snacks; no phones interrupt the process. The cook can turn toward the work at hand—creating the dish. When I prepare to meet with a client or have a conversation with a friend, I often call to mind this image. The television cooking show reminds me that the work I do can be creative and nourishing when I take the time to properly prepare to listen.

Try

Create rituals or practices that will support you in setting aside your own personal preoccupations and focusing on the people you are with. Use these rituals in your conversations this week, then reflect on the following questions:

- In what ways did the rituals support you in being more present and able to listen to the person you were with?

- What additional practices might support you in being able to listen well?
- What are signs to you that you are preoccupied and cannot listen well? How might you communicate that to another person?

Talk

1. Share an experience of speaking with a person who cannot focus on you. What was that like? What messages did it communicate to you?
2. Talk about how you prepared to be present with and focus on other people this week. What worked? What didn't?

---

23 ❀ Use Listening Tools

A wise old owl sat in an oak.
The more he heard, the less he spoke;
The less he spoke, the more he heard.
Why aren't we all like that wise old bird?

Mother Goose nursery rhyme

And the whole time I was talking, Gloria Dump was listening. She was nodding her head and smiling and frowning and saying, "Hmmm," and "Is that right?"

I could feel her listening with all her heart, and it felt good.

India Opal Buloni in *Because of Winn-Dixie*

I used to require that my confirmation students write sermon notes. Some of my most discouraging afternoons were spent reading those notes. Either I wasn't communicating clearly or they weren't listening well, because more often than not the young people heard many things I did not say. Now that I sit in the pew more Sundays than I stand in the pulpit, I realize how difficult it is to hear what the preacher is truly saying. My mind wanders to the book I am writing. The children who wiggle beside me pull my attention away from the words. My own need to hear a certain word of hope hampers my ability to hear the sermon being preached. These challenges remind me of how difficult listening well is.

Most of us are not simply "good" or "bad" listeners. Instead, we have developed listening habits. Some of these habits are helpful and contribute to our ability to listen supportively. Other habits hinder our ability to pay attention to the speaker. Sometimes our ability to listen has more to do with the situation—how we feel or the time and location of the conversation—than our skills. This chapter looks at both helpful and unhelpful listening habits as a way to explore how we can become better listeners.

How Not to Listen

In the middle of a high school faith crisis, I went to my Campus Life leader to talk. Ten minutes into our conversation, it became clear to me that he was most concerned that I understood what salvation meant and how to get it. He did not seem to care much about my questions. He was preoccupied with my eternal destination. This man has become a helpful example to me of how not to listen. Sometimes it is easier to understand how we can become supportive listeners by defining poor listening skills.

Here's my tongue-in-cheek advice for practicing poor listening skills. Perhaps it will point to the ways we fail to be good listeners and turn us toward better attentiveness. As you read the list, evaluate your own listening skills. Are some of these habits that you practice?

MULTITASK

Yes, listen to the speaker's story—but do something else, too. Wash dishes or pick up the trash left by the confirmation class. It's great if you can make the listener really work to get your attention. Maybe even let them follow you around and talk while you do other stuff.

LET YOUR MIND WANDER

When the speaker's story gets boring—he tells about an event that seems familiar or she worries over a theme you have visited a gazillion times before, think about your own life or your last appointment or what you might have for dinner.

LOOK AROUND

Look around to see who else might be in the room. This is especially good after church or at parties, but it also works in any public place. Don't focus your eyes or your attention exclusively on the person you are with. Look around to see if there is someone more important to talk to. It's great if you can do it surreptitiously, but don't worry too much about that—crane your neck if it helps you see better.

WATCH THE CLOCK

Remind the speaker that your time is limited. The best way to do this is to constantly look at your watch or the clock while they speak.

LOOK AT INTERESTING STUFF

Look at the interesting stuff in the room. Pay more attention to the décor or to the books on the shelf than to the person you are speaking to.

PLAN WHAT YOU WILL SAY NEXT

Once you get the gist of their point, plan to say something that will make you look good—smart or funny or helpful.

PREPARE A LIST OF STOCK ANSWERS

You don't need to treat every person like an individual. Really, how many different problems can there be? Create a bunch of stock answers like, "God loves you" or "I'll pray for you." Whenever the speaker appears to be going down one of those familiar paths like, "Life isn't going so well," deal up one of your truisms. It usually cuts some time off the conversation.

MAKE ASSUMPTIONS

You're smart. You can usually figure out what a person is getting at or where they are coming from before they do. Why waste time waiting for them to process it out themselves? Assume you get what they are saying and plow ahead with your solutions.

PRETEND

Say you understand when you don't. Say you get what they are saying when you haven't the foggiest idea. Shake your head knowingly when you have lost their train of thought.

LISTEN WITH AN AGENDA

Go into every conversation with a purpose. Common agendas including fixing, instructing, correcting, judging, advising, approving, and sharing your own story.

LISTEN FOR AGREEMENT

Listen to hear the speaker confirm your point. Listen only for the information or narrative that agrees with what you believe to be true.

LISTEN FOR AN OPENING

Listen for an opening to tell your story. Don't worry. It doesn't have to be really obvious. Even a passing reference to a place you once visited or a holiday you celebrate can be an excuse to interrupt and shift the focus to your own life.

INTERRUPT

Sometimes it is hard to wait for a person to finish talking. If you are feeling like you need to be the center of attention for a moment, well grab it! Just interrupt!

TALK INCESSANTLY

One of the best ways to practice poor listening is to simply monopolize the conversation.

SILENCE THE SPEAKER

Once you get the sense of what the listener is looking for, give them the opposite. If the listener is looking for acceptance or understanding, shame them. Say things that will lead to their silence. Discredit them. Dismiss them. Make them wrong. Make yourself right. Put down their ideas. Laugh at them. There are really thousands of ways to do this—be creative.

How to Listen Well

A supportive listener is similar to a great dance partner: you cannot always see the technique but the dancing seems effortless. These are some techniques that turn distracted listeners into devoted ones.

SET ASIDE DISTRACTIONS

A series of techniques relating to this step was discussed in the previous chapter, "Prepare to Listen." This step includes setting aside anything that distracts you from the task of listening, such as

- personal preoccupations;
- personal agendas—our need to save the other person, look smart, get something accomplished, or convince the other person of our point of view;
- the desire or need to be the center of attention.

DEAL WITH RELATIONSHIP BLOCKS

Sometimes our preoccupation with something hurtful that has happened in the relationship can get in the way of our ability to listen. When our mind and energy are busy working over old pains, we cannot be present. It's important to take time to confront and dismantle the relationship block. For example, during one council meeting a member said something that was particularly hurtful to me. When she called two weeks later to discuss a church issue, I found it difficult to listen to her. I had not been able to let go of her hurtful words. Instead of pretending or stewing, I asked her about them. After several minutes of talking about what had happened, we were both able to move past the unfortunate incident and concentrate on the current conversation.

ASK FOR GUIDANCE

As a coach, I want my client to set the agenda of our conversation. I often ask my clients to tell me what they want me to listen for or what sort of feedback or help they are seeking.

LISTEN FOR CONTENT

This process is akin to "reading for plot." My son's main interest in reading a book is discovering what happened. He doesn't care so much about how a character was feeling or what motivated her, he wants to know "whodunit." This skill is about being able to understand what happened. What is the story the speaker is telling you? Listen for the main parts of any story. The simple plot is basically discovering what happened, how it unfolded, and why it occurred.

LISTEN FOR EMOTION

Behind the bare bones of the plot—who did what to whom—we can hear how the speaker is feeling about the events. Here are several ways to listen for this.

Pay attention to nonverbal cues. When looking for emotion, watch the speaker's eyes. Do they tear or light up when she speaks about something? Does he look at you or stare into space? Also pay attention to hand gestures and body posture. All of these things can suggest mood and emotion.

How does the speaker's voice sound when telling the story? Pay attention to volume, inflection, energy level, tone, and pacing. Noticing changes in any of the above is especially important, as they may indicate the speaker is experiencing or sharing an emotion that is extraordinary for him or her.

Pay attention to the words the speaker uses to tell the story. What sort of emotional content do you hear within the words? Powerful words like *hate* or *passion* suggest strong feelings and perhaps indicate that the speaker understands herself as the aggressor or rescuer. Passive words like *disappointed* or *pleased* may indicate sadness or even depression and might reveal that the speaker thinks of himself as a victim. Consider how the speaker expresses action. Does he or she use active verbs like *seek* and *dare* or passive verbs like *is sought* or *was dared*? Action words suggest that the speaker feels some energy or passion for what he or she speaks about. Passive verbs might indicate that the speaker feels less in control of the events in his or her life. Listen for how the speaker uses descriptive words. Does the speaker use many adjectives and adverbs like *super, horrid, marvelous*, and *disgusting*? Using adjectives can suggest that the speaker feels strongly about the topic (or is simply a dramatic person). Does the speaker relate only the bare facts? This may indicate that the speaker is detached from the events in some way, perhaps because of sadness. It may also reveal that the speaker is a big picture thinker who is not very interested in details.

LISTEN FOR INTENT

The intent of the speaker is what the speaker is truly saying—sometimes in spite of the thoughts and feelings he or she seems to be communicating. In a conversation with my coach, I spoke for almost 10 minutes about why I needed to enter a family-therapy training program. When I finished she said to me, "You are very convincing, but I sense that you don't really feel any passion about going. It's just what you think you should do." She was dead on. For me, listening for intent is about seeking the truth that hangs at the inter-section of thoughts and feelings. Susan Scott, executive educator in communication and cultural transformation, calls this listening "for the scaffolding on which a story hangs."[1] When we listen for intent, we are straining to see what this scaffolding looks like. Intent can often be discerned by listening for how the speaker's thoughts and feelings interact. Are they congruent? Does the speaker's affect match her words and vocal tone? Is any one part of the whole pic-ture off? In what ways? Learning to read intent takes time. In the end it may be more about listening to your gut than learning a set of techniques.

CLARIFY

Even the best listeners do not always clearly hear the speaker's thoughts, feelings, and intent. Never assume you know what the speaker thinks, feels, or intends. Asking clarifying questions can help you gain a deeper understanding of what the speaker is saying or what the speaker means by his or her words. Asking questions can also support the speaker in getting clear about the topic. Common clarify-ing questions include:

- Can you say more about that?
- Can you give me an example of what you mean?
- Could you tell me how you are feeling when you say that?
- What is behind your strong words?
- You sound really upset. What's that about?

SHARE HUNCHES OR INKLINGS

As a coach, I often get inklings of what the client is talking about. An inkling is a vague insight or suspicion about something. Inklings come to me like an intuitive flash. In reality, inklings or hunches are the prod-uct of the marriage between good listening and experience. I will of-ten share my hunch and then invite the client to either discredit or affirm it—giving evidence for each.

TAKE NOTES

I have found that making sparse notes helps me to focus on the client's words. If I try to take thorough notes, though, I get caught up in what

I am writing and miss the gist of what the person is saying. My own thoughts, questions, or ideas can also distract me from listening. If a thought occurs to me while a client is speaking—a question, challenge, resource, or exercise—I write it down in the right-hand margin of my notepaper and, if appropriate, raise it later in the session.

Become the Dance

Dancers learn both the steps of each dance and the techniques that will support them in being strong, healthy dancers. The best dancers learn the techniques and the steps so well that they can dance without thought. They enter into the process and in a sense *become* the dance itself. A similar thing happens for me when I write. In some blessed moments, I get so engaged in telling the story that I forget to worry about the details—the grammar and the form and content that I have learned and practiced for years. I cannot hear the college students screaming outside my office window (or my own children's matching shouts outside my door). In these moments, I get the sense that God's spirit is with me, supporting me in doing what God has called me to do.

Supportive listening takes practice. We need to learn the techniques and let go of our bad habits. But, in time, we become like the dancer or the writer, entering into the conversation and instinctively, intuitively moving with its rhythm. We do not think so hard or worry very much. Instead, we let God's spirit move over and within our conversations—gracing us with the ability to listen well.

Try

For this exercise you will need a partner. Ideally, it will be the person you are working through this book with. Set aside one to two hours for this exercise. You will need to be in a private place where you can talk openly. In each of the first two phases of the exercise, you will tell each other a story about your life. It is helpful if you use a story that the other person has never heard.

1. While your partner tells a story, practice as many of the poor listening skills as possible. Switch roles. When you have each had a turn, take a short break.

2. Your partner will tell another story. This time, practice as many of the supportive listening skills as possible. Switch roles.
3. Reflect on the following questions:

- What emotions did you experience as the teller in each of the above situations?
- What emotions did you experience as the listener in each of the above situations?
- What did you find difficult in each of the above exercises? In what way?
- What are some of the things you appreciated about being supportively listened to?
- Give feedback to your partner. What did he or she do especially well as a listener?
- What did you gain when you were the supportive listener?
- What did you learn about your own listening habits from the above exercise?

Talk

1. Review the list of poor listening skills. Name and describe others.
2. Review the list of supportive listening skills. Name and describe others.
3. Share an experience when you struggled to listen to someone. What happened? What would you do differently now?
4. Share an experience when someone listened well to you. What happened? What did they do that was especially helpful?

---

24 ❀ Practice Silence

A time to keep silence, and a time to speak.

Ecclesiastes 3:7

I used to be uncomfortable with silence. In my first years as a parish pastor, when I invited the congregation to keep silence during the

weekly prayers, I counted out the time in my head—10, 30, 60 seconds. The time crawled by. I wanted and needed to move forward, to
get to the next thing I had to do. I could hear the wiggles of fidgety
children and impatient adults. I forced myself to experience the discomfort of being still, of facing my need to fill every moment with
words. I made myself listen for the Holy One in those brief moments
of silence—but mostly all I heard was my own restless spirit and anxious thoughts.

Silence doesn't scare me so much anymore. As a coach, it has
become a valuable tool in the work I do with clients. Primarily, the
practice of keeping silence keeps me from morphing into Molly McFixit.
As a coach who began her career in parish ministry, I am afflicted with
the "helping" gene. When my clients hurt, I want to comfort them. My
first instinct is always to be helpful—to find a way to fix their problems. But as a coach, I know that clients learn to take responsibility
for their own lives by sitting with the mess they have created or tripped
over and then choosing how to cope with it. When I feel the urge to
comfort or fix, I sit on my hands and shut up. Sometimes the client
ups the ante by asking me to step in. "What should I do?" he might
ask. Or, "How do I make this right?" she might ask. Of course I have an
idea—sometimes several. Instead I ask, "What do you think?" and then
I count as the moments of silence tick by. It takes time—sometimes
lots of it—and often the client will try more than once to hook me into
fixing. But in time the client steps in to play.

A second benefit of practicing silence is that it keeps me from
imposing my agenda on the client. As a coach, I certainly hold buckets full of hopes and dreams for my clients. I care about them and
want to see them succeed. But my hopes and dreams are just that—
mine. I might have ideas (even good ones) about what my clients
need. Many clients come to coaching expecting that I have an agenda
or a program to give them. And I could do that, easily. But I have
noticed that the clients who do the best work are the ones who set
their own agenda and work toward achieving it. One client of mine
struggled over a busy schedule that got in the way of some of her life
passions. "I don't know what I should do—give up or find a way to do
it all or what. What should I do?" she pleaded. I had some ideas. I
could have set forth an agenda that would fix it in a way that worked
for me. Instead I asked, "What do you think?" We sat silently for many
minutes as she struggled with what to do next. Finally, she came up

with a starting place: "I think I need some sorting mechanism to decide what works and what doesn't in my schedule." Bingo! We had an agenda, and it came from her.

Third, the practice of silence is essential in the face of life's deep questions and sorrows. Words sometimes fail us. Words do not always adequately embrace life's richest moments. What do we say in the face of death? How do we answer the deepest spiritual questions—who am I, what has God called me to do, or who has God called me to love? These situations and questions tend to be the heart and soul of both ministry and coaching. Inside them, silent presence can be a healing balm. I spoke with a client who was struggling to understand and to grieve the end of a significant relationship. She spoke and cried and spoke some more. I asked some questions. Mostly, though, I practiced silence. Though I was intensely present to her story, I wanted her to have the space to feel what she was experiencing without having to apologize for it or rush to a place of closure.

In my coaching work, silence has become a holy place where I am wholly present and without anxiety. Still, I know that silence has a contrary side. The practice of silence can be an act of passive aggression. We refuse to participate in a group conversation. We give another person the silent treatment. We refuse to provide answers or opinions. Sometimes our silence is coupled with self-deprecating remarks like, "You wouldn't care what I had to say anyway." At other times we use aggressive statements, "I refuse to speak because when I do you twist my words." Our silence is the tool we use to convey a variety of messages:

I am angry with you.
I dislike you.
I do not care what happens.
I am bored.
I am disappointed in you.
I am confused.
I am too tired to fight.
I wish you would notice me.

Obviously, this side of silence is not holy. This sort of silence is aggressive, manipulative, and hurtful. This type of silence needs to be confronted. Asking the person who is silent what their silence is about can be helpful. If the person refuses to answer, we can move on. We tried to engage and the person refused to respond. It is not healthy or helpful to cajole a person out of silence.

Probably the most famous biblical passage about silence is Elijah's encounter with God at Mount Horeb. Elijah looked for God in many fierce displays of nature only to encounter God in silence. The passage reads, "Now there was a great wind, so strong that it was splitting mountains and breaking rocks in pieces before the Lord, but the Lord was not in the wind; and after the wind an earthquake, but the Lord was not in the earthquake; and after the earthquake a fire, but the Lord was not in the fire; and after the fire a sound of sheer silence" (1 Kings 19:11-12). Sometimes in our anxiety to find God, we talk too much. This happens when we get together with other believers but also in our time alone. We ask questions, propose theologies, and offer words of comfort. When we get quiet, we face the anxiety and discomfort that often bubbles up inside the unfilled spaces of life. Like Elijah, we encounter God inside these silences.

Try

Take a 24-hour silent retreat. Abstain from speaking; listening to the radio, compact discs, or tapes; watching television; reading or writing; using computers, personal digital assistants (PDAs), or cell phones; and any other practice that engages you with speech, music, or words. When you finish, reflect on the following questions:

- What feelings did you experience during the 24-hour retreat? How did your feelings change?
- What were the hardest practices to give up? Why?
- What did you learn about yourself?
- How might this experience inform your relationship with other people?

Talk

1. Talk about your experience making a silent retreat. How did it affect your work or life?

2. Talk about the role of silence in your life and ministry. In what ways has it been helpful? In what ways has it caused harm?

3. Talk about the ways you deal with people who use silence as a tool to hurt other people.

25 ❀ Prophesy

I could have been a priest instead of a prophet. The priest has a book with the words set out. Old words, known words, words of power. Words that are always on the surface. Words for every occasion. The words work. They do what they're supposed to do; comfort and discipline. The prophet has no book. The prophet is a voice that cries in the wilderness, full of sounds that do not always set into meaning.

Jeanette Winterson, *Oranges Are Not the Only Fruit*

My young daughter sat on my lap, facing me. I was speaking with her. She did not like what I had to say. She tried to educate me: "Mommy, you're supposed to say I love you." When that didn't work, she touched my lips and said, "Mommy, I like you better when you say nothing." You're not the only one, I thought!

Hearing the truth is not always a pleasant thing. It may uncover the less-than-beautiful parts of our behavior. It calls us to be accountable for our lives. It pushes us toward choices that may be uncomfortable or even frightening. In the book of Isaiah, the prophet characterized the people of Judah in this way: "For they are a rebellious people, faithless children, children who will not hear the instruction of the Lord; who say to the seers, 'Do not see'; and to the prophets, 'Do not prophesy to us what is right; speak to us smooth things, prophesy illusions.'" (Isa. 30:9-10). My daughter preferred that I not speak; the people of Judah wished blindness for the seers. They wanted the prophets to flatter them, to tell stories that would flow smoothly over them instead of truths that would knock them over like ocean waves.

As a coach, I've found it necessary to leave my priestly role behind—much like the character in the above quote from Jeanette
Winterson's book. This means that I rarely use the old words, the
words of "comfort and discipline," even though clients and others I
meet may expect it. I'm still an ordained minister, after all. When
people hear I'm a pastor, they stop using profanity. They tell me the
things *they* think I want to hear (how much they go to church, how
often they read their Bible). They look to me to say the right words,
the truisms that have come to be associated with ministers. (God
won't give you more than you can handle. When God closes a door,
God opens a window.) I can tell my clients are talking to "Pastor Rochelle" instead of "Coach Rochelle" when they preface their words with
phrases like:

> "I know that this isn't the right thing to say, but . . ."
> "To be politically correct, I'd have to tell you that I want . . ."
> "I know I *should* say . . ."

When I can, I stop the speakers at the ellipsis. "Red light," as my
kids would say. I can tell the client the politically correct thing (Yes,
you should stay in your ministry position for at least three years; yes,
you should work 55 hours a week). I can offer truisms (It must be God's
will). But I don't. In the coaching relationship, I am not the defender of
the status quo. I will not be the one who tells the client what they
"should" do—based on the agenda of an institution, a theological frame-
work, or even my own ideology. I will, however, share my inklings. In
that way, I function more like a prophet than a priest with my clients.

The root of the Hebrew word for *prophet* means, "to bubble forth,
as from a fountain." The word almost has the sense of an uncontrol-
lable utterance, like a belch. Coaches pay attention to their inklings,
the whispers of God in their ears. An inkling is an unbidden nudge. It
bubbles up or springs forth on its own. It cannot be teased out. It
simply appears. Inklings are like tiny prophecies, small chunks of truth
that describe the situation or suggest a direction for the future. In
seminary, a friend shared her inkling with me: "You can do this seminary thing—but I think you'll eventually end up writing books." It was
an odd thing to say. She knew I loved books, that I created stories for

her children. She didn't know that I wrote. But the words popped out anyway. That's what an inkling does—it appears.

Often these inklings come to me when a client is speaking, but only if I am listening well and not formulating a response in my head. When I first began coaching, I needed to work on dismissing the priestly thoughts I had cultivated over the years as a pastor. Most of us get inklings about our own lives. They often come when we are doing something relatively repetitive and mindless—like walking, folding towels, washing dishes, or knitting. In time and with practice, we will learn to pay attention to these inklings for ourselves, then for the people we minister to.

Love is the most important ingredient in prophesying. There's a guy in town who prophesies. He pasted large prophetic messages all over his big black station wagon. He drives around town shouting out of a public address system. His words always condemn. Little of what he says communicates love. When Jesus shared his inklings, he did so with love and compassion. When the rich man approached him asking how to inherit eternal life (Mark 10:17-22), Jesus knew the problem. Before Jesus shared his inkling, he chose to love the man, "Jesus, looking at him, loved him and said . . ." (Mark 10:21a). We need to pray for the same compassion, the same willingness to speak the whispers of the Holy Spirit out of God's love.

Try

1. For one week, spend 15 minutes a day in silence. If it helps, do something repetitive like walking or crocheting. Pay attention to the inklings that come to you. Ask of each one, "Is this a priestly word? A story I have created? A truth?"

    In the same week, pay attention to the inklings that come to you while engaged in conversation. Ask these questions of each one, "Is this a priestly word? Does this reflect my agenda in some way? Is it true?"

    In what ways does spending time in silence, listening for God's whispers, change the way you experience life?

2. After you have done both of the above tasks for a week, practice sharing your inklings in conversation. Then reflect:

- How were they received?
- In what ways did it change the way you listened to the conversation?
- In what ways did it change the conversation?

Talk

1. Discuss the benefits and difficulties of being prophetic within a priestly setting. Share an example of when each was appropriate.
2. Share your thoughts about how love (or its absence) might affect prophecy sharing.
3. Share your experiences of listening for and sharing inklings. What happened? In what ways did it shift your approach to conversations? In what ways did it shift the conversation?

---

26 ⊛ Encourage Accountability

We need not only God's help to lead accountable Christian lives, we also need the support of our faith community. Therefore, the newly baptized are often welcomed with these words: "We receive you as fellow members of the body of Christ, children of the same heavenly Father, and workers with us in the kingdom of God."

"Yes," says the faith community to the newly baptized. Yes, we are one with you in Christ. We're all in this together. As we welcome you, we promise to be accountable to each other as members of the community of faith.

Rochelle Melander and Harold Eppley,
Our Lives Are Not Our Own: Saying "Yes" to God

Jesus was passing through town, on his way to Jerusalem. Ten lepers approached him (Luke 17:11-19). Now they had to keep their distance because by Jewish law they were unclean. So they called out, "Jesus, Master, have mercy on us!" (v. 13).

And Jesus did. He healed ten lepers that day. One of them returned. Only one knelt before Jesus. Only one said thank you. The text says,

"And he was a Samaritan" (v. 16). So, not only had this man been un-touchable because of his illness, he was untouchable to Jesus, a Jew-ish male, because he was a foreigner, an outsider, a Samaritan.

Jesus had some questions. He said, "Were not ten made clean? But the other nine, where are they? Was none of them found to return and give praise to God except this foreigner?" (vv. 17-18).

Jesus showed up to heal ten lepers. He turned around the life of these lepers—from outcast to acceptable, sick to well, broken to whole. One leper returned. One leper showed up to say thanks. Afterwards, after the thank you, after the questions, Jesus said to the foreigner: "Get up and go on your way; your faith has made you well" (v. 19).

This story is about showing up. Jesus showed up to heal. One leper showed up to say thanks. Jesus sent him on his way to show up for the rest of his life. Our life is about "showing up" as well. At my church, we talk a lot about showing up—for school, for church, for your life, your kids, your family, and your friends. During the children's sermon one Sunday, the pastor invited a young girl to stand up. She is a fifth grader at the neighborhood school, just around the corner from the church. The pastor congratulated Gabrielle on having achieved perfect attendance since she entered school at three years old. This is a kid who knows how to show up! The pastor and the congregation honored Gabrielle and her parents for being responsible, for doing what was necessary so that Gabrielle could show up every day for school. That morning, Gabrielle stood as a reminder to all of us that much can be accomplished when we show up.

Life is about showing up, too. Showing up may not sound like such a big deal. But showing up is crucial to any endeavor. In high school, I marched with the band for six summers. We were known as the award-winning Marching Blues. We even captured a place in the Cherry Blos-som Festival Parade in Washington, D.C. My nonmarching friends heard about the trip and said, "Wow, you're lucky." Luck had nothing to do with it. We won awards and placements in parades by showing up. Every summer morning for six summers I dragged my butt out of bed to march around town at 7:30 AM. I wasn't the only one. My classmates showed up, too. We showed up because we felt accountable to one another, to our band teacher, and to the art we created together.

In our lives, accountability happens on at least four levels. We are accountable to God, ourselves, our significant others, and our com-munity. In the coaching relationship, we become accountable to one another—promising to show up and pay attention. Still, clients are not ultimately accountable to their coach. I do not want them to accomplish their goals in order to please me. Instead, I am present as a reminder to them to be accountable to God and to God's call to show up for their lives. I ask my clients: how is God calling you to show up for your life? I want to know how my clients are honoring their promises to themselves—perhaps to make art or to eat well. We think together about how they can keep their commitments to both their significant others and their communities.

Accountability Tools

As a coach, I use several tools to support my clients in showing up for their lives: regular coaching sessions, e-mail updates, goal setting, pointing out traps, and encouraging them.

SET REGULAR COACHING SESSIONS

Most people respond better to external rather than internal deadlines. We are more likely to finish writing a sermon if there are going to be 200 people sitting in the pews who will care very much if we show up. It may be difficult to write a book if the only pressure is our own desire to put our thoughts onto paper. In this case, the coach and coaching sessions can become a form of external pressure. In addition, clients working on specific goals often seek out a buddy or group with a similar goal for daily or weekly support. For example, one of my clients wanted help committing to daily exercise. She found it helpful to have a walking buddy.

INVITE E-MAIL UPDATES

Most clients choose to report their progress to me via e-mail before each session. They write from prompts such as:

- This is what I accomplished this month.
- This is what I hoped to accomplish but didn't.
- This is what I want to work on in the next session.

Clients who seek additional support often arrange to e-mail me between sessions as a way of staying accountable. For example, one client who was working to finish several papers between monthly coaching sessions e-mailed me each time he finished a paper.

ENCOURAGE GOAL SETTING

Each client comes into coaching with one or two goals to accomplish. In addition, I encourage clients to set yearly and monthly goals. We regularly review these goals. Goal setting helps clients avoid getting stuck inside a life that isn't working anymore.

POINT OUT TRAPS

People who are accountable take responsibility for themselves and their actions. People who avoid or have difficulty with accountability often fall into several traps. These include:

Making excuses: I could have accomplished my goal of exercising every day if the weather was better.

Blaming others: If my coach were better, I would have achieved my goals.

Avoiding: I need to spend this session complaining about work; I can't focus on my goals.

When we get inside these traps, we get stuck. We cannot achieve our goals when we avoid taking responsibility for ourselves. My job is to point out the traps and nudge the client back to the place of responsibility. For example, I might say to the excuse-making client, "So what choices might you make so that you could exercise no matter what the weather?" This question reminds the client that ultimately she is in control of her exercise—not the weather. The goal is to get the client to *manage* his or her own life.

ENCOURAGE

When Gabrielle was honored at church for her perfect attendance, the whole congregation clapped. I am certain that the applause was encouraging to Gabrielle and the other children who hope to follow in her footsteps. Perhaps the next time it is cold, the memory of that applause will encourage them to get out of bed and go to school!

In my own life, it sure helps to know that people care about what happens to me. When I was struggling to start this book, a friend wrote, "It will be lovely when it's finished and it will be a help to a lot of people." Her words reminded me of my goal (finishing the book) and my purpose (to help others) as well as encouraging me about its quality (lovely). Now when I sit down to the blank paper, I hear these encouraging words—and the writing goes a bit easier.

As a coach, I hope to give the same encouragement to my clients. I want to remind them of their goals and their purpose. I want them to know that I believe in them—and their ability to accomplish what they desire to do. I want to give them applause for a job well done.

A Final Word

I want my clients to know that no matter what happens—what they do or fail to do—Jesus will love them. In the story of Jesus healing the ten lepers, nine lepers failed to show up to say thank you to Jesus. Only one returned. I am struck that the response of the lepers—grateful or not—did not change the fact that Jesus healed ten lepers. Jesus shows up whether we do or not. For my clients—for all of us—this means that we have nothing to lose. Jesus blesses us no matter what we do. So we can show up for our life and see what happens. We have everything to gain.

Try

Think about one area of your life where you struggle to be accountable. Together with your partner, take turns sharing stories about this struggle and using the tools above to support and encourage one another to "show up."

Talk

1. What other biblical stories teach about accountability?
2. What is the relationship between accountability and grace?
3. Talk about how being accountable has supported you in "showing up" for the life God has called you to.
4. As a spiritual leader, in what ways do you encourage and support the people you minister to and with to be accountable?

27 ⊛ Encourage Discernment

> Sometimes we must leave our fixed abode and become sojourners in
> uncertainty. We need to learn that no place, however hallowed in
> our memories, is more holy than any other.
>
> Elizabeth Watson, twentieth century
> Quaker, feminist, and spiritual writer

> One does not discover new lands without consenting to lose sight of
> the shore.
>
> André Gide, twentieth century
> writer, humanist, and moralist

I love clarity. When I am beginning anything new—a book, a job, a relationship—I usually spend too much time pining for a road map. Maybe because my freelance life often leaves me feeling adrift, I have frequent conversations with people about the experience of being adrift. For many of us, the process of discernment means setting sail from the land of clarity. We become caught between what we once knew (our fixed abode) and what we have yet to discover. As Watson says, we become sojourners in uncertainty. Scary!

Most clients seek coaches because they seek clarity around an issue or a part of their life. They want to practice discernment. People of faith often seek out spiritual leaders to help them discern what God is asking of them or calling them to do. In working with clients on discernment, I have found the following approaches useful.

Affirm the Process

From the outside, most everyone's life looks like smooth sailing. We do not know the secret terrors people confront each day. I remember a colleague once put this Henry Wadsworth Longfellow quote on the bottom of each of his e-mails: "If we could read the secret history of our enemies, we should find sorrow and suffering enough to disarm all hostility." Because we don't always share our struggles with one another, people can feel as if they are the only ones who have ever gone through this sort of process of discernment. One of the first things

I do with clients is affirm them for their courage in setting sail! Moving forward is always hard. I ask clients to write kind things to themselves on sticky notes and put them everywhere. If they don't have kind things to say, I say them and make them write them down! I encourage them to repeat this mantra from Julian of Norwich: "All will be well, all will be well, all manner of things will be well." It takes great bravery to even look at one's life and I commend them for doing so!

Encourage Balcony Space

Balcony space is a term used by Ronald Heifetz, director of the Leadership Education Project at the John F. Kennedy School of Government, Harvard University. According to Gil Rendle and Alice Mann of the Alban Institute, "Balcony space describes taking a position sufficiently distant from day-to-day operations and worry in order to see the larger picture. The opposite of balcony space is *reactive space*, in which the leader must constantly deal with the immediate person or problem that confronts him or her."[1]

For me, balcony space is like time on an airplane—time when people and responsibilities of daily work and home life disappear. There are not piles of dirty laundry that need to be washed, phones that need to be answered, and e-mail that needs to be read and responded to. Balcony space creates time, room, and energy for us to ask new questions, dream new possibilities, and discover new solutions.

In a sense, coaching time is balcony space. It's set apart enough from daily life to provide the opportunity for coach and client to look at the client's life and begin to see it from more than one perspective. On top of the coaching time, though, I encourage clients who are in the discernment process to make time for balcony space each week. This is time spent outside home or work environments in which the client can read, write, think, and process his or her life. Princeton scholar Julian Jaynes suggests that three locations inspire us the most: bed, bath, and bus.[2] I encourage clients to spend balcony time resting, near water, or on a moving vehicle.

Examine the Details

As I packed client folders in a bag, my daughter handed me her Dora the Explorer magnifying glass. "Take this," she said.

"Why?" I asked.

"It might help you find things."

I did take it. I showed it to each of my clients. One of the things we do in coaching is look at one's life using the magnifying glass of our conversation. Often a coaching process that is about discernment will begin with the crisis, what led the client to seek coaching. From there we will look at both what is and what might be. Each of these bigger themes gets broken down into a series of smaller themes. Smaller themes and life experiences get put under the magnifying glass and explored in any way that is helpful to the client. Remember, the client always directs the process. The client can say no to any coaching suggestion. For example, one client came into coaching to discern a new career direction. In the first coaching session, he told me that his rocky marriage was affecting his discernment process *and* he was not ready to talk about it. I suggested that if it was affecting his discernment—it might be helpful to look at it. He said no. So we didn't look at that part of his life until he was ready.

Time management speakers used to tell a riddle about how to fit a series of objects into a glass jar: large stones, small stones, pebbles, sand, and water. The solution to the riddle was a metaphor for setting priorities—if you start with the big pieces of your life (the large stones)—then everything fits. Using this metaphor, I encourage my clients to put the biggest pieces of their lives under the magnifying glass first. Questions that might be raised include the following:

- What are the big pieces in your life (for example, life partner, location, work)?
- In what ways do these pieces work? Give examples.
- In what ways do they not work? Give examples.
- How does each of these parts of your life define who you are?
- How is each of these parts of your life inconsistent with how you define yourself?
- Are these the pieces you want to keep in your life?
- What about them do you want to keep?
- What about them do you need to let go of?
- What purpose do these pieces of your life serve?
- In what ways is this part of your life pleasing to you? To someone else?

- What excites you about this conversation?
- What scares you?

Offer a Reality Check

Magnifying glasses, like those mirrors that make prominent every fine line and gaping pore on our faces, tend to connect the client to reality. But sometimes clients are so used to saying what will please their parents, spouse, friends, the institution, or anyone in the room that they don't even know when they are telling the truth or lying. They need to conduct a reality check. But how? How do you get the client who is a practiced political schmoozer to tell the truth? Here are a few ideas:

- I simply ask: Are you telling me the truth?
- I ask, "What if status, money, your parents, your spouse, what anyone else you love thought, the church's polity, all of that external stuff didn't matter—then what would you do?"
- I mirror their story back to them, "I hear you saying that this is what you believe to be true." Then I ask a question I borrowed from coach Martha Beck, "Tell me how I'm wrong."
- If a client is intuitive and reads situations with his or her "gut," I ask them what their gut knows about this. Does your gut feel like this is a true statement?
- If the client is more of a sensor—someone who makes decisions based on evidence and external stimuli, I ask them to tell me how they know when something is right or not right. What sort of evidence do they use to discern? Then I ask them to use that tool to tell me what is true.

Observe Patterns

Life coach Debbie Ford has observed that we create stories about our lives when we are young (I am the victim; I am a loser; I am a user), then we look for situations that fit our stories. In fact, we repeat these stories again and again and again. Clients in the discernment process are usually hoping to move into new territory, into a place that is healthier than that defined by their old stories. To do that, I encourage clients to think about the patterns in their lives.

I often invite clients to use an exercise described in great detail in the book I wrote with my husband, Harold Eppley, called *The Spiritual Leader's Guide to Self-Care*. The exercise invites the client to create a map of his or her life. From birth to the present, the client records visually each major event in his or her life. Some people who have done this exercise with me have used a sort of graph-type representation of high and low points. One person represented his life with a tall building. Still others have made it look like a hiking trail, allowing it to branch off into winding paths or to follow the straight and narrow. I've used this exercise with many groups over the past several years. Most participants get a sense of the patterns of their lives: high points followed low ones, best friends appeared at the worst times, and what looked like wandering was actually purposeful. I want the clients who use this exercise to be able to reflect on questions like:

- What stories or patterns repeat in my life story?
- What sorts of roles do I play in my life story?
- What factors have gone into my decision making?
- What self-sabotaging actions have I done? How many times?
- What healthy practices have I engaged in? How much?
- In what places do I now see that God was present to me? How?

Encourage Prayer

When I was in seminary, we had long conversations with our professors about the process of discerning a call. One of our professors made it utterly clear that our denomination only recognized the external call—that which comes from the community of faith. Although he thought it might be good to also have an internal call—the kind that makes your soul leap for joy—it wasn't necessary in our tradition.

Over the years, I have come to disagree with that professor. I have seen the absolute necessity of having an internal sense of call as well as an external one. In my work as a coach, I have been interested in supporting clients in paying just as much attention to the internal discernment process as the external discernment process. Prayer is an important tool in our discernment. In prayer we place our dilemma in God's hands. As we wander through our maze, we know that God goes with us. Like a shadow, God sticks by us during the (sometimes) confusing process of figuring out where to go next in life.

Since adulthood I have struggled to pray regularly. Most of my prayers tend to be those 911 calls to God, "Help! I'm lost!" Several years ago I actually made a 911 call by accident. I was trying to call a similar number and failed. Minutes later, a fire truck, ambulance, and police car showed up and the officers wouldn't leave until they could clearly see that I was OK (and wasn't going to be hurt by an angry husband or intruder). This comforted me. It reminded me that God shows up not only in response to my 911 prayers but also to my mutters of frustration, meandering thoughts, late-night tears, and complaints to others. God shows up whether I dial the right number or not.[3]

Do What Works

There are more ways to discern than there is time. I'm always collecting tools for discernment and inviting clients to do the same. In some cases, the tools I offer most readily, such as the ones described in this chapter, are the tools that work for me. They will not work for every client. I ask each client to first try a tool that I suggest. If it doesn't work for them, I invite them to abandon it in favor of something that does work. In the end, if we cannot find tools that work, sometimes it is because I am not the right coach for this particular client. I will happily work with the client to find a coaching relationship that fits.

A Final Word

When I was pregnant with my first child, my husband and I took a trip to Rehobeth Beach, Delaware. To get there, we had to cross the four-point-three-mile Chesapeake Bay Bridge. I hate crossing bridges. They terrify me. All I wanted was to get to the other side. As my husband marveled at the view, I closed my eyes and said, "Please, just keep *your* eyes on the road!" Crossing bridges is a good metaphor for moving through a discernment process. In the midst of it, I encourage my clients to keep their eyes open. Seek beauty each day. In the spring, I make a daily morning pilgrimage to a house that has dedicated its front lawn to bulbed flowers. This riot of color gives me such hope and joy each day. People in the midst of discernment need hope. Encourage them to find it—in flowers, in the smile of a child, or in the tight grip of an elder's hand. It will make the process seem less scary!

Try

As a leader, it can be helpful to see how discernment tools work in your own life before using them to help other people. Choose one or more of the tools above and use it as a way of discerning what you need to do or decide in an area of your life.

Talk

1. Quakers use "clearness committees" to practice discernment. What biblical verses, theological ideas, or practical tools from your own spiritual tradition do you use with those who are seeking discernment?
2. Describe a time that you were in the process of discernment. What tools helped you? What didn't?

28 ❂ Tackle the Tough Stuff

Sooner or later we will come to the edge of all that we can control and find life, waiting there for us.

Rachel Naomi Remen, *My Grandfather's Blessings*

I'm a member of a cabinet, a four-person coaching group. We meet monthly on the telephone. Each of us speaks for twenty minutes about our struggles and successes and then the rest of the group can question, challenge, or encourage us. I don't know about the other participants, but I signed on for the encourage part. That and the accountability piece. I always do better if I know that people are expecting me to do the work. Accomplishing stuff on my own is more difficult. So there I was at the second meeting, chatting away about my goals, expecting the response to be a cake walk when—*Wham!*—the conversation turned into a pie toss. Each cabinet member hurled challenges at me. Kindly, gently, but very firmly they questioned me about the stuff I had said—stuff that most other friends would have bought without any kind of guarantee or warranty. These women did not. It peeved me. How dare they doubt that I was being truthful with myself? My ruse went on for several months. They weren't deceived, but I continued to try to deceive myself and others. Finally, I was able to face the truth of what they had said and make some necessary changes.

Hearing the truth may be difficult. But it is even harder to have an authentic relationship without committing to telling and hearing the truth. In my first call, I was troubled by what people indicated they wanted from me: niceties. They wanted me to affirm the status quo no matter what it was. Pastoral care and counseling professor Patricia Davis, in her book *Beyond Nice: The Spiritual Wisdom of Adolescent Girls*, wrote this about the problem of nice: "Niceness is the opposite of spirituality. Niceness is, in fact, the opposite of what is required to build any genuine relationship—with God or with others. While niceness can smooth superficial human interactions, it is devastating to true intimacy. Niceness requires putting away genuine feelings, avoiding conflict, swallowing hurts, denying pain, and being untruthful."[1]

The effective coaching relationship requires that participants tell the truth. In part, this means that the coach commits to confronting the client on the tough stuff. This might include discussing a client's self-destructive habits or behaviors, helping a client face the truth about an illusion he or she holds, or talking with the client about getting serious medical or psychological support. This chapter considers some approaches for dealing with tough stuff.

Covenant

All relationships have rules. The rules of most relationships are not written in a contract or covenant. Still, inside the dance of relationship, people make all sorts of agreements, occasionally conscious but mostly unconscious. In some relationships, every topic is fair game while in another the parties might only talk about their jobs or their health. Some relationships allow for emotional intimacy, others do not. Some tolerate one person being the center of attention all of the time while another might demand parity. In the coaching relationship, the parameters of the relationship are set up in a contract or covenant. Both parties agree to behave in a certain way. One of the things most coaches promise and require in all relationships is truth telling. Coaches vow not only to tell the truth but also to confront "the hard stuff." Clients promise to tell the coach if something he or she says is uncomfortable or unhelpful. Agreeing to these principles lays the foundation for a healthy relationship.

Some congregations and congregational working groups have also developed covenants or codes of conduct. These agreements support spiritual leaders and congregational members in having healthier relationships.[2]

Do It Sooner

In her book, *Fierce Conversations: Achieving Success at Work and Life One Conversation at a Time*, consultant Susan Scott lists this as one of her seven principles of conversation: "Tackle your toughest challenge today."[3] When it comes to confronting difficult things, waiting to talk about it often buys anxiety and not much else. When a difficult issue comes up, confront it right away. One's silence in the face of unhelpful behavior can seem like tacit acceptance.

Use "I" Statements

"You are driving too slow. You do everything wrong. You can't be my mommy. You're fired. You need to get me a new mommy." My daughter and I were on our way to visit a friend. Shortly after this speech, my daughter named this friend her "special new mommy." When we arrived, I was tired of the accusations and quite ready to trade jobs with my friend as my daughter had suggested.

Evidently, my daughter never got the memo on "I" statements. She was caught in the deadly "you" trap. "You" statements place the responsibility for the speaker's thoughts, feelings, and needs on the shoulders of the hearer. Hearing a blast of "you" statements has always made me feel like I'm a magician's assistant, pressed flat against the wall while the magician tosses knives at me. You! You! You! There's no escaping, nowhere to turn, no one else to blame. The spotlight is on you!

"I" statements allow the speaker to share what she or he is observing, experiencing, feeling, thinking, needing, or desiring. Examples include: "I think you are driving too slow. I feel like you do things wrong. I need a new mommy." Phrasing an observation or a need with an "I" statement provides space for the hearer to listen to the content of the message and also to hear the care of the speaker. "I" statements are especially important when the content of the message may be challenging for the hearer to absorb.

Be Specific

"A lot of people are mad at you, Pastor."

"You're hard to talk to."

"You don't seem spiritual enough."

These are the kinds of accusations that drive me mad. Besides being phrased in a "you statement," they are about as wide as the side of a farmer's barn. Because these accusations are so general, they are absolutely useless. They provide no real information. They give no indication as to how the hearer might improve. They are simply too big and general to be helpful.

Specific feedback with examples can lead more quickly to change. So "You're hard to talk to" might become, "When I came in to talk to you last week, I wanted you to sit down and pay attention to me instead of answering the phone and doing office chores." The second statement is actually something clear and fixable.

Avoid Labels and Categories

"You're such a slacker."

"You act that way because you're an introvert."

"If you were younger, you'd get this."

In confronting difficult issues, using labels or categories as a sort of short cut can be tempting. Labels and categories can provide a picture of what we find difficult, but they are usually pejorative. And while *we* may be clear on why the label describes the situation, the hearer usually isn't. Plus, a label or a category reduces the beautiful individuality of a person to a subset of characteristics. Finally, labels and categories usually are not specific enough to convey helpful information.

Instead, be descriptive, explain your feelings, and ask questions. In the heat of an argument about theology, one of my colleagues called me a "modernist" and a "baby boomer." I had no idea what he meant by the first statement and I didn't get why the second was a slam (and the category didn't quite fit me). He thought it was funny. It seemed unkind to me. I wanted to shoot back, "Well, you're just a postmodern, Gen X slacker looking for someone to blame." I didn't. I can never think that fast. Later I thought saying something like this might have been helpful: "I heard you using labels and categories instead of telling me how or why what I said upset you. It hurt my feelings. I'm wondering if you can tell me what was going on?" This sort of a statement allows the two parties to move the conversation beyond name-calling to a deeper level.

Avoid Making People Wrong

One of my clients complained to her child's school about the fact that his bus had been repeatedly late or absent over the past month. "You should have told us," said the secretary. My client patiently explained that she had mentioned it to her each time she had called to let them know her son would be late for school. "Well, that's not how you make a report," said the secretary. "You should have . . ."

I call this the "you idiot " form of communication. It's when we let another know how wrong and stupid they were for thinking, doing, or assuming something. In my coach training program, instructors encouraged us to avoid the right-wrong continuum when approaching difficult situations. Instead, they taught us to simply describe what is. For example, when a client is consistently late with his or her payment, pointing to the contract and the evidence and declaring them wrong is tempting. "You promised to pay by the first of each month and you haven't." A better approach might be to simply state what is, "I've noticed that your checks have been coming about the middle of the month instead of the beginning of the month. It would be helpful to me to understand what's going on." This opens the conversation without assigning blame.

Get to the Point

So many of the most painful conversations I have had were the ones where someone started by telling me they "had a bone to pick with me," then talked endlessly about nothing and everything while my heart leapt from my chest until finally they told me what I had done to offend them. Yikes! Talk about trying to give another person a heart attack. If you have to have a tough conversation with someone, get to the point. Be clear, concise, and quick. It's like the old Band-Aid analogy—quicker is always better.

Expect Resistance

When I studied family-systems theory, one of my teachers would tell me that when I was experiencing resistance from a client or a family member it was probably because I was on the right track. In other words—I was shaking up the status quo and that was causing anxiety in the system. I imagine it is like fishing. If there's nothing on the end of the line, then there isn't much resistance when you pull on the line. Resistance means that you have caught a fish. In a conversation, resistance can mean that you have hit on a difficult topic.

When my colleague group confronted me, I certainly resisted. I have noticed that my clients have a similar reaction when I confront them with hard truths. They deny the existence of a problem. They refuse to talk about it. They may even cut short the conversation. Or worse, they ignore it and move on. Whatever happens, usually something lodges in their brain. Later, one of my clients said to me, "I was pretty angry with you when you said that. But now I am glad that you did."

Let Go of Your Need to Be Right

In the end, we can only say what we need to say and then let go of everything else—especially our need to be right. The members of my coaching group were kind enough to question me, to confront me with hard stuff. But they didn't seem to need me to react or respond in a certain way. They said their piece, and we moved on. Their willingness to let go of being right gave me the freedom and personal power to allow them to be right.

A Final Word

Jesus told the truth—even when the truth was not popular with his hearers. He drove those who were selling goods out of the temple. He made it clear more than once that he wasn't going to play games with the scribes and Pharisees (see for example Matt. 19:3–12; Matt. 22:15–22; and Luke 20:1–8). He recognized and valued the truthfulness of others, such as the honesty of the Samaritan woman he met at the well in Sychar (John 4:1–42). In Matthew's Gospel, Jesus set forth a method for dealing with difficult behavior within the community of faith (Matt. 18:15–20). His first recommendation was for a person to go alone to the one who had hurt them and speak with them.

The truth can be a scary country. Because we fear the consequences of being truthful, we stay bound to our carefully constructed web of lies and half-truths despite Jesus's words about the truth: "If you continue in my word, you are truly my disciples; and you will know the truth, and the truth will make you free" (John 8:31–32). But healthy relationships must be built on the truth. That is what makes it possible for people to move freely with one another. Yes, it can be painful at times. But in the end, the truthful relationships are the ones we value, not the ones built on politeness and niceties.

Try

Find a partner to role-play a difficult conversation with. Take turns confronting and being confronted. It can be helpful to do the exercise twice, once doing everything wrong and once doing as much right as possible. Afterward, talk about what each of you found helpful. How could each of you improve your skills?

Talk

1. What biblical stories or theological beliefs speak to the practices of telling the truth and having the difficult conversations?

2. Share a story about a difficult conversation that went well. What made it work?

3. What are some things that you have found to be unhelpful in the course of a difficult conversation?

29   ✸   Offer Comfort

Perhaps the most basic skill of the physician is the ability to have comfort with uncertainty, to recognize with humility the uncertainty inherent in all situations, to be open to the ever-present possibility of the surprising, the mysterious, and even the holy, and to meet people there.

Rachel Naomi Remen, My Grandfather's Blessings

For two years I worked as a chaplain at our local children's hospital. My title was Chaplain PRN, an abbreviation often used in medicine that means "as needed." The PRN chaplains worked nights and weekends, wearing beepers in case something happened. It didn't take long to realize that we were never needed for the regular stuff, if there is such a thing as regular stuff at a children's hospital, such as praying with frightened children or sitting with parents while their children underwent tests. Instead, we were always called to the extraordinary situations—serious injuries and sudden deaths. We met family members who had had their whole world turned inside out in seconds. As nun and popular writer Joan Chittister says in her book *Scarred by Struggle, Transformed by Hope,* "Struggle begins with shock. With loss. With radical interruption of what just minutes before had been certain and sure and drowsily eternal. It would never end. It could never end."[1] But it did end. And there I stood, next to family members who had lost so much in the last hours that they couldn't even articulate what they might need from anyone, let alone a stranger.

I walked into each of these situations with some measure of terror. Despite my pleas to God to be useful in the situation, I felt absolutely helpless in the midst of these great tragedies. I could do the things I had been trained to do—listen, hold, pray. I offered talismans—prayer rugs, teddy bears, prayer beads. There were practicalities I could attend to, find their home pastor, bring them beverages, find toys for the siblings. If their child had died, there were prayers and rituals we did as a way to begin saying good-bye. None of these words or actions felt big enough to help heal these enormous, deep wounds. They seemed more along the lines of tossing Band-Aids at a broken leg. As Chittister said, "Other people commiserate, of course, as they watch us struggle with the pain of losing, the meaning of endings, the shock of great change, the emptiness of the present. But they cannot really share our pain because what we have lost, however significant to us, is not really significant to them. What we lose is ours and ours alone: our dream, our hope, our expectation, our property, our identity."[2]

Chittister's words bring me great comfort. They acknowledge what I know to be true: we are often clueless in the face of great suffering. Who we are or what training or life experience has taught us does not matter. Whether we are spiritual leaders, coaches, counselors, hospice workers, members of the faith community, family members, or friends, we all begin from this place of helplessness. Knowing this has helped me understand, first as a spiritual leader and now as a coach, that any good I happen to do depends on God. In my professional role as a coach and in my life as a member of the faith community, I am still called upon to offer comfort. Before I do or say anything, I ask God for help. God is the only one who can bring a measure of peace in these awful moments. As my friend said when speaking about a beloved family member's death, "In the horrible loss we faced, with the burden of grief upon us, what else could we do but seek God's love knowing that God's love was seeking us?"[3] In the midst of suffering and loss, God is the beginning, middle, and end of all help. In many ways, I see that God works through us to extend this help to one another.

Ways to Offer Comfort

Here are some of the tools I use to comfort other people in my work as a coach.

SUPPORTIVE LISTENING
Much of my work centers around listening—bearing witness to the life of another person. When someone is in crisis, this is the most crucial skill we can offer. Whether the crisis is job loss, illness, a tumultuous relationship, death, emerging identity, or midlife

transition, people need to talk. Young adult author Maia Wojciechowska records this phenomenon in her book, *A Single Light*, "[The women] let her moan and cry. They let her talk without interfering, without giving a word of comfort, because they knew that with the talk, the tears, and the moans, her grief would come and go. Later it would leave the woman alone."[4]

Never assume there is someone else who can hear the story; who will listen without judgment; who will be patient in the face of repetition, never saying, "You told me that before;" who will listen with love. Never think that your listening is not enough, that you should be jumping in to fix or advise or say wise things or even quote Jesus. Your listening is one way of telling the person that God loves them, that no matter how they feel their life slipping away from them, no matter what they have done, nothing can change the fact that God's love seeks and embraces them.

PRESENCE

Akin to listening, a ministry of presence is the willingness to sit with a person in crisis through awkward silences, sobbing, anger, frustration, helplessness, and the ugly side of illness. A ministry of presence means that you show up even when you feel helpless, even when being there makes you sick, even when it feels so awkward and frightening that you want to throw up. Feeling comfortable with being present in the midst of someone else's suffering takes time. See chapter 17, "Be a Fierce Presence," which is devoted to this topic.

THE "THOU SHALL NOTS"

We usually learn what doesn't work by doing it. We say the stupidest thing and someone tells us so. We experience that deathly silence in response to our inappropriate question or action. Here are a few things that don't really help when someone is in crisis:

Offering unsolicited advice—especially in areas outside your expertise. If someone asks you what helped you when a parent died, by all means share. The problem occurs when we share advice without the permission of the advisee. Even though my clients have hired me to support them, asking first if I can offer advice, instead of just assuming that they want it, always seems appropriate.

Telling unsolicited horror stories about your own experience of whatever the person is going through. Again, the difficulty is with the word unsolicited. Sometimes people want to hear about your experiences. Sometimes they don't. And you can pretty much guarantee that no one wants to hear a story that ends badly. You know, saying you knew someone who had the same disease and then died young: *not* so helpful!

Taking charge without permission. This is the "I know what you need and I'm going to make sure you get it whether you like it or not" form of so-called comforting. When I was in labor with my second child, I had a nurse that I called, "The Nazi Nurse." She knew best and barked orders according to her own ideas and without any consultation with me. If I hadn't felt like my body was being ripped in two, I might have fired her. Instead I had to add the work of negotiating to the already challenging job of giving birth.

Saying that you know exactly what they are going through when you don't. We empathize with people, and so we say we understand what they are experiencing. But, of course, often we don't and we cannot. We may have similar experiences, but because they are our experiences and we are different people, we cannot really understand another's experience fully. Saying that we cannot imagine their loss is helpful. When my daughter was ill, a friend very helpfully said, "I have only a small window into what this might be like for you." In her words I experienced her sincere empathy and understanding as well as her willingness to admit her limitations.

There will be times when you work with people who are going through similar experiences as you. Letting them know of the parallel and offering either to be a listening ear or to share your story, if they would find it helpful, can be appropriate. In a sense, this is the foundation of support groups. People who have experienced similar life experiences—illnesses, loss, abuse, addiction—gather to tell their stories and console and encourage one another.

Not listening to or respecting the wishes of the person you are ministering to. This might include staying too long; praying when they don't want you to or not praying when they do want you to; or sharing confidences with other people.

Resources

In most situations, as I've mentioned before, I know that my ministry is woefully inadequate. I will sometimes offer resources that extend my ministry beyond my presence. These include prayer tools, media resources, and talismans.

PRAYER TOOLS

Besides praying for those you minister to, provide prayer cards or send specifically chosen prayers to people. I have made it a habit of sending written prayers (either by traditional mail or e-mail) to clients and friends both at times of crisis and during culturally and spiritually significant times, like the beginning of Lent.

MEDIA RESOURCES

Books, articles, films, and music can sometimes speak to the depth of a person's difficult experience. If I have encountered something I think might be helpful to a client, I often will mention it to them or give them a copy of it.

TALISMANS

Stuffed creatures, notes of encouragement, necklaces, stones, shells—any of these things can be helpful reminders of God's love and care, as well as your own care, to the people you work with. At one church I know, the minister gave each person she visited a prayer stone—a smooth stone with a word like hope or peace etched into it. Another congregation makes prayer shawls and gives them to people in crisis. As mentioned in an earlier chapter, I have recently begun stringing prayer beads for friends. When my daughter was ill, a friend brought by a small statue of two angels, mother and daughter. My daughter often holds that statue saying, "This is us, Mommy; this is us!" When I see it, I am reminded of my friend's care for us.

Creature Comforts

What is it they used to say—the way to anyone's heart is through their stomach? In fact, we are powerfully affected by sensory experiences. Who hasn't encountered a familiar childhood smell and felt deeply connected to the past? In times of great stress, creature comforts that engage our senses can be very nurturing. One of the best ways we can support those we minister to is by encouraging them to engage in creature comforts or actually giving them something comforting.

I often ask my clients to tell me how they plan to take care of themselves in the midst of a difficult time. We speak about eating, sleeping, engaging in sensory pleasures (like listening to music or lighting candles), and taking care of their bodies (exercising and getting massages). I take this just as seriously as I take creating and accomplishing any goals. I invite clients to name two or three ways that they will take care of themselves; then ask them to let me know via e-mail if they have done them. Often just taking this seriously is enough to get clients to actually engage in comforting themselves.

From time to time I will give clients something to support them in taking care of themselves. For the most part, these gifts are small and act as tokens, reminding them that engaging in sensory comforts is important. I might give a client a chocolate bar or a small scented candle. My own coach sent me cookies once. Another coach I know gives coffee-shop gift cards—with her reminder to take time for reflection.

A Final Word

There's a quote that I used to keep on my desk as a reminder of God's presence in uncertainty. It went something like, "When you come to the edge of all that you know, you will either be given a place to stand or you will be taught how to fly." In a sense, anything that we do to comfort or care for others is in that place at the edge of all that we know. We depend on God to give us either firm ground or wings.

Try

Review the above list of tools for helping people in the midst of crisis. Choose one or two that you find especially difficult and try to use them this week in your ministry. If you do not have the opportunity to offer comfort this week, ask your partner to role-play this process with you.

Talk

1. Share a good experience of someone helping you in a time of difficulty. What did they do that worked? What did it teach you about comforting other people?

2. Share a less-than-helpful experience of someone helping you. What did they do that didn't work? What did their mistakes teach you about comforting others?

3. List additional tools for comforting. Also make a list of the ways we fail to offer comfort by our actions and words.

4. Share with one another the biblical passages, hymn texts, prayers, and other resources that you have found useful in helping others.

---

30 ✹ Practice Curiosity

Befriending life is less a matter of knowledge than a question of wisdom. It is not about mastering life, controlling it or exerting our will over it, no matter how well intentioned our will may be. Befriending life is more about harmlessness than it is about control. Harmlessness requires connection. It means listening to life from the place in us that is connected to the wholeness around us. The place in us that is also whole.

Rachel Naomi Remen, *My Grandfather's Blessings*

"Why did her mommy name her Holly?"

"What did you have for lunch? I had skapettios!"

"Why did you say that?"

These questions come from my four-year-old daughter. She has the gift of curiosity and she uses it regularly. It doesn't matter where we are, grocery store, doctor's office, church, or hair salon. The subject of her curiosity could be a person, place, or thing. The object of her questions might be a family member, friend, or stranger. When she wonders, she asks. She explores. She's a curious girl.

As we consider practicing curiosity, we need to address our conversational habits. We develop conversational patterns throughout our lives. Most of us have developed ways of approaching or responding to people in conversations that get in the way of being curious. Learning to express curiosity is a two-step process. First, we need to notice and interrupt our automatic responses to people in conversations. Second, we need to learn how to offer prompts and ask good questions. This chapter will cover the first step, noticing our automatic responses; the next chapter will be about asking good questions.

Many of us were socialized not to express our curiosity about other people. Our questions about an adult's burgeoning belly or gold teeth were hushed. Later we may have been told, "It's rude to ask people things like that." Our parents warned us with adages like, "Curiosity killed the cat" or even, "A bird in the hand is worth two in the bush." As adults, we may recall these childhood cautions and hesitate to ask questions. Although we feel curious about those we relate with, our automatic response is to remain silent. We fear that our questions are either impolite or nosy.

As trained professionals, we may approach conversations with our own agenda—something that needs to be expressed, discovered, answered, or decided. As busy people, we might want to get to the point of the conversation fairly quickly, exchanging information or making a decision. Our agendas and schedules might impede our ability to be open to other people. We need to know when we can hold the meeting. We want to learn how our colleague is doing in the midst of a recent loss. Stating an objective for a conversation can help it to go well. Still, our agendas can narrow conversations and halt curiosity. For example, many of us approach new acquaintances with the agenda of categorizing or contextualizing. Putting people in categories can help us see the very basics of how we relate to one another and the world. It also makes it difficult to learn who another person is aside from these narrow categories. I met a young woman at a Protestant writer's conference. Given the context, I assumed that she was a life-long member of the denomination we were meeting with. Later over lunch, I learned that she simply worked for the denomination. She had grown up in the Unitarian Universalist church and still considered herself to be a member of that denomination. She both fit and didn't fit the category I had assigned her to. Asking questions helped me to better understand her and opened up the possibilities for us to actually connect with one another.

Most of us have habitual ways of responding to people that grow out of our own needs and values. We do what the golden rule recommends, treat others as we wish we would be treated, often giving others the kind of attention and response that we desire for ourselves.

We may also respond to people in ways that relieve our own anxiety or help us to feel good about ourselves. We may interrupt someone in order to share an experience or story because our need to be heard at that moment is greater than our desire to be curious about someone else. In addition, those who work with people all the time may simply feel too tired or overwhelmed to be curious.

Still, curiosity has its benefits. Curiosity allows us to let go of our assumptions, categories, and stories about other people. Our questions and prompts create space for our conversation partner to tell his or her own story. Our openness may free our conversation partner from the pressure to be right or to please us. We learn new things about the people in our midst. As they answer our questions, they may even discover something about themselves!

The first step in practicing curiosity is noticing and letting go of unhelpful conversation habits. As discussed above, our automatic or instinctual responses to people often quash our ability to be curious. Some of these habits are simply unhelpful, such as gossiping or demeaning another person. But not all of these responses are all bad all the time. However, when they become habitual responses, dished out without regard to the person in front of us, they impede our ability to be curious. These habitual responses include when we:

- advise
- comfort
- correct
- fix or solve
- help
- inform,
- present a connected experience
- label
- gossip
- demean
- one-up yourself
- give an automatic response

"One-up yourself" means to make a statement that indicates how you are in some way better than or more powerful than the speaker. "An automatic response" refers to phrases that we use all the time without thought or meaning such as, "That was thoughtful of you," or "I will pray for you." These are not bad phrases, but using them habitually gets in the way of being curious about another person.

When we become aware of these habits, we can begin to let go of them. We see that we tend to respond to every person as a problem to be solved and we work to quiet this need. We notice that we tend to approach a conversation with an agenda—and we let it go. We feel a question stirring inside us and ask it, despite the inner parent voice warning us that polite leaders don't ask personal questions! We feel our need to comfort, to say the one thing that will fix the situation. Instead, we stay silent, waiting for the other person to finish. We might offer a prompt such as, "Tell me more about that." We may ask a question like, "What does that mean for you?" We may simply lean forward and ask, "What do you think?"

A Final Word

Every Christmas, my family and I attend a performance of *The Nutcracker*. I was five years old the first time I saw a live performance of this ballet. Since then I have seen many more stagings, both live and televised. I know the story and the music well enough that not much about it surprises me. Until the Christmas my four-year-old daughter sat on my lap and I saw the ballet through her openly curious eyes. We clung to each other when the Nutcracker was hurt, wondering what would happen next. Could he be fixed? We jumped when the Rat King emerged from the fire and again when he was shot. We sat on the edge of our seats during the second act eagerly awaiting each new dance. It was a whole new ballet for my daughter and, thanks to her, for me, too.

The gift of curiosity lets us step down from our know-it-all grown-up roles and approach the world like a child. Suddenly we don't know the right answer, we do not hold the truth, we have no idea what to expect, and we couldn't begin to tell you what's best. In that place of open wonder, God can surprise and astound us. Sometimes I look at the biblical stories and wonder how a healthy dose of curiosity would have changed things. Perhaps Jesus's childhood friends and neighbors would have considered the possibility that the boy who played on the streets of Nazareth with them might indeed be the one God sent to bring good news to the poor. Maybe the disciples would have had less trouble trusting that Jesus could feed thousands with a few morsels of bread and fish. I wonder if Thomas would have had an easier time believing that God had raised Jesus from death to life. It seems that the people who Jesus transformed were the ones willing to move toward Jesus in curiosity, open to the possibility that Jesus might be a source of hope and healing, among them the paralytic (Luke 5:17–26), the woman who anointed Jesus (Luke 7:36–50), and Zacchaeus (Luke 19:1–10).

Practicing curiosity changes how we encounter other people and the world. We let go of our visions of what must be, of what seems logical and expected and obvious. We open our hearts to the possibility of God's abundant blessings. We welcome whatever life brings, knowing that often God shows up in the most unlikely places. As the writer of Hebrews put it, "Do not neglect to show hospitality to strangers, for by doing that some have entertained angels without knowing it" (13:2).

Try

What are your habitual responses? In the next week, observe how you respond to other people in conversations. What are your most instinctual responses? Once you have noticed these, try letting them go.

Talk

1. This chapter offers several possible instinctual responses within conversations such as informing and comforting. What are others? Give examples.
2. Has anyone approached you with the kind of openness explored above? How did that affect you?
3. Talk about how the practice of noticing and letting go of habitual responses changed or affected the conversation.

31 ❀ Ask Questions and Offer Prompts

"The answers aren't important really. . . . What's important is—knowing all the questions."

Ivy Carson in *The Changeling*

I met Ava at a bookstore's café on a wintry evening in March. She was starting a book group, and this was to be our first meeting. As we waited for the other participants we chatted. After getting through the basics—age, living arrangements, significant others, jobs—we started on the deeper questions. Or rather, Ava did.

Tell me how you decide what kind of a book to write next.

What made you want to become a coach?

What books have really changed your life?

In between answering Ava's questions, I got in a few of my own. Mostly I marveled at the quality of her questions. They made me look at my life with new eyes. Her excitement and interest in me got me excited about myself. Toward the end of our evening, I said to Ava, "You ask really good questions. How did you learn to do that?"

"I'm just curious about people. I like to listen to their stories. Sometimes the only way to get at someone's stories is to ask them questions."

Questions serve an important function in conversations. At the most basic level, questions help us gather information about another person. They also can elicit stories and personal history. On a deeper level, questions get at the emotions and reasons behind our actions and behaviors. Questions push us to open up to new ways of thinking about our behavior, beliefs, and relationships. This chapter will explore the use of questions and prompts in conversation.

Questions

There are basically two types of questions: closed and open. Both closed and open questions are necessary in conversations and serve a purpose in the development of a dialogue. Let's look at each in turn. Closed questions lead to specific, informational answers. This means that closed questions can be answered with yes, no, or a brief piece of information. In some cases, closed questions expect a "right" answer. These are examples of closed questions:

Do you like your job?
Where do you live?
Did you like the class?
Why is God against premarital sex?

Closed questions can be helpful when you want to obtain specific information from a conversation partner. This information can be especially useful at the beginning of a relationship. We want, and may need, to know certain information in order to place our conversation partner within a context. For example, when I begin working with a client, having some basic information about the client—his or her age, location, occupation, job situation, and relevant personal circumstances, such as a significant personal relationship—is helpful for me. In developed relationships, closed questions can be useful in gathering information about a specific happening in another's life.

Open questions allow the recipient to tell a story, share feelings, or explore his or her reasoning behind a decision. Open questions allow the person to take his or her answer in more than one direction. These are examples of open questions:

What is your job like?
What drew you to choose your neighborhood?
What was that experience like for you?
What do you think the Bible says about sexuality?

While a closed question may garner information, an open question will tell you what the answer means to the recipient. For example, the question "Where do you live?" invites specific information: "I live in Andersonville, a neighborhood of Chicago." The question, "What drew you to choose your neighborhood?" allows the recipient to tell you something more than the basic information. For example, the Andersonville resident might say, "I chose Andersonville because the first time I visited I saw that right there, on the same block, I could shop for two things I love: books and Swedish cookies just like Grandma used to bake."

Prompts

Prompts are another tool for opening up dialogue. A prompt is a word or phrase that encourages the speaker to say more. Prompts include statements like

> Tell me about . . .
> Describe . . .
> Say more about that.
> Tell me what you mean by that . . .
> How so?
> Is that all?
> Why not?
> Why?

Prompts can be helpful in several ways. First, prompts ask for clarification on confusing or incomplete answers. Second, prompts give your conversation partner the opportunity to expand his or her answer. Many people are used to giving only brief informational answers and prompts encourage them to say more. Third, prompts encourage your conversation partner to move his or her answer into new territory. When you ask someone, "What do you mean by that?" or "Tell me why?" you encourage him or her to give you a deeper, more thoughtful answer.

Looking back at my bookstore conversation with Ava, I see how she made use of all three techniques: closed questions, open questions, and prompts. She began by asking closed questions. They were simple to answer and put me at ease. As the conversation grew, and with it our comfort with one another, Ava asked more open-ended questions. Toward the end of the evening, Ava pushed me to give more weighty answers. Her later questions were followed up by prompts to say more or to explain my answer. Ava's ability to ask a variety of questions created a healthy dialogue between two strangers and laid the groundwork for future conversations. We can only hope that our questions do the same!

A Final Word

Ava gave me more than an entertaining evening and the possibility of a new friend. Ava offered me a rare and deep gift that night. She invited me to move with her beyond the social dance of, "Hi how are you what do you do okay good good-bye." Her questions and prompts welcomed me to open up, to dig deep and share my story. Ava invited me to engage with her on a soul-level about the people, ideas, feelings, and truths that mattered to me. In doing this, Ava communicated that she valued me. She honored me instead of simply recognizing her construction of me or engaging with the part of me that reminded her of herself. When we can do this for one another, we honor not only the soul before us but the Christ that dwells within him or her.

Try

Notice the types of questions you ask. In what ways do your questions reflect

- your agenda for the conversation?
- your automatic responses within a conversation?
- your assumptions or stories about your conversation partner?

Make an effort to ask more open than closed questions in the next week. How does this change your conversations?

Talk

1. In what ways do you see open questions, closed questions, and prompts as necessary and helpful to your conversations? Give examples.
2. Talk about questions that you have seen open up or close down conversation. What were the questions? What happened? Why do you think they had a dramatic effect on conversation?
3. Make a list of questions that you have found helpful in conversation.
4. Share your experiences with using open questions and prompts. In what ways did these techniques improve conversations? In

what ways did the techniques make conversations awkward or uncomfortable?

---

32 ❀ Provide Models

Knowledge will not always take the place of simple observation.
                              Arnold Lobel, *The Elephant and His Son*

The first time I visited Hephatha Lutheran Church the woman in front of me helped me follow the service. After I'd been there for a few months, I heard the pastor instructing the adults to help children with the service. By then my children and I had collected some pew mates, a whole family of children ages four to thirteen. I did as instructed, opening hymnals to the proper page and passing them to the children. After two Sundays of that, I noticed the older children helping the younger children to follow along. Then the younger children helped the even smaller ones. There had been no instruction, no lecture about helping. The children had experienced helpful adults and did the same.

We learn how to do things in many ways: hearing, reading, watching, talking, and doing. One way we learn is by imitating other people. Children learn how to be in the world by imitating the big people around them. When they play at cooking, raising children, teaching school, and being in relationship, they are learning by mimicking other people. I learned how to dance by imitating my dance teacher. She would stand in front and model the steps for us. We would watch and copy. I learned how to crochet in the same way, by observing a friend. Even my training for ordained ministry included modeling. Field education placements and internship gave me the opportunity to shape my own ministry in light of the work of more experienced ministers.

As both a coach and a spiritual leader, I have noticed that modeling can be a helpful way to educate, inspire, motivate, and encourage other people. Sometimes modeling just happens. We get repeated exposure to a behavior, like hand washing, and by observing others, we learn to do likewise. But very little learning just happens. For modeling to work, these things need to be present:

- A clear example
- Repeated exposure to the example
- Conversation about the example
- The opportunity for the learner to choose to follow or reject the example

At Hephatha, the adults who helped the young people every Sunday provided the clear example. The children who came to church more than once got repeated exposure to the example. Each Sunday, the pastor repeated her instructions, providing some conversation about the example. From time to time, she would point out how children were helpful to others (more conversation). Some of us adults would thank the helpful children for their service (even more conversation). Of course, the children had the opportunity to choose to help or not. No one was forced to be helpful.

In coaching, models often take the form of stories. And for good reason—we connect better to stories than we do to treatises. I can give my clients 10 reasons to lose weight or to start exercising or to set goals. And even if they are very persuasive reasons, logic does not always motivate. But we do respond to the real-life stories of people who have done what we hope to do in a way that works. Flesh and blood motivates. Emotion motivates.

The stories used in modeling can be either positive or negative—kind of like the cartoon characters Goofus and Gallant in the magazine *Highlights for Children*. In any situation, Goofus always goofs up—reminding the reader what *not* to do. Gallant makes the better choice, giving the reader some insight about how to behave well. I have always found the positive stories to be more helpful than negative ones. Positive stories provide the bricks to build a road with, to make a way in the world. Negative stories just point out the many holes in the road. In my own life, it has been the positive stories about how other people have overcome difficulties that I cling to in my own tough times.

Story Sources

Here are some of the sources you might use for modeling stories.

THE CLIENT'S STORIES

The best stories in the coaching conversation come from the client. In the midst of the coaching relationship, clients share stories that call attention to their strengths and successes. Retelling the stories of a client's success can connect them to their strengths again. A few years ago I worked with a client who had the courage to make a decision that was good for her health but unpopular with her superiors and colleagues. Over the two years that we worked together, I often pointed to that story as a model for her. I would ask:

- What does that story teach you about you?
- In what ways is that a helpful model for you?
- How might that story influence the way you handle this situation?

My coach has been good about using my stories to help me achieve things in the present. In the fall of 2004, a friend and I wrote a book together in less than two weeks. The actual writing process took nine days. My coach lived through those two weeks with me. A year later, I am writing another book—this one—under a tight deadline. When I am discouraged or feeling stuck, my coach holds up the story of the nine-day book as a model for me. She focuses on the part of the story that relates to the situation at hand. When I was stuck, she talked about the strategies I had used to overcome blocks a year ago. It worked. Her words connect me to the best parts of me.

OTHER CLIENTS' STORIES

Coaches sometimes use the stories of other clients as models. For the most part, these stories work well when a client faces a situation that another client has handled well. This might include handling a difficult boss, beginning an exercise program, or setting up a Web site. There are some rules when using other client's stories:

If possible, ask permission. When a client tells me a story that stirs me, I often ask if I can use it in my work with other clients.

Eliminate identifying details. If gender, age, and location do not matter to the gist of the story, don't use them.

Use stories judiciously. In close-knit communities, eliminating a few details won't hide the identity of the story's subject. In those situations, using client or parishioner stories feels like gossip. Only use the stories of people who are strangers to the person you are speaking with.

CULTURAL STORIES

Cultural stories are those that exist in the public domain. They include news stories, community stories, colleague experiences, and even the happenings on popular television shows. These have been helpful tools for modeling because the clients often know these stories as well as or better than I do. As we discuss how a client might handle a tricky relationship issue, I might share a vignette from a *Desperate Housewives* episode or a story I saw on *Oprah*. We might unpack a story we heard on the radio about how a person overcame extreme poverty to get an education. In each instance, the story holds up a way of being or acting that I think might be helpful for the client to consider.

LITERARY STORIES

In my own life, I often turn to books to discover how other people have handled their lives. In coaching, I use scenes from memoirs, novels, spiritual nonfiction, poetry, song lyrics, and magazine articles as models for my clients. One spiritual leader I knew used index cards to keep notes on book passages he liked. Arranged thematically, he was able to use these for sermons and counseling. I keep a "commonplace book," a journal filled with the quotes and stories I like. In the coaching relationship, I tend to use the literary stories that are fresh in my mind. So if I happen to be reading a book on, say, the lives and times of turtles, then I may have a turtle story for every client that week. After a client session, when I have some time to think, other stories may come to mind as being helpful to a client. I usually e-mail them with recommendations saying, "This might be a helpful model for you as you consider your next step."

BIBLICAL STORIES

Many of my clients are spiritual leaders who share with me an interest in biblical stories. Biblical characters can be helpful models, almost metaphors, of how a client might handle a situation. A client coping with feeling overwhelmed might benefit by a conversation about the attentive Mary and distracted Martha story from Luke 10. Thinking about each of these people as a model for ministry can support the client in discovering how he or she wants to live life. A client wrestling with her call might benefit from thinking about the call of Abraham in Genesis 12. Someone considering how to move forward after the end of a life stage might benefit from looking at how the disciples coped with Jesus's death. When I do not have a biblical model for clients, they usually do. I often ask, "What biblical story do you relate to in this situation?" or "What biblical characters are you drawn to right now?"

YOUR OWN STORY

Your own life stories can be powerful models for those you minister to and with. In my own relationships with my coaches, leaders, colleagues, and friends, their life stories have been like a helping hand over a puddle of water. When I was still in parish ministry and longing to create a life that included ministry but looked very different, I spoke with many other clergy persons in specialized roles. Their stories about how they created their life became invaluable to me as I created my own new world.

In using my own life stories with clients, I follow these guidelines:

Other stories first. Because of the weight that clients can give a coach's story (or people can give to their spiritual leader's story), I try to use other stories before I use my own. Once a client asked me to share with her how I built my speaking and writing career. I promised that I would—after she interviewed two other people.

A little goes a long way. Less is more. You know the clichés. To avoid becoming Molly McGuru, use your life stories sparingly. To me, sparingly means one story every four to six sessions.

Insert disclaimer! All models need a disclaimer: what worked for me or this person or Lydia, seller of purple goods, may not work for you. Disclaimers are especially important when it is the coach's story because, again, any leader's story runs the risk of being treated as more godly than it deserves.

Again!

Every Friday morning when my daughter was in four-year-old kindergarten I would read to her class. After reading poetry every Friday for the whole month of April, National Poetry Month, I thought they'd be sick of it. No chance. Weeks later, after I finished my stack of storybooks I would hear, "Can you read a poem?" I would read a few and hear, "Again!" The children wanted to hear the same poems again and again. I would hear them repeating lines to each other in the morning as they hung up their coats. Hearing the words repeatedly helped them to learn them "by heart."

In using stories as the basis for modeling, the four basic elements are present: a clear example, repeated exposure to the example, conversation about the example, and the opportunity for the learner to choose to follow or reject the example. We learn from stories by living with them—moving in and out of them over time, taking metaphors and examples from the narrative and applying them to our own life journey. When a story is presented in coaching, the conversation loops in and out of it, sometimes for more than one session. This provides both repeated exposure and conversation. The client is always free to reject the example as being unhelpful to him or her. The coach can underline this choice by asking the client, "In what ways does this example work or not work for you?" After several sessions, there are often slices of the story that the client has learned by heart and integrated into his or her own life.

Line Leaders

Every Tuesday afternoon the children gather at my church for learning, prayer, and snacks. At the beginning of our time together, the children share something from their day and a thought about God. One particular Tuesday, my young friend Abby shared that she had been a line leader at school that day. At Abby's school, when the children move from their classroom to anywhere else, they walk in a line, following the red, blue, and yellow lines taped on the school floor. The line leader holds the important job of sticking to the appointed line color (no jumping from red to blue) and leading the class to their destination. The pastor said, "This world needs line leaders." In a sense, modeling is pointing to the line leaders in our midst.

Try

Review the types of modeling stories listed above. Choose one or two to use in your conversations this week. Then reflect on the following questions:

- In what ways were the four facets of modeling present in your conversation?
- In what ways did using a model support the person you spoke with?
- In what ways was the technique limited?
- What other tools did you use as a companion to this technique?

Talk

1. Share a story about someone or some event that has served as a model for you. In what ways has the model been helpful?
2. Share with each other examples of how you have used modeling in your preaching, teaching, and conversations with other people.
3. Share with each other resources that you have found helpful in finding stories of models for other people.

---

33 ❁ Remember Life Stories

> I have thought sometimes that the Lord must hold the whole of our lives in memory, so to speak.
>
> Rev. John Ames in *Gilead*

When my friend's uncle died, she got out the family photo album. Together, she and her family told stories about this beloved family member. She wanted to remember.

Every November I can count on one friend to send us a wedding anniversary card. She never forgets this day. Her remembering that day makes it more special.

I have a college friend who reminds me of how I used to be. Spicy, she'll say. Her stories of those early days call me back to a part of myself I too often forget.

One of the gifts we offer to one another is our presence. We bear witness to the twists and turns of each other's life journeys. When we cannot bear direct witness, we can be present to the stories of each other's lives. When we carry some of that other person's story with us and remember it to them later, we offer a second gift. This is the gift of remembering.

Part of the job of the coach and the spiritual leader is to bear witness to the life stories of people. We hear about their griefs and tragedies as well as the long-awaited pleasures. We bring a deeper gift to those we minister with and to when we are able to remember parts of their stories to them. We become like the ghost of Christmas past—reminding them of how it used to be. When we remember a once-voiced dream, our words might call someone to accountability. When we remind a person of how God has been present in the past, our memories might bring hope or comfort. Our stories about someone's past triumphs might encourage him or her to be courageous in the present moment.

Remembering the stories of other people comes fairly easily to me. But I still need to work at it. I listen intently. I take notes and review them before each session to help myself remember the stories of my client's lives. When the person I am speaking to appears moved by his or her story—either with joy or sadness—I take notes about these transforming moments. I also record client goals. Other items I tend to record include:

- phrases that seem meaningful to the person
- metaphors
- Bible verses, stories, or images
- dreams
- repeated words, phrases, goals, or metaphors

Hansel and Gretel left breadcrumbs to help themselves find their way home. Our memories of each other's lives become like these breadcrumbs, guiding each other to the place God calls us to be.

Try _____

Be intentional this week about learning the stories of other people. If you can, remember a story, phrase, or goal to someone. What effect does this have on the relationship?

Talk _____

1. What are some of the theological and biblical meanings of remembering?
2. Share a story about how other people remembering your story has supported you. Talk about how that was helpful to you.
3. Share the techniques you use to remember the stories of other people's lives.

---

34 ❂ Nudge

Meg is traveling to the dark planet Camazotz to free her brother from IT:

The momentary vision and faith that had come to Meg dwindled. "But suppose I can't get Charles Wallace away from IT—"

"Stop." Mrs. Whatsit held up her hand. "We gave you gifts the last time we took you to Camazotz. We will not let you go empty handed this time. But what we can give you now is nothing you can touch with your hands. I give you my love, Meg. Never forget that. My love always."

Madeleine L'Engle, *A Wrinkle in Time*

When my daughter was learning to walk, I would sometimes provide tiny nudges to keep her from harm. I never changed her direction. I let her go where she wanted to (for the most part). I did do some gentle adjusting—away from ledges, steep stairs, and sharp edges. Sometimes I would gently nudge her toward something she loved but could not see—a pile of toys, a pretty flower, a soft place to land.

As I look back on my life, I see people who have nudged me toward my passions. One of my favorite professors, Timothy Lull, was one of my nudgers. In seminary, Tim encouraged me to write. It's rare to find someone who encourages you to do what *you* are good at instead of what *they* are passionate about. Tim Lull was one of those rare people. For my final paper in his Theology 3 class, I wrote a short story. He spoke to me about getting it published. Every time I saw him on campus that spring, he asked if I had submitted it yet. He sent it to one of his friends, a well-known theologian and author. That was one of the first times someone had given credence to my passion for writing.

There are other nudgers in my life. A friend reminds me to eat, sometimes bringing over a tub of chicken noodle soup and a pan of Rice Krispies Treats. My coach asks me about my goals, nudging me to keep at the weight lifting and walking. My daughter stands at my door each night at about five and whispers, "Pssst" until I come out and play. The words and actions of these nudgers gently prod me to do what God calls me to do and to care for the body God has given me.

Most of the spiritual leaders I coach and consult with are faithful, hard-working individuals. They do what's required of them and much more. These leaders extend their caring beyond the confines of the parish, serving in their community and caring for their neighbors. In addition, they do their best to attend to their families and friends. The one person these leaders tend to ignore? The face in the mirror. These leaders got the "love your neighbor" part but forgot the "as yourself." One of my colleagues has a term for this practice: "deferred maintenance."

As a coach, I have learned to be as much nudger as prophet. *Nudger* seems to be an appropriate term for the kind of prophet that sticks beside us, pushing us each day to follow God's call. My favorite biblical nudger is Naomi. She nudged Ruth toward Boaz, providing helpful hints about appearance and behavior.

In the entire Bible, only one passage actually uses the term *nudge*. It's in Eugene Peterson's paraphrase of the New Testament: [Jesus said,] "That's why I tell stories: to create readiness, to nudge the people toward receptive insight. In their present state they can stare till doomsday and not see it, listen till they're blue in the face and not get it" (Matt. 13:13).[1] Nudge works here—Jesus's words and works nudged people toward faith. (Of course, sometimes Jesus also pushed people towards insight, but that's another chapter!) As a coach, I also work to create readiness, to gently nudge my clients toward "receptive insight." As a nudger, I want to be like my professor, Tim Lull, gently prodding people to follow the dreams and passions they have articulated to me. With one of my clients, a spiritual leader and visual artist, I remind her of one of the reasons she came to coaching. "You said you wanted to make more art. Are you making art?" As a nudger, I sometimes gently guide my clients into a better position, so that they can see their lives with more clarity. I might ask them to reframe their story, shifting the focus. "What if you saw yourself as an artist who preaches instead of a preacher who makes art? What might your life look like then?" As a coach, I am that little voice of sanity, reminding people to care as deeply for themselves as they do for other people. When clients articulate self-care goals, I will often end the session by asking, "Tell me about how the exercise is going. Tell me about your eating."

As a nudger, I know that there are rules for nudging. Nudgers can quickly morph into naggers when they

- promote their own agenda or the agenda of an institution, group, or other person;
- voice personal complaints about the client's behavior or appearance;
- encourage actions or goals that cause the client discomfort or anxiety or go against his or her personal integrity;
- persist in promoting a plan of action after the client has said no, I am not interested.

I do not want to be the voice for deferred maintenance. Nor do I want to encourage a client to follow my vision for his or her life. My goal is to support the client in following God's call. And so I listen—and listen, and listen, and listen. I take notes. I ask questions like, "Clarify this for me: are you telling me that if you had one year to live you would go to the opera once a week?" I review my notes. I listen for patterns. I listen for the clues. Then I begin to nudge.

To nudge, I do what my children did when they were learning to speak—I echo. When children first start to vocalize, they simply mimic adult sounds and words. When I would say "cookie" to my daughter, she would say it back to me: "cookie." Back and forth, like voice and canyon, we would play at echoing. In coaching, I echo the words of the client back to him or her in some way. I ask a question. I tell them a story from their own lives: "I remember you telling me about the first time your dad took you fishing." I call attention to how their face lights up when they talk about their passion. I give them an article on healthy walking. I send them a postcard that asks, "How goes the writing?" I remind them of why they came to coaching in the first place. I ask them to talk about the consequences of this or that choice. I push a little here, prod a little there, and hope that one of these nudges puts them in a place where they can listen to the voice of God.

Try

1. Make a list of your "nudgers" and note how each nudges you. How do you see their words and actions as a sign of God's presence in your life?
2. Who do you nudge and how? Make a list.
3. Practice nudging. Note that the best nudges come not from your agenda but from the expressed desires and dreams of the person you are nudging.

Talk

1. Make a list of biblical nudgers. How did they fulfill God's call by nudging others?
2. Discuss how nudging might be an important part of ministry.

35 ⊛ Pray

Somebody prayed for me,
had me on their mind,
took some time to pray for me.
I'm so glad they prayed,
I'm so glad they prayed,
I'm so glad they prayed for me.

Traditional

I'm a shy Scandinavian Lutheran from Minnesota. We take seriously Jesus's teaching about prayer: "But whenever you pray, go into your room and shut the door and pray" (Matt. 6:6). When I got to California for my internship year, I was immediately challenged by the practice of public praying. Not only did people hug a lot out there, they also held hands while they prayed. I could have crawled under the table the first time a leader said, "Let's join hands and pray together."

In the Quaker meeting I attend from time to time, the congregation forms a large circle at the end of the meeting. This time is set aside to ask the community to hold people "in the light." The divine light is the presence of God within each of us. To hold another in the light is to hold another's concerns in our hearts, asking God to take care of the person whose need we offer. When I was going through a difficult time in my life, a Quaker friend would end each of our calls by telling me, "I am holding you in the light." That image of being embraced by a friend and the light of God carried me through many dark and lonely moments.

Prayer is one way we support each other in the community of faith. The congregation I attend publishes a long prayer list on the back of each Sunday's bulletin. We regularly sing the song that opens this chapter and talk about our commitment to pray for one another. Each year our pledge sheets contain a section of questions where we can pledge to pray during the day and for the people of the parish and the world. And we pray—during church, after church, between services. Sometimes we hold hands, at other times we lay hands on those in need. One Sunday a parish friend laid her hands on me during the Lord's Prayer. I don't know how she knew I needed that kindness. I regularly attend a Tuesday night communion service at my church that gives a small group the opportunity to hold hands, pray, and share in Holy Communion. These practices have become guideposts for me, like those posts that keep hikers on the trail instead of wandering in senseless circles through the forests. These prayers are places that I can grab onto for a moment, holding onto the light, resting in God's abiding grace. These are places that show me where I need to go next. As the Indigo Girls sing, "I must say around some corner I can sense a resting place."[1] The last time I stopped at the church to drop off some things, my daughter went into the pastor's office and said, "Can we hold hands and pray?" She knows about guideposts, too.

As a coach, prayer has become one of the ways I show care for my clients. This includes

- Asking clients for prayer requests or concerns
- Praying with clients at the beginning or end of a session
- Sending prayers to clients via e-mail or snail mail. These mark special occasions, times of celebration or difficulty, seasonal changes, health concerns, losses, and other events.
- Sending cards or e-mail notes that say, "I am praying for you"
- Including clients on the prayer list at church, with their permission
- Inviting clients to pray for me
- Encouraging clients to participate in services or other prayer practices. This might include walking the labyrinth, participating in a Taizé service, doing art, or dancing.
- Giving clients prayer beads, a prayer book, or another tool for praying

Last year, one of my clients went through a particularly difficult stretch. We live thousands of miles from one another, so I had never met this client in person. In many ways, I knew that I could not support her as I might if I were present. I couldn't take her hand and pray for her. At the time, I had begun taking weekly walks by the lake, searching for heart-shaped stones. Every time I find one, I am amazed at what water can do. For me they are a powerful reminder of how God slowly and gently shapes our lives and our hearts over time, perhaps without our even knowing it. I sent a stone to my client as a reminder of my presence with her in prayer.

I have begun using these stones pretty regularly as a gift to those in need of prayer. I gave one to a client who was taking a difficult trip. Another went to a friend after the death of her sister. I painted one pink for a friend who had just celebrated her fifth year anniversary of recovery from cancer. The rest sit in my dining room, in a bowl given to me by my mother, as a reminder of the people I need to pray for—especially those, as an old prayer goes, "who have no one to pray for them."

Try

Try a new prayer practice this week. If possible, choose a prayer practice that involves another person, communicating to them your love and care.

Talk

1. Talk about how prayer has affected you.
2. How do you pray for the people you minister with or to?
3. Share a prayer form or a written prayer that has made an impact on your life.
4. Share creative ideas for praying for the people you minister with and to. One leader I know sends out postcards to her members at the beginning of the week she plans to pray for them. Another gives out bookmarks to the people she prays for.

36 ❀ Coach to Transform

"It makes you wonder. All the brilliant things we might have done with our lives if only we suspected we knew how."

General Benjamin in *Bel Canto*

Every weekday morning, I drop off my daughter at school and then head to the Y. The YMCA in my neighborhood houses both an athletic center and a leadership academy for young people. I arrive just as the children are leaving their morning assembly and going to class. The halls are packed but not chaotic. The children move with military precision, marching along taped lines on the floor. If one student steps off a line or gets out of step, the instructors bark out military commands. I have often wondered if this method inspires the children or only terrifies them into behaving well.

What transforms people? Those of us who work to serve others hope to be about the work of transforming. Transforming seems to happen along a continuum: motivating, inspiring, empowering. I use all three tools to support my clients in transforming their lives. This chapter will consider how a coach or spiritual leader might use these skills with the people they serve.

The differences between the three actions—to motivate, to inspire, to empower—can be explained with a personal illustration. In

January I received an invitation to my high school reunion in August. The idea of seeing old friends *motivated* me to exercise. In other words, the reunion gave me an *incentive* or *stimulus* for firming up my wiggly parts. Transformation had begun.

The gift of *inspiration* came in the form of two friends. The first told me about her daily workouts—how she had shifted from walking to running and had a training program planned out. Her skin glowed as she spoke about it. "I could never run," I confessed. "I'm too wimpy." "I think you could," she said. Her words *breathed hope* into my dream of attending my reunion looking fit. Another friend spoke about her history as a weightlifting competitor. I had recently read about a woman who had started competing in her forties. "Do you think I could do it, too?" I asked. "Yes," she said. I rolled up my sleeves and showed her my stick-like arms. "Tell me the truth," I begged. "Look at these arms. I've been called Twiggy since I could walk. Do you honestly believe that these arms could get Popeye-sized bumps on them?" "Yes," she repeated, emphatically. Two short conversations later, I believed I had the ability to *transform* my body. That belief came from the *inspiring influence* of my friends.

These friends also *empowered* me. The first friend gave me a book about running, which told me everything I needed to know about beginning a training program. The second friend took me to the gym and taught me a simple and an effective weightlifting program. These simple actions *enabled* me to work out. My body was not yet transformed but my life certainly was. I began to go to the gym five days a week. With each passing day, I became more of what I was hoping to be, thanks to some clear motivating, inspiring, and empowering.

Motivating

A motive is anything that "causes a person to act." To motivate is "to provide with a motive."[1] Motivations can be external (such as my high school reunion) or internal (such as an individual's desire to lose weight). Often motivation is connected to incentives—a reward, punishment, goal, or even a feeling. Different things motivate each of us. In the confirmation class at my church, the pastor has a five-dollar question each week. The question is derived from that evening's lesson. At the end of the class, the pastor draws a name out of the hat. If the person can answer the question, he or she wins the money. This reward motivates the children to pay close attention in class. At my son's school, students have a list of rules to follow. The teacher has given them consequences for not following the rules: a warning, a missed recess, a call home, and finally suspension. My son dreads missing recess more than anything in the world. These punishments motivate him to not break the rules. For some people, a goal like getting confirmed or graduating from college is enough to keep them attending class and studying. Some people are motivated by their feelings, such as fear. For them the fear of failing or disappointing their parents may be the motivator. For the blessed, the sheer joy of acquiring knowledge becomes their motivation. They love learning, and so the process is enough to motivate them.

One summer during college I lived at home. My parents would leave long notes about what they needed me to do during the day (vacuum, dust the baseboards, do your laundry) and I would ignore them in favor of my favorite hobby—reading. My mom would yell and I'd whine, "But I didn't feel motivated." She'd snap back, "Well, *get motivated*." As a coach, part of my job is to support people in doing just that, getting motivated to do the things they need to do but maybe don't feel like doing. I do that by helping them to place in their lives things that will motivate them—joy, accountability, deadlines, rewards, and the endgame.

JOY

Okay, we know that some people just love doing all that stuff the rest of us don't like so much, such as exercising, eating green stuff, going to the dentist, and cleaning out the gutters on the house. We suspect they're crazy, but we cannot prove it. Getting motivated to do something that seems pointless or loathsome is hard. Really. So I ask people how they might *better* the task—how can they make it more joyful. When I first started working out, the minutes on the treadmill ticked by in slow motion. I bettered the experience for myself by making a compact disc of my favorite music to listen to while I exercise. Now I look forward to getting on the treadmill. A client of mine bettered her new food regimen by creating a menu of really tasty meals and snacks. Now she does not dread eating. (Though she would still rather be eating more brownies and donuts!)

ACCOUNTABILITY

For most clients, simply having a regular coaching meeting motivates them to make changes, especially if they are paying for the time. The relationship provides some level of accountability: the client feels responsible to the coach for achieving what he or she promised to do. As one client said to me recently, "I couldn't just show up here without having done anything." Additional accountability can be built into the coaching process by inviting people to report in through e-mail or short phone calls.

DEADLINES

Someday. Most of us dream of that magical someday when we will be able to accomplish all the things on our eschatological to-do list. The truth is, though, that unless we have a deadline, someday rarely comes. Asking people to set deadlines will make it more possible for them to achieve their goals.

REWARDS

Of course I'd rather my clients give themselves rewards than punishments. So I encourage clients to make a list of ten delectable rewards—small, inexpensive gifts and activities that they can use to motivate themselves. One of my clients rewards herself for writing chapters of her book with a trip to the sewing and craft store. She rarely buys anything; she simply enjoys making the trip and appreciating the colors and textures of the materials. Another client treats herself to a bath by scented candlelight after she finishes a speaking presentation.

ENDGAME

I often ask my clients to imagine what it would be like to cross their own personal finish line—to lose the weight, get the degree, finish the paper, or write the book. I ask them to articulate in great detail how this achievement will change their life, how it will change what they will do, how they will look, whom they will relate to, what they will eat, and how they will feel. Then, I invite clients to create a visual reminder of the endgame, something that they can see each day. This vision can give hope to those trudging down the long path toward the endgame.

Inspiring

According to organizational strategist Lance Secretan, the "word in-spiration is derived from the Latin root spirare meaning 'spirit,' to breathe, to give life—the breath of God."[2] Often inspiration is con-nected to the divine, how God affects humankind. God breathes life into our deadened spirits. Consider the valley of the dry bones—a desperate situation, a pile of bones cut off from flesh and breath. All hope was lost. Then the prophet proclaimed God's promise, "Thus says the LORD GOD to these bones: I will cause breath to enter you, and you shall live" (Ezek. 37:5). The breath came from the four winds and breathed life into the bones. We all have dry-bone days, dry-bone dreams, dry-bone places when our life seems to be more about dying than growing. Then God inspires us, breathing life into the dead places, and we are reborn. God inspires through modern-day prophets—chil-dren, friends, spouses, spiritual leaders, and even coaches.

When I began writing this book, I felt a bit lost. I could not find within me what I needed to put flesh on the ideas for this book. None of the usual things inspired me, not my favorite music, movies, or poems. Finally, at the point of nearly giving up, a couple of things hap-pened. First, I had a long talk with my editor. I can't remember the details of the conversation, but something in it breathed life into my confidence. Somehow she articulated her belief that I could write this book, and it mattered. Then, I borrowed a stack of sermons from a friend. Her ability to articulate how God works in our lives resusci-tated this skill in me. Both of these events inspired me—and I started to write again.

Like motivation, inspiration is unique to every individual. As a coach, I would love to think that something about what I do or what is created in the coaching conversation inspires my clients. But I don't think inspiration can be orchestrated. Setting out to inspire another person is akin to trying to force cheer on a grieving person. It patron-izes them. That said, we can and do inspire people.

LIVE INSPIRATION

We inspire other people by the way we live our lives. Hearing that both of my friends had set and achieved their goals for physical health inspired me to do the same. According to Lance Secretan, "We experience inspiration and inspire others when we live authentically and are aligned with a clear sense of our higher purpose and a commitment to building soulful relationships with all those whom we serve."[3] Coaches often call this "walking the talk." In a sense, we need to be who we hope to become. When I was more of a wannabe than a writer, "being who I hoped to become" meant writing daily and submitting my work even in the face of constant rejection. As a wannabe athlete, it means showing up at the gym five days a week. As leaders it means considering our life purpose and living into it each day. As people of faith, we work at being who God hopes us to become. This means doing our best. It means making meaningful connections with other people—speaking kindness, offering encouragement, and giving care. When we work each day to be who God hopes us to become, we may inspire others to do the same.

COLLECT AND SHARE INSPIRATION

I collect inspiration. Look around—it's everywhere. Stories in the newspaper, television profiles, movies, music, poetry, photographs, the ballet, a whimsical snowperson, the kindness of strangers, the stories of friends and family members, a beautiful sunset, an amazing meal—all of these things can inspire. When a client is having a dry-bone kind of day, I will share some of my collection with him or her. I might pass on the lyrics to a song or recommend a movie. I may tell a story about an event that inspired me. I hold up this or that piece of my collection until a window opens and the breath of inspiration begins to blow again.

CREATE AN INSPIRATION PRESCRIPTION

When an irritant or allergen triggers my asthma, I know what will bring back my breath. I grab my emergency inhaler. I drink water. I close my eyes and stay calm, imagining that the breath is easily moving out and in. Just as I know what will bring air into my lungs, most of us know what breathes life into our weary souls. I encourage clients to create a list of the things that inspire them and then set up their lives to include regular doses of this medicine.[4] For example, I just ordered a copy of *Spirited Away*, a Japanese anime film about a young girl who needed to develop her internal resources in order to free her parents from the spirit world. When I watch this film, I feel inspired to dig deeper inside myself to discover my inner strengths.

Empower

In the middle of my pastoral internship year, my supervisor died. For the next month, I worked as the solo pastor. The congregation's lay leaders supervised my work in weekly meetings. At one of these meetings, the leaders changed many of the worship decisions I had made for the upcoming Holy Week services. After that meeting, I realized that although my responsibilities had grown considerably, I had little or no authority to make decisions. The leaders had given me responsibility but little authority or power.

The literal meaning of the word *empower* is "to give official authority or legal power to."[5] In the above situation, I may have been capable of doing the assigned tasks, but I did not have the power or authority to make binding decisions. In other situations, the power we need might be legal, physical, intellectual, emotional, or spiritual. Our ability to empower another person varies with the role we have in the other person's life. For example, I have much more ability to empower my children than I do my clients or acquaintances. Still, as with motivation and inspiration, we can and do empower people. The following are some of the tools that can be used to empower others.

SUPPORT

We can be empowered by the support of other people. My daughter was diagnosed with epilepsy about a month before starting four-year-old kindergarten. When she entered school, I became her advocate. I negotiate between the school staff and the physicians to create an atmosphere for my daughter that will be both safe and conducive to learning.

In the face of serious illness, most of us feel pretty powerless. Although I had taken the advocate role for others as a spiritual leader, I hadn't felt prepared to take on this role as a mother. I wanted a Wonder Woman cape or a bionic brain or something. That didn't happen. Instead, my power came from the support of others. A teacher told me that other parents who had dealt with this would help me fight for my daughter's care. A friend prayed and prayed for us, for my strength and for my daughter's wellness. Another friend who had been through this with her child passed on her own superpowers by telling me that not only *could* I do this, I *had* to do the work. These simple acts supported me and empowered me to keep fighting at a time when I wanted to go back to bed! All of these tools of support—presence, prayers, and encouragement—are easily translated to the coaching or ministry relationships.

CONNECTING TO RESOURCES

We are empowered by having the financial, educational, and spiritual resources we need to achieve our goals. At our congregation's annual meeting, the treasurer spoke about how ministry needs resources to be effective. She encouraged congregational leaders to ask for the resources they need to make a program or project work. Financial resources make it possible to gain an education. Cookbooks give us the recipes we need to bake. Spiritual directors support us in learning how to be better connected with God. Resources like these can make the difference between dreaming and doing. As a coach, my job often is to support a client in identifying the resources they need, then discovering how to get these resources. The process is as simple as asking *what* and *how*.

EDUCATE

Education empowers us. When I started lifting weights, I needed some very specific empowerment—education. My friend was able to provide that for me. As a coach, moving into the role of educator, consultant, or advisor is sometimes necessary in order to empower the client. Of course, this only works if the client is looking for empowerment in an area of the coach's expertise. Otherwise, the coach or spiritual leader can work with the client in finding the education that will support his or her needs.

Being Transformed

Life is about growing—being transformed again and again into more of who God has called us to be. On one Martin Luther King Jr. Day, social activist and pastor Joe Ellwanger preached about transforming moments. He spoke about the text for the day, Jesus's calling of Philip and Nathanael (John 1:43–51). He told us about his own transforming moments—some of which happened while marching and working with Martin Luther King Jr. He said to us, "An encounter with Jesus will transform you."

I hear that same message from people at my church. "Jesus changed me," they tell me. I see it in their lives. Jesus has transformed what they do with their money, time, and skills. As I learn the stories of their transforming moments, I hear how Jesus worked in their lives through the hands of teachers, pastors, and community members to motivate, inspire, and empower change.

Ultimately, only Jesus's love can transform people. We cannot work miracles on our own lives or the lives of those we serve. We need to trust that Jesus has his hands in the lives of those we love. Still, Jesus does use our lives to motivate, inspire, and empower these changes in other people. Our stories, our service, our gifts, our loving—even our very lives—transform people.

Try

Make an inspiration collection. Find a container you love and fill it with ideas and things that inspire you and that you can use to inspire others.

Talk

1. What stories in the Bible show how we might motivate, inspire, and empower other people?
2. Share a story of a time when someone motivated, inspired, or empowered you. In what ways did his or her action make a difference in your life? How did you see the hand of God in this action?
3. What are some of the ways you work to motivate, inspire, or empower yourself?

37   ❋   Coach to Support

> Trouble can always be borne when it is shared.
>
> Katherine Paterson, *The Tale of the Mandarin Ducks*

One Epiphany, the pastor gave each of the children two small flashlights that said, "Jesus is the light of the world." She encouraged each child to give the extra flashlight to someone who might need to see the light of Christ. When the sermon ended, my daughter rushed back to the pew and handed one of her flashlights to the friend we were sitting with. Our friend's face lit up with a bright smile. Later I told my daughter what a kind act that was. She said, "Well, the pastor said if you have a friend, give it to them. Besides, that's what best friends do. They make each other feel better. They help each other out." A few weeks later, my daughter had a seizure just before the end of the school day. She waited in the gym with the rest of the children who were to be picked up. When we got there, she was leaning against the wall, resting. Her classmate said, "She doesn't feel well. If she falls down, we're supposed to catch her."

The words from Elly and her friend about helping reflect the ideas in this passage from Ecclesiastes: "Two are better than one, because they have a good reward for their toil. For if they fall, one will lift up the other; but woe to one who is alone and falls and does not have another to help" (Eccles. 4:9–10). We have all been there, needing the help and support of another to accomplish a large task or to struggle through a difficult period in our lives. If we're lucky, we will have family members and friends we can count on to share their flashlights with us and to catch us when we fall. But there will always be experiences that we feel uncomfortable sharing with those we are closest to. Perhaps we worry that they would disapprove or we feel frightened or embarrassed about our situation. Maybe we do not believe that anyone would want to help us. Sometimes it seems that someone who is not already involved in our lives can better support us. That's when we call professional help, perhaps a mentor, coach, or spiritual leader.

When a client needs support beyond the typical support offered in regular coaching conversations, the coach needs to gauge the type of help the client needs at the time. There are basically three stops on the support continuum beyond the supportive coaching conversation: supportive presence, collaboration, and assistance.

Supportive Presence

When my clients are experiencing a difficult time, I often will ask them: "What sort of support do you need to get through this time in your life?" Almost always, clients will name the coaching relationship as being a crucial part of their support network. In my conversations with clients, they name two things as being helpful. First, the client gains support from the coach within the conversation. The coach's fierce presence, supportive listening, and questioning supports the client. Second, the client experiences support between sessions simply by knowing they have a coach they can turn to. All of my clients know that they can call or e-mail in an emergency situation. Almost none do. But some will say that having this as an option is like having a safety net just in case they need it. One of my colleagues suffers from some difficult medical problems. On a recent trip overseas, she packed a whole bunch of "just in case" medicine. This extra medicine was designed to help her just in case she got into trouble. It made her and her family rest easier. In a sense, the coaching relationship works like this just-in-case medicine; its existence provides a measure of comfort and support.

During my coach training program one of my instructors demonstrated supportive presence in a unique way. She invited us to be present with and for one another on an entire Saturday. Each of us chose a task we believed to be difficult. I planned to work on clearing out a large storage area and sorting through the boxes. My goal was to get rid of half of the stuff. One woman wanted to figure out the technology in her life, namely her cell phone and Palm Pilot. Early that Saturday, we met together on a telephone bridge line to introduce our goals. We met again two hours later to report our progress. Throughout the day we met at regular intervals for conversation and encouragement. At the end of the day, most of us had achieved our goals.

"I almost quit this morning," admitted a woman from California.

"Why didn't you?" asked the coach.

"Because of you all. How could I let down the whole group?"

Most of us felt that way. We achieved our goals because we knew we had support. The presence of the group was good support for us.

Collaboration

My friend still talks about the day her sister came over and helped her to sort through her overstuffed clothes closet. Her sister's brutally honest opinion got her to finally throw out some of the clothes she had stored since high school. She now swears by this method of closet cleaning, believing that we can never be really truthful about our stuff on our own.

Collaboration can be a helpful way of supporting someone who faces an overwhelming task. Clients will often use their coaching time to collaborate with me on tasks that they have found difficult to do on their own: completing goals, creating a resume, working through an assessment, or putting together a book proposal. Working on a task with another person releases the pressure and opens up room for the client to think creatively.

A second way for the coach to support the client through collaboration is to encourage the client to find a partner to collaborate with. Perhaps the client wants to clean her basement or learn a difficult skill. Sometimes the client will benefit by scanning his or her network of acquaintances for someone who might be willing to barter skills (for example, "I'll teach you how to make a bookshelf if you teach me how to knit") or attend a class together.

Assistance

When I was seven months pregnant with my first child, I fell while walking to church. The next day was Christmas Eve. Not only did I have to preach that evening, I was expecting a whole houseful of guests for supper. I needed support. Not the "kind friend on the phone" support or even the "let's do it together" support but the "sit your butt down while I do the work" assistance. Thankfully, a friend was willing to come over and begin meal preparations while I put my feet up and rested. Without her assistance, I could not have survived the night's agenda!

Sometimes those we serve need assistance; they need our physical presence and help negotiating life. People usually require this assistance in one-time emergency situations. In my own ministry, I have helped people get proper medical and psychiatric care, enter shelters, and get food when the cupboards are bare. My colleagues share similar stories. As a coach, I have had little opportunity to offer this sort of assistance, but I know that there may be times when it is absolutely appropriate.

Codependent Behavior

In a helping relationship such as coaching or spiritual leadership, considering the challenge of codependent behavior is important. People who act in codependent ways demonstrate an unhealthy responsibility for the behavior and feelings of other people. They may feel a need to rescue another person, to do more than their share in and for the relationship. Support can easily become unhealthy. It's the responsibility of the coach or the spiritual leader to keep healthy boundaries and to watch for signs of codependent behavior. Here are some signals to watch out for:

- Needing to help out of fear of another's disapproval
- Consistently doing more than your share in the relationship
- Feeling like another person's success or failure depends on what you do or do not do (say or do not say)
- Difficulty setting or keeping boundaries
- An extreme need to be approved of or recognized by others

The typical reaction to feelings of codependency, either your own or another's, is either to cling or to run. Both are less than healthy reactions. When you see signs of codependency in yourself, evaluating your own behavior can be helpful. Review your patterns of codependent behavior. Once you know the situations and personality types that trigger these moments, you will have an easier time recognizing that your impulse to rescue is part of your own set of relational habits and not a healthy response to those you work with. Then, plan strategies to cope with these feelings. Sometimes the best strategy is

simply to learn how to sit with the discomfort of not helping, res-
cuing, saying yes, or whatever behavior characterizes your
codependency. This can take time and may require the support of a
therapist.

When you notice codependency in another, you may want to
create a plan for addressing this. In my experience, clients who act
in codependent ways benefit from a combination of regular affirmation within the confines of the coaching conversation and strong
boundaries. For example, a client who insists that she cannot do
a task on her own might not benefit by collaboration or assistance.
Instead, the coach might work with the client to come up with a list
of strengths that indicate that she can successfully complete the
task. They might create a plan of action together, but then the client
will do the task alone, perhaps reporting to the coach when it is
finished.

Defining codependent behavior can be especially confusing for
people of faith. Some of Jesus's words, such as "love your enemies
and pray for those who persecute you," sound codependent (Matt.
5:44). But Jesus's life practice was one of balance between indepen-
dence and connectedness—hardly codependent. Jesus said no and
disagreed with others, as he did when Peter rebuked Jesus about his
prediction of his own death and resurrection (Matt. 16:21–23). Jesus
changed his mind about healing the daughter of the Canaanite woman
(Matt. 15:21–28). He spoke and acted for the truth, even when it was
unpopular (see the cleansing of the temple, Matt. 21:12–17). Jesus also
took care of himself, taking time to be both alone in prayer and with
friends. Jesus's life embodied healthy relationship.

A Final Word

Jesus encouraged supporting one another. In fact, he linked our support of one another with our love and care of him. He said, "for I was
hungry and you gave me food, I was thirsty and you gave me something to drink, I was a stranger and you welcomed me, I was naked
and you gave me clothing, I was sick and you took care of me, I was in
prison and you visited me" (Matt. 25:35-36). When we care for one
another, we care for Jesus.

Try

Choose a project or situation and take turns working through the four phases of support with a partner:

supportive conversation
supportive presence
collaboration
assistance

When you have finished, reflect on the following questions:

- When your partner was supporting you, what was helpful to you at each stage on the support continuum?
- When you were supporting your partner, what did you notice about each stage?
- How did you discern when to offer each stage of support?

Talk

1. Discuss your experiences of offering support to others. How do you judge what sort of support is necessary in each situation?
2. Share your experiences with codependent behavior. Using the list of signals found on page 179, consider the following questions: When have you acted this way in a relationship? What happened? How did you handle it? When has someone behaved in one of these ways with you? How did you deal with it?
3. Share biblical texts and theological ideas about helping.

38 ❀ Coach to Advise

Please give me some good advice in your next letter. I promise not to follow it.

Edna St. Vincent Millay

One Sunday afternoon my daughter Elly and her friend Helen created their own superhero costumes. Helen jumped from the window seat to the floor and shouted, "I'm Super-Helen. I'm here to save the day!" Then Elly jumped and declared, "I'm Super-Elly. I'm here to save the world!" As a child, I also imagined that I had superpowers. I fantasized about how my special knowledge or power would save my teacher, classmates, and even the school from utter destruction.

As spiritual leaders, we may have similar fantasies. We want to help people. It feels good to offer concrete answers and directions to life's quandaries. I have the same need as a coach. I want the client to tell me that something I said supported them in making a key shift. Clients also want me to offer some bit of wisdom or advice to hold onto.

When coaching first emerged as a profession, its leaders wanted to distinguish it from consulting and therapy. For that reason, some of the first coaches and coach training programs argued against any kind of directive work with clients, including consulting and advising. As the coaching profession has developed and matured, coaches have seen the value of interacting with clients using a variety of styles, including ones that lean more toward advising. This chapter will consider how leaders can make use of the three steps on the advising continuum: reflecting, educating, and advising. Note that though we will treat each tool as a separate entity for the purposes of clarity, the distinctions are somewhat arbitrary. Most coaching conversations use a combination of the three tools.

Reflecting

When my young daughter heard that she could not spend the night at Grandma's house, she was brokenhearted. She sobbed for two hours. For much of that time, I held her in my arms and talked to her. I knew that offering a list of the fun things I had planned for us to do together would simply fall flat when she felt this much loss. Instead, I used a technique I had learned from therapist Harville Hendrix while watching the *Oprah* show many years ago. I listened to Elly's story of why she felt sad and I empathized with her. I said, "I bet you feel really sad that you can't go to Grandma's." She would sob her agreement. Together we did this repeatedly, Elly remembering what she would be missing and me expressing my empathy. Much later, we got to the solution stage—the ways we could make her time at home fun for her. I have used this process for years with my children and have modified it to use with my coaching clients. This four-step process is designed to help clients feel heard and find a solution to their dilemmas.

Step 1: Listen. The client tells his or her story. The coach listens intently and says things like, "Is that all?" and "Tell me more."

Step 2: Reflect. The coach reflects the story back to the client asking, "Is this what you are saying?"

Step 3: Empathize. The coach empathizes with the client's experience saying, "I can imagine that the experience must have been _____ for you."

Repeat as needed. The coach and client repeat the first three steps as often as necessary until the client feels ready to move from storytelling to solving.

Step 4: Solve. The coach and client work together to find a solution. The coach asks the client, "What do you want to happen?" The coach may have some clues about what the client wants from listening to the storytelling process. The client talks though a strategy for solving the situation with the coach. The coach listens and reflects, but the solution comes from the client not the coach.

Educating

Educating is the next step on the advising continuum. My pastor speaks frequently to the young people about the importance of education. One Sunday she asked various members of the congregation to stand up—an eye doctor, a teacher, a licensed practical nurse—and she spoke about the education that paved the way to these careers. She pointed out several college students as an example of what to aim for. She then encouraged the children to talk to these young people after church to learn about how to prepare for college.

In order to get to where we want to go, we need to learn how to get there. Some things we can learn on our own by reading and observing. But sometimes we need to be taught. Many of the children at my church do not come from homes where the parents are college educated. They need someone to teach them how to prepare for college. Those of us who work as spiritual leaders did not emerge from the womb with a bunch of theological and biblical knowledge—we needed to be trained. I didn't just sit down and write a book one day.

My writing career is the product of much teaching and coaching by professors, mentors, editors, and coaches as well as years of my own hard work.

Most often, the people I work with have all the tools they need to figure out how to get from here to there—with a little coaching. But sometimes they honestly don't know. They want to manage their time better but do not know how. They dream about writing a book but do not know how to get started. They need to lead a congregation through conflict and do not have the tools to do so. This is when coach becomes both consultant and educator. If possible, the coach uses his or her knowledge to meet the client's need.

In one of my therapist's offices, there was a white board on the wall. Whenever she wanted to present a concept that might help me, she would leap up and write it on the board. Suddenly my therapist became my teacher. This therapist understood that part of her job was to gather resources that might help her clients better understand and manage their lives. I do the same. A good portion of my work time is spent learning new tools to support my clients in getting from here to there, wherever their "there" may be!

In the advising continuum, educating is the step where clients are offered some type of information instead of direct advice. Coaches who educate clients offer a variety of types of information.

EXPERIENCE

The coach shares with the client his or her own experience. For example, I have many clients who struggle with juggling the constant interruptions of modern life, including e-mail and telephone calls. I share the same struggle. I may tell them about my experience, how I've tried this or that method and now use clustering. I no longer answer the phone when it rings or look at e-mail as it comes in. I save it all for an hour later in the day. In essence, the coach functions as a mentor, saying, "This is how I have learned to do it. Maybe it will work for you."

INFORMATION

The coach shares pertinent information. For example, one of my clients was struggling to process a difficult job situation. I had recently read the book, *Asthma Free in 21 Days*, which cites the landmark medical study that proved that writing about stressful experiences can reduce the symptoms of autoimmune disorders such as asthma and rheumatoid arthritis. Forty-seven percent of the patients who wrote about a difficult life experience for 20 minutes a day, three days a week showed "clinically relevant changes in lung function."[1] This brief educational moment set my client on a course of daily journaling that brought some closure to a difficult life experience.

CONCEPT

The coach teaches a concept that is pertinent to the client's situation. One of my clients was frustrated by her coworker's inability to remember the information she presented at team meetings. I shared with her the concept of "the recency effect"—psychologists have proved that we are better able to remember what we last learned. I wondered if it might help to end their meetings with a summary of what happened so that her colleague would leave remembering his tasks. She tried the tactic and, while it didn't solve everything, it certainly improved the situation.

TOOL

The coach teaches the client a tool to use in addressing a specific situation. One of my clients was struggling to write her first book. The sheer size of the project—sixty thousand words—sent her into a panic. Though she diligently set aside time to write, she spent the time staring at the blank screen wondering where to start. I taught her a tool I had learned from Anne Lamott's book *Bird by Bird* and have taught many writers: take short assignments. I encouraged this client to make a list of all the topics she needed to cover in the book and simply write about one topic at a time. In the end, she'd be able to take the pieces and arrange them into a book. This is how novelist Janet Fitch wrote *White Oleander*—one scene at a time. The tool worked, and my client finished her first book with ease.

RESOURCE

The coach shares a resource that will support the client in making necessary changes. One of my clients began coaching needing to get organized. Her house and office were strewn with stuff—and she needed some quick relief. I gave her the name of my favorite organizing book, Julia Morgenstern's *Organizing from the Inside Out,* and shared some of the book's key concepts. By our second session, she had taken 20 boxes of clothes and books to the secondhand store and was well on her way to a more orderly life.[2]

STORY

The coach tells a story about how someone got from here to there. When I work with clients who want to write a book but feel that they're too old, I tell them about Harriet Doerr who was 73 when she published her first novel, *Stones for Ibarra*, which won the National Book Award. When a client moans about the stack of rejection letters collecting in her mailbox, I tell them that Madeleine L'Engle's Newberry Award-winning book, *A Wrinkle in Time*, was rejected by 26 publishers before Farrar, Straus, and Giroux published it in 1962. Small inspirational stories can offer a client hope.[3]

EXERCISE

Clients who are experiential learners—who learn by doing instead of listening—often learn more through completing an exercise than listening to a story.[4] One of my clients wanted to have a better attitude about his job as an associate pastor in which he often functioned as the senior pastor's flunky. I asked him to think of his job as an independent-study class. I gave him the assignment of creating a set of learning objectives, a reading list, and a set of assignments. In addition, I asked him to put together a list of how his senior pastor, other staff members, and congregational members might be helpful teachers in completing this program. This exercise put the client back in charge of his own experience, offering him the ability to make choices that would help him get as much as he could out of a difficult situation. In addition, his shift in attitude from disgruntled to curious associate minister affected the way the senior pastor treated him. Without breathing a word about his learning objectives, the associate minister was able to move into a more collegial role with his colleague.

REFER

I don't know everything. I do know how to connect people with the institutions and people who know more than I do. Often, my role as an educator is to refer clients. One of my clients wanted to start a speaking career. I have done some speaking, but I do not do it enough to offer this client concrete tools about building a career. Plus, this client lives two thousand miles away from me and operates in a whole different field of study—I cannot begin to know her network or her market. I referred her to people who would know. I gave her the names of two speakers I know who make a full-time living doing this. Then, I asked her to make a list of the people in her field who are doing what she wants to do. I instructed her to interview each of these people about how they got started and what advice they would have for her.

Advising

Someone once said that we only ask for advice when we want to hear that what we plan to do is the right choice. Maybe so. I have noticed that people give the advice they most need to hear themselves or that affirms their own choices. The biology professor who regrets not becoming a doctor advises his students to go into medicine. The consultant who has lost a lot of weight using a specific program tells everyone to use this program; "It's the only way to go." Some people give advice about everything—whether you want it or not. I often ride the bus with a know-it-all prophet who walks up and down the aisle advising his fellow riders on everything from our outerwear choices to our romantic lives. I don't know what's worse, that he thinks he knows everything or that he dishes out his advice without our permission!

Giving advice is tricky. The very nature of advice giving is hierarchical. It puts the advisor in a "one-up" position over the advisee. This position may suggest that the advisor is in some way better than the advisee—wiser, more spiritual, or more learned. At the very least, the advising role assumes that the advisor knows some truth that the advisee needs to know in order to move forward. The practice of advice giving can have the effect of leaving the advisee feeling less competent. Because of this, advising can seem contrary to coaching, which values mutuality and depends on the strengths of both client and coach. Still, even with these cautions, advising can be a helpful tool if used judiciously.

I have noticed that clients ask for advice more frequently in the early part of the coaching relationship. In fact, clients often show up because they want advice on managing work, significant relationships, or balancing their own lives. I attribute this to our cultural fascination with experts and the plethora of television and radio shows that dish up advice on everything from marriage to money. Because of the culture, clients want advice and direction. As the coaching relationship matures and clients feel more confident about their own strengths, clients look for advice much less frequently. Here are some guidelines for offering advice.

STICK TO WHAT YOU KNOW

I once met someone at a conference dinner who offered her dining partners advice on everything from medical problems to confirmation programs. Not that she had expertise in any of these areas—she just liked to tell people what to do. When it comes to advising, stick to the topics you know well. Never offer advice that could be harmful to others, such as medical or financial advice. I often will offer advice to clients about publishing. After working in the publishing industry for fifteen years, I have some knowledge about how to write a book proposal, connect with publishing houses, and work with editors. I am more than willing to advise clients in these areas. One client asked me if she could write off her coaching as a work expense. I had no idea and offered no advice. Her question fell into the vast area outside my expertise.

USE "I" LANGUAGE

As you offer advice, make it clear that this is how you would do it and not how everyone should do it. Often writing coaching clients will want my advice on whether they should self-publish their book or go with a traditional publisher. I explain each path, offering them the pros and cons of each. I then talk about what I did and why. I want them to know that though my decision worked for me, it would not be right for everyone.

LET GO OF OUTCOME

Several years ago a former professor of mine sent me a note congratulating me on the publication of a book. The note was mostly kind and generous. But one part grated at me. He said, "I always thought you'd become a professor. I see you've chosen to write books instead." His words made me realize how hard it is to offer our advice as a gift instead of a prescription. The most helpful advice comes with the caveat to "use as you choose."

A Final Word

One of the things I admire about my daughter is her ability to ask for what she needs. One night as I carried her upstairs to bed, I rehearsed what we had to do: brush teeth, find pajamas, say prayers, and tuck her in. "Two more things," she said. "What?" I asked. "Cuddle more and read a book together." We did. Ask and receive.

It's tough to know just what kind of support a client needs. Instead of guessing, I ask, "What kind of help do you need?" If a client is confused about what would be most supportive, I might offer the steps on the advising continuum as a sort of menu of choices. This gives clients the opportunity to ask for what they need. As Jesus said, "Ask, and it will be given you; search, and you will find; knock, and the door will be opened for you" (Matt. 7:7).

Try

With your partner, practice the step on the continuum that is most difficult for you to do. Take turns being coach and client.

Talk

1. As you look at the advising continuum—reflect, educate, advise—what other steps would you put along the way? Why?
2. As you look at Jesus, where did he most often fall on this continuum? Give examples.
3. Do you have some gauge as to when you will reflect, educate, or advise? What is it? Give examples.

39 ✹ Support Strategic Assessments

Always listen to experts. They'll tell you what can't be done and why. Then do it.

Robert Heinlein, *Do It! Let's Get Off Our Buts*

When I worked as a chaplain at a children's hospital, I often entered the lives of people I had never met. Our training taught us to make an immediate assessment of the situation, sort of like filling out a mental "who, what, why, when, where" checklist. In chaplaincy training, we had already assessed our purpose and anxieties. In each situation, we assessed the context—the needs of the patient and family members. From this information, we created a plan for ministering to the family. This assessment process became immensely helpful to me as I began to work as a coach. From it I learned that the first step in creating any strategy is assessing the situation. As I work with clients, I teach them to begin strategizing by assessing their own values and needs, the situation, and the desired outcome.

Personal Assessment

When I teach classes on creating daily spiritual practices, I encourage participants to do a body scan several times a day. I invite them to close their eyes, take three deep breaths, then scan their body from top to toes. I encourage them to use the scan as a way to discover any stress or anxiety resting in their body. The scan gives them an opportunity to purposefully relax that part of their body, bringing them a peaceful feeling. The body scan is a good image for what I ask clients to do as they begin to strategize.

The personal assessment is basically a scan of what one needs to have happen and what one can let go of in this particular situation. It assumes that the client has done some foundational work on his or her life purpose, passions, values, needs, assets, and so forth. Later in the process, the client will put together a statement of purpose. To begin the assessment process, we consider two basic questions: (1) What do you need to hold on to? (2) What can you let go of?

WHAT DO YOU NEED TO HOLD ON TO?
In my first call, I worked more than 70 hours a week. In strategizing with the church council about how I might reduce my working hours, one of the members suggested I could buy sermons. I knew that this strategy would not work for me. I could not let go of writing my own sermons. I valued the time I spent working with the text in the context of the ministry I did. I also valued the opportunity it gave me to

communicate to the congregation. As we continued to talk about reducing my work hours, I began to make a list of the ministry tasks I valued and needed to hold on to. The question to ask the client at the beginning of every strategizing process is "What do you consider to be nonnegotiable?"

When considering what the client needs to hold on to, it can be helpful to create three levels: what is absolutely necessary, what is preferable but not necessary, what would be glorious but isn't at all necessary. Think of this in terms of cake:

Necessary: the cake
Preferable: the frosting
Glorious: the decorating

WHAT CAN YOU LET GO OF?

My mother always said, "Choose your battles." Good advice. As we look at what we need to hold on to, we can also look at what we are willing to let go of. Letting go can create room for us to make creative strategies. One of my clients was working to develop a strategy to get her family to participate in housework. The challenge for her was always her very high standards. She needed help but had difficulty with the way her husband cleaned toilets and her son folded towels. I encouraged her to make a list of five to ten tasks she could let go of controlling in the house. Once she had that list, we could think about how she might enlist family members to assume responsibility for these tasks. The question to ask is this, "What are you willing to give up?"

Situational Assessment

One fall I delivered the same retreat material in two different settings. Both groups had asked for a retreat that would help participants see God's hand in their life and think about how God might be present in the future. The first retreat group was a small gathering of 11 women in a country cottage. As I talked through my opening dialogue, the women stared straight ahead, barely engaged. No one laughed at my jokes. When I instructed the group on creating life maps, one participant after another whined about the task. "It's too hard." "My life is boring." "Mine's sad." "We can't do this." At the second retreat, more than one hundred women gathered in a church basement. I approached the day with more than a little fear. After all, I had failed so miserably the week before. But everything that had bombed the previous week succeeded. They laughed at my jokes and enthusiastically participated in the exercises.

What happened? Had I just done a poor job the first time around? Or was the first group a bunch of mean women? Neither was true. As I evaluated the two retreats, I realized that my material was more suited to a large group. In addition, members of the first group had recently been through some traumatic events that made the retreat work scary to them. I had not known this but perhaps should have asked more questions before beginning. I vowed to do better assessment work before leading another retreat.

Assessing the situation is valuable in any kind of strategic planning. Congregations that plan to do visioning work or call a new leader often do assessments of the values, beliefs, and desires of their membership as well as studying their community. Here are some things that need to be considered when making an assessment of a situation. As we look at each element, we will use my retreat experience as our example.

HISTORY

Is there historical information that is relevant? As a retreat leader, I want to know about the group's retreat history. What topics have been covered? What were successful retreats? Why? Which ones were not successful? Why not? Is there any congregational history that would be helpful to know?

CULTURE

What is the culture of the group, individual, or situation you are encountering? When I prepare to lead a retreat, it is helpful for me to know some things about the participants:

   age
   gender
   race
   cultural background
   socioeconomic status

educational level

professional interests

individual or group norms (For example, it helps to know if the group is comfortable with participating in discussions or used to lectures.)

CURRENT CONTEXT

What's happening right now? What values or fears guide the current behavior of the individual, group, or institution? Is there an economic, leadership, or health crisis that is determining the behavior of the individual or group? In preparing to lead the retreat I described above, knowing that several of the members were experiencing a life crisis would have helped me. It's also helpful to know about community pressures, political agendas, and any other significant shift that might affect a community.

Assessing the Purpose

Once the client has made a personal and situational assessment, it is time to assess the client's goal for the outcome of the situation. What does he or she want to happen? One of my first clients was a high-level magazine editor who had failed at five job interviews when he came to me for coaching. John is an expert at putting together content that sells magazines. He's also intelligent and a bit impatient with others. At job interviews, John wanted to prove his expertise. John often did that by criticizing a magazine's current editorial decisions. Instead of sounding smart, John appeared arrogant and rude. He offended the very people he needed to win over: his potential employers.

I asked John about his purpose for interviews. John wanted to show his knowledge. While that may be part of what needed to happen in an interview, this purpose didn't seem to be working. I thought John might benefit from shifting his purpose from showing his expertise to building relationships with the interviewers. Once John had shifted this, he was able to shift his strategy for interviewing.

Consider the client's personal purpose. What does he or she want to happen? John approached his strategy with a purpose or goal. He might also have made a statement about what he needed to accomplish. Simplistically, he wanted to get a job. But, he might also have said that his purpose was to develop a trusting relationship with the magazine staff so that they would be more likely to hire him.

Some people find it more useful to create a guiding question. Phrase the client's purpose or result in the form of a question you can use as a sort of measuring stick while creating a strategy. For example, John's guiding question might be, "Is this strategy going to help me build relationship?" As he developed a strategy, he would then ask that question of every step in the plan he was creating.

Putting It All Together

When I first learned to drive a car, every action required a whole lot of thought. It's as if I had a mental checklist for everything that needed to be assessed, starting with my own posture and ending with the situation on the road. In those days, driving took a lot more mental energy. I do the same tasks today, but because I've been driving for so long, these assessments have become almost second nature to me.

I would say the same thing about this process of preparing to strategize. When I began coaching, I almost wanted to create a cheat sheet of the assessment questions I needed to ask when a client needed to strategize. Now this assessment process comes more easily. The length of time it takes to complete each assessment will vary depending on the client-coach history, the complexity of the situation, and the personality of the client.

THE CLIENT-COACH HISTORY
It may take longer to do an assessment in a new coaching relationship because the trust level is still developing. Once coach and client have assessed one situation, the next one will go much quicker.

THE COMPLEXITY OF THE SITUATION
It's much easier to do an assessment for a personal goal than it is to complete an assessment for a client who will be interacting with an institution that has multiple layers of authority such as managers, coworkers, operating committees, and advisory boards.

THE PERSONALITY OF THE CLIENT
Some clients love this stuff and are good at it. Some clients have difficulty making assessments or simply do not like it. For clients who

connect with the work, the process can go fairly quickly. For clients who have difficulty, each step might require more time devoted to educating and exploring examples.

As a leader, it may take some time to learn each step in this assessment process, but once you have done it several times, it will be like driving a car. You won't need to run through that mental checklist. You'll just zoom ahead.

Try

With your partner, take turns coaching each other through the work of assessing a situation. It will be helpful if you can use a real situation from your life.

Talk

1. In what ways has your training and work as a spiritual leader prepared you to assess situations?
2. What assessment tools or questions have you found helpful?

---

40 ❀ Strategize

> The method of the enterprising is to plan with audacity, execute with vigor; to sketch out possibilities; and then to treat them as probabilities.
>
> Christian Nestell Bovee, American lawyer and author

When the first churches I served began to experience serious conflict, I looked for help. As a new pastor, I needed someone to work with me in developing a strategy for leading. One leader encouraged me to "let the criticism roll off your back." He offered to give me a hug. Another pastor asked me if I loved the congregation enough. A third had a list of tips for avoiding conflict. All of these people intended to help me. Not one was able to give me what I needed—someone to strategize with me.

This changed when I attended the Center for Family Process in Bethesda, Maryland, with family-systems instructor Rabbi Edwin

Friedman. Spiritual leaders, therapists, coaches, and consultants gathered to strategize about how to work with individuals, families, congregations, and other institutions. Individuals would present a situation and together the group would strategize about it. The process changed the way I looked at problems or conflict. In the past, I had seen life's challenges as something to:

- avoid
- complain about
- make me stronger (what doesn't kill you, you know!)
- reinforce my status as a victim, rescuer, or persecutor

These challenges became opportunities to think creatively. Like playing chess or figuring out a Sudoku puzzle, I could develop strategies that would help me more successfully do anything from creating an exercise plan to working with a family in crisis.

As a coach, much of what I do involves supporting clients in developing strategies. In addition, I want the client to learn to use the process of strategizing as a tool in their life and work. This chapter will cover some of the tools I use to support people in developing a strategy. Although each of the tools is presented separately, I almost always use them in combination with one another.

Coaching the Gap

Often when I work out in the mornings, I listen to a song by the rock group Switchfoot that says, "This is your life, are you who you want to be?"[1] This song reminds me to evaluate the present and consider the possibility of a new vision for some aspect of my life. Often a vision will emerge over several mornings. Lately I've been wanting to learn how to make movies. I spoke with a friend about this desire. "What would you need to do to learn how to do that?" she asked. "Take some classes," I said. She pushed me on this, asking, "How about just getting a camera. Maybe do an online tutorial. Why do you need a class?" Back and forth we went, talking through various options for gaining experience. Her words began to help me lay out the steps that might build a bridge across the gap of my ignorance to the place where I could actually shoot a film.

"Coaching the gap" is a tool I use to support clients who experience a gap between where they are and where they want to be. The goal is to help them create a strategy that gets them from here to there. In a sense, the coach functions as a sort of travel agent, supporting the client in creating a TripTik travel plan that moves them from place A to place B. My friend helped me begin do this with my filmmaking goal just by asking some simple questions. Coaching the gap involves three basic questions:

- Where are you?
- Where do you want to be?
- How can you get from here to there?

The coach then works with the client to discover how to create the bridge that links here and there. I once worked with a client who wanted to write more regularly. Unfortunately, her husband moved every year or so, and her writing plans (as well as her files) often got lost due to the pressing agenda of resettling a household. By the time I met her, she had a clear idea of what she wanted to accomplish: to write 20 hours a week without losing more than a week to a move. "What do you need to do to make that happen?" I asked her. We spoke some about the problems she had encountered with frequent moves: she had difficulty getting connected to a writing group, and it took her some time to establish a routine and locate files after she moved. We developed a strategy that included

- Joining an online writing group.
- Developing an e-mail relationship with a writing buddy. They could provide each other with e-mail and phone support, even in the midst of a move.
- Creating a writing routine that did not depend on a stable physical space.
- Creating a writing box that could hold all of her current projects and be easily moved with her in the car.

These simple strategies helped this client close the gap and do what she had dreamed about, write professionally. This strategy took only one session to develop. Other coaching-the-gap strategies may take longer. They may require that the client do more work research-ing the options that would help him or her move across the gap.

Do What the Client Knows

My client, who I'll call Robert, was finishing his PhD dissertation. When Robert contacted me for coaching, he was tired, overbooked, and need-ing to figure out how to finish this dissertation in the next two months. Robert's work was complicated by the fact that he had a difficult topic and was writing in a language that was not native to him. We began our coaching work together by making a list of the writing habits that had worked for Robert in the past. Obviously, he had developed some research and writing skills to get this far into a graduate program. We made a list of the actions that made writing doable for Robert, such as taking frequent breaks, pushing himself to write even when he did not feel ready, and tackling the hardest work first thing in the morning. We also looked at what life support pieces—like daily exercise, plenty of rest, and a good diet—had strengthened his ability to work in the past. We then developed a strategy for approaching the dissertation based on his previous good experiences.

Often the best way to develop a strategy is to get the client to come up with a list of the actions that worked in the past. Sometimes in the midst of a new and challenging situation, we forget that we are actually quite accomplished at this task called life. I invite the client to list the strengths or strategies that he or she used in previous simi-lar situations. Often a client needs to fish around in his or her memory bank to come up with a story or two that reveals these strategies. At times, I need to help the client see the strategies embedded in the story. One client told me of her love for shooting the breeze with her parishioners. She told it to me as a way of illustrating how bad she was at wasting time. I saw it differently. This woman's love of conver-sation demonstrated her gift of developing relationships. Her goal, though, was to use her time to communicate her ministry purpose to the congregation she served. She had created a list of ways that she thought she should do this. I wondered aloud, "What if this thing you're already doing became your strategy?" Meaning, what if you spoke about your purpose in these conversations you're already having. It worked.

When clients have difficulty coming up with strengths or stories that reveal strengths, I ask them to make a list of the ten achievements they are most proud of. If clients have time, I may ask them to create a list of five achievements for each decade of their life. Then I ask them to make a list of the strengths and strategies that helped them reach each of these goals. I usually invite them to review the list with me, thinking aloud how they might use each of these in whatever challenge they are currently strategizing about. The motto of this tool is: when you don't know what to do, do what you know how to do!

Do What the Coach Knows

After my daughter was born, I sat down to finish writing a book. Because I was breastfeeding, I continued to eat for two. When I finished the book four months later, I *looked* like I had been eating for three. For the next two years I complained about my bulging belly. Doing aerobics with the television helped a bit, but my workout times were sporadic. On most days napping seemed much more inviting. When I finally threw out my maternity pants and bought a pair of jeans, I was stunned to see that I had gained four pant sizes. Finally, I began working with a wellness coach. This woman had spent her life getting healthy and now helped others do the same. We began to strategize about the situation. "What's your goal? What's doable?" she'd ask. I wanted to be able to chase after my daughter without being short of breath. Being able to fit into my old clothes also sounded good. But I was too busy to do anything but work and eat! My coach suggested that a pedometer would measure my current level of activity and help us strategize how I could increase it. The pedometer got me into an active relationship with my health. After seeing that I was easily walking five thousand steps each day in the house, I set the goal of walking ten thousand steps a day. My coach had worked with hundreds of women in similar situations. She wore a pedometer herself. She didn't waste our time having me try to figure out how to make my goal. She told me what had worked for her and her clients. From her collection of tips, we created ten strategies for achieving this goal (take a daily walk, park as far from the door as possible, make more trips than necessary up and down the stairs). It worked. Watching the pedometer became a game, and I worked hard to increase my steps, proud of every step past ten thousand. A year later I had dropped those four pant sizes.

Over time, people in the helping professions develop strategies that work. As a coach, I am always seeking new strategies to help my clients with the situations they experience most frequently. Sometimes the most efficient method of supporting a client in strategizing is presenting two or three strategies to the client. The coach and client can talk about which of the strategies might work. Then the client promises to try one or more of the strategies (sometimes in combination). This is exactly what my wellness coach did with me. After a few weeks of working with her strategies, we had a session in which we spoke about what worked and what didn't work. My feedback allowed her to offer new strategies and adjust the ones I was using so that I could continue to achieve my goal.

Coaching by Committee

A few years ago my family went through a difficult time. We had just purchased a new house when my husband's job ended suddenly. My work was nowhere near full time. I could not imagine how we would pay our mortgage, fund our health insurance, and feed the children. To supplement our income, I had added several part-time jobs. Keeping track of my various jobs, a seven-year-old, and an eighteen-month-old was enough to drive me bonkers. Since my husband's job was with a church, we also lost our community of faith. A friend invited me to attend the Quaker meeting with her. It sounded good. The hour I spent at meeting each week was the only slice of peace I knew. After one meeting, my friend said, "Did you know that you can request a clearness committee?" A clearness committee is a group of people who will meet with someone facing a dilemma and support them in finding clarity. As I mention elsewhere in this book, coaches call this a "research and development team"[2]—a group of people we gather to help us strategize around a situation or issue. This is exactly what we did with Rabbi Edwin Friedman and his staff at the Center for Family Process. When clients experience a predicament that seems confusing, I often suggest they form a clearness committee. Here are some suggestions I offer clients for this process.

SET A GOAL

Write down your goal for the clearness committee session (for example, to explore my interest in pursuing this job with corporation XYZ). If articulating a goal is difficult, create a list of guiding questions. Then decide what kind of support you need, questions, advice, or storytelling.

SELECT PARTICIPANTS

Choose people you trust. A clearness committee works best when populated by people who offer a variety of opinions and expertise. When you make the invitation, be clear on what you are asking group members to do. Tell them both the goal and the kind of support you are looking for (for example, questions, advice, challenge).

CHOOSE A FACILITATOR

A facilitator will help the conversation move forward appropriately. It can be helpful if either you or the facilitator sets ground rules for the meeting. Ground rules can cover anything from setting a time limit for the meeting to how participants interact with you. For example, at clearness committee sessions, participants only ask questions and do not make statements.

Ask someone to take notes for you so that you can be present in the conversation. Or, if the members of the group agree, make an electronic recording of the meeting.

REVIEW

A day or so after the meeting, set aside time to review the meeting notes and to develop your strategy. Meeting with a trusted friend or coach to review the content of the meeting and your reactions may help the process.

An alternative to the clearness committee is a group coaching session. In group coaching, several people with a common interest meet with a coach. The time is divided up into a variety of tasks, including individual check-in and updates, a coach presentation on a topic of interest, coaching individual members around a specific situation, and giving homework assignments. This process can be helpful for supporting people in similar situations to create and use new strategies.

Some coaches will gather a group of clients who are all facing similar challenges (for example, setting priorities) to work together. This can be a helpful way to offer a strategizing session to a group of individual people.

The "Let's Suppose" Game

When I was growing up, I never wanted to be lassoed into working in the kitchen with the women. So during family gatherings, especially the ones without kids my age, I would hang out with the men. They usually gathered somewhere out of the way, holding beers and shuffling their weight back and forth from foot to foot. The men would start with a few rounds of stories about odd happenings around town— you know, talking about poor Elmer Lamppinen who was just trying to do his business in his outhouse when some nasty teenaged boys came along and tipped it over. Each story would end with a staccato of "Well, how about that!" Then it was time to tackle the big stuff, imagining how to fix everything from their snowmobiles to the state of the country. When someone had an idea to pose, they would introduce it by saying, "Well, I suppose a guy could . . ." The rest would echo, "Jah, I suppose a guy could do that if they had a . . ." And on it went until the men came up with a strategy for doing whatever it was they were talking about doing.

These afternoon sessions taught me a valuable strategizing tool— supposing. Supposing is the art of imagining possibilities. Those who suppose are willing to ask the question, "What if?" This form of strategizing can be playful, asking the person to consider his or her wildest dreams. Here are some ways to strategize by playing the "Let's Suppose" game.

Propose a bunch of strategies in a row, using the phrase "What if you . . ." Don't edit them for realism or propriety: the wilder the better. Sometimes it's the odd strategies that pave the way for the workable ones.

Switch roles and ask the client to coach you about the issue. Use the same technique of proposing strategies using the phrase, "What if." It can be easier to think of strategies for another person.

Up the fun and creativity of the above two games by adding action to the ideas. Have the person who is offering the "what if" suggestion toss playing cards with each suggestion or perhaps clap, hop, take a step, or toss a ball or small beanbag. Using one's body while playing the "what if" game can sometimes loosen up the mind (or drive you crazy!).

Ask the person to create a mind map of possibilities for action. A mind map is simply visual brainstorm. Draw a circle in the middle and label it with the dilemma. Using spokes and more circles (and as many colors as you like) write down as many strategies as possible. Which one feels most helpful? Most inviting? Which one are you drawn to? Which one can you justify doing?

Ask the person to come up with strategies from another person's point of view. For example, I once asked a client how they might approach a conflict on their congregational council as a circus clown, a military strategist, and Mother Teresa. Each persona gave the client an opportunity to craft unique strategies. This tool also works well if the person making the strategy chooses two or three people they admire to use in the exercise.

Ask the client to think about the situation metaphorically. It often helps if the metaphor mirrors either something the client is skilled at in his or her life or the situation they are creating a strategy for (or both). For example, for a client who happened to be a mother of young children and was dealing with an antagonistic member of her parish, I asked, "What would your strategy be if this were your three-year-old who was shouting at meetings?" For a client who was able to cook fabulous meals every night but couldn't settle down to write his sermon each week, I asked: "What strategies do you use to get that meal from conception to completion each night?" Here are some other metaphors that have worked. What would your strategy be if you were

- Trying to catch a fish?
- Planning a party?
- Designing a piece of jewelry?
- Teaching a group of kindergarten students?
- Preparing to perform a solo in a concert?

Some of the best supposing happens by people who are not tied to the past or the future. As a professor of mine used to say, "I'd rather work with the under eight and over eighty crowd any day." I agree. When all else fails in the game of supposing, ask the experts. I currently have two people I contact regularly for supposing: an eighty-year-old friend from my book group and my four-year-old daughter. The eighty-year-old has seen enough come and go in her lifetime to be able to think beyond the obvious or the expected. My daughter hasn't seen enough to be bound by reality or rules. And both of these wise ones know the value of taking breaks to play and have treats.

The Value of Waiting

Internal and external pressures can make emergencies where there are none. We become driven to come up with a strategy both by our own need for closure (or at least movement) and by the pressures of people and institutions. Still, strategizing, like most other things in life, depends on good timing. When strategizing doesn't seem to be working, we tend to start blaming others and ourselves:

- They are not committed to the process.
- They don't really care about me.
- They do not understand the seriousness of the issues.
- They are stuck in the past.
- She does not have any good ideas.
- He doesn't know how to help me.
- I'm not smart, creative, or imaginative enough to do this.
- I'm too tired.
- I don't have enough power in the system to make a strategy.

Blaming solves nothing. When all other pieces are in place, and even when some are not, those involved in strategizing need to consider the timing. Just as it's helpful to go with what's working, it's also helpful to stop doing what's not working. When strategizing isn't going anywhere, stop and try again another time.

A Final Word

I've always loved that quote about the best laid plans of mice and humans going awry. Strategies are meant to be revised and even broken. God's spirit can blow over us, something "epiphs," and suddenly the strategy doesn't make sense anymore. So we change things around and it works better.

One Christmas my daughter had fun rearranging the figures in each of the nativity sets. Sometimes the shepherds watched the baby Jesus while Mary had a conversation with the wise ones and Joseph took the sheep for a walk in the field. Each time I'd put the figures back into a traditional arrangement, my daughter would move them around again. "Mom, you're messing up their conversations!" she'd chastise me. Her willingness to play with my arrangements reminds me daily to make my strategies and then let go, always asking God to continue making miracles and epiphanies!

Try

With your partner, take turns coaching each other through the work of strategizing, using one or more of the tools above. Just like in the last chapter, using a real situation from your life if you can will make it most helpful.

Talk

1. What biblical passages or historical stories show people of faith strategizing?
2. Who has helped you to strategize? What happened? What did they do that worked?
3. Share a story of a group strategizing process that worked well. What factors made it work?

41 ✸ Address Difficult Behavior

Any silly little soul
Easily can pick a hole.
Nursery rhyme

My colleague's outburst took me by surprise. This person had much to say about my presence and performance at a recent meeting, and none of it was positive. My colleague perceived that my message undermined his objectives. This person communicated by labeling, blaming, and demeaning me. I felt blindsided and flabbergasted. Suddenly I was in a competition that I had not entered. Because I didn't know how to respond, I didn't. I told my colleague that I needed time to think. In the following days, I saw several clients. In an odd sort of serendipity, many told of encountering difficult behavior from people at work and in the community. They knew nothing of my experience, and yet their stories mirrored mine perfectly. We all encounter people who behave in ways that are difficult. We do not always behave well. We struggle to understand and then respond in the best way possible. This chapter looks at that dilemma.

Identifying Difficult Behavior

A wide variety of behaviors can qualify as difficult. These behaviors include:

- criticizing
- making jokes at another's expense
- making sarcastic remarks
- belittling things, activities, or people that another values
- demeaning another person's performance, experience, training, or values
- calling someone names or labeling him or her
- refusing to celebrate another's successes
- disagreeing with the majority of another person's ideas, suggestions, or behaviors
- not listening
- giving unsolicited advice
- verbally abusing
- taking advantage of another person
- bringing up another's past mistakes
- failing to respect boundaries
- encouraging someone to engage in self-destructive behaviors
- sabotaging plans or efforts to take care of oneself or one's needs
- breaking promises
- expecting another to meet one's unspoken needs
- threatening

- attempting to control another person
- using praise to manipulate
- gossiping to or about another
- refusing to take responsibility for one's own life
- complaining
- blaming other people for one's problems
- physically or sexually abusing
- making a catastrophe out of daily events
- lying
- refusing to engage as a way of punishing[1]

If you're like me, you probably read that list and thought, "Oh crap! That's me." Yup. The list describes behaviors that *all of us* practice. We are human. We fail to love one another as Jesus commanded. Out of our fears, insecurities, and bad habits, we hurt other people, even those we love. For that we reason we practice confession and forgiveness. We apologize to God and to those we hurt. We ask for forgiveness. We try to transform our lives and relationships so that they reflect God's love and hopes for us. As we transform our lives, we try to identify and change the behaviors that do not work, such as those listed above. Recognizing the severity or toxicity of the difficult behavior in our lives, relationships, and in the institutions we work in can also be helpful. The level of toxicity depends on factors such as:

- the type of relationship
- the frequency of the behavior
- the type of behavior
- the connection between type of behavior and a person's areas of sensitivity

All difficult behavior hurts. Difficult behavior from someone who our culture expects to be loving and supportive—such as a parent, spouse, or child—can be especially painful, even toxic or damaging. When the people we depend on to give us safe harbor instead become the storm, we can feel like we are drowning.

The more we are exposed to toxic behavior, the deeper it affects us. Psychologists discovered that post-traumatic stress disorder can result from a severe trauma (witnessing a murder, being raped) or from experiencing a long siege of traumas (fighting in a war, growing up in an abusive environment).

All difficult behavior can damage us. Some behavior, such as verbal, physical, and sexual abuse, is toxic. It leaves deep and abiding wounds and can destroy us.

Each of us defines normal behavior differently. To some of you, this list might look like the script for your family's Thanksgiving dinner. Others may think the list describes the behavior of monsters in a horror movie. Many factors influence your understanding of what behaviors are difficult or even toxic, including your family system, the systems you live and work in, faith tradition and practice, emotional maturity, education, and so forth. For example, a friend grew up hearing her parents call her stupid. Because of this, encounters that demean her intelligence upset her more than they might upset another person. As you begin to identify and discuss toxic behavior in your life and relationships, it's helpful to keep in mind that people will have different definitions—and unique responses.

Responding to Difficult Behavior

Triage means the sorting and prioritizing of patients in an emergency situation. Often patients are treated at multiple levels—by a team of first responders on site, the emergency room workers at the hospital, and their own personal physicians.

Triage might be a helpful concept for thinking about how to respond to difficult behavior. Level one is making the first response—what do you do when difficult behavior happens or comes to your attention? This is the stage for making immediate decisions, much like the emergency medical technicians do when responding to an accident. Level two can be compared to the work done both by emergency room physicians and personal physicians. This is the stage when we need to analyze the situation, identify the goal, and outline a treatment plan. Level three puts the plan into practice.

THE FIRST RESPONSE

You walk into the office, and the secretary greets you with an angry scowl and the words, "I'm angry with you. Really angry." At the monthly board meeting, you learn that the board members met privately last week and have developed a list of complaints about your work. You call your friend to hear how he is doing and he lashes out at you for not calling sooner. You have come to expect this behavior from him about once a month.

Toxicity happens. Sometimes it takes us by surprise. At other times, it becomes a familiar part of the relationship, as regular as breathing. How we first respond to difficult behavior, whether it occurs within our professional or personal relationships, can impact its level, duration, and effect on us. Here are some thoughts on what has worked for me and for my clients as we coped with difficult behavior in a variety of relationships, including those with colleagues, clients, parishioners, friends, and family members.

Get safe. In cases of difficult behavior that threaten your physical safety, get out. This is not the time to think about being nice or worrying about offending another person. If you or the people you are responsible for are in physical danger, get to a place of safety and get help.

Take a time out. Ever try to reason with a small child throwing a temper tantrum? It's not wise. One is liable to get kicked or punched in uncomfortable places. When my daughter throws herself on the floor in a rage, I leave her there to work it through. When she has calmed down, we usually make better progress at understanding one another. In children and adults, difficult behavior is matched with high emotion. We become like a kicking and screaming child, held captive by our needs and emotionality. When we encounter people who are acting like that, it's often best to simply ask for a time out. Ask the person who is attacking you to talk again when he or she is feeling calmer.

Someone who is in the middle of an attack can only see the target. The attacker cannot think about the consequences of their behavior. And they certainly cannot listen or reason well. A time out can give both parties the needed space to approach the situation with more resources.

Avoid reacting. When I was a child, I was terrified of dogs. At five, I'd been jumped on and pinned to the ground by the neighbor's German shepherd. Afterwards, I had trouble telling the difference between friendly and aggressive dogs. Any dog made me want to perch on top of my mother's head. My parents and other adults tried to teach me that the dogs could sense my anxiety and that made them more effusive. They encouraged me to remain calm. When I could do it, it worked. My calmness often diffused the dog's aggression.

In the face of an attack, our brains respond with a fight or flight response: attack back or get the heck out of the way.[2] We may want to match the attacker's behavior with similar behavior of our own—yelling, complaining, gossiping, or demeaning. Our reactivity can be like yeast, doubling the size of the altercation. Instead, remaining calm and responding as little as possible is helpful. It is always okay to say:

- I need to think about what you said.
- I need to get back to you on that.
- Thank you for sharing. I'll take your opinion under consideration.

Diffuse the situation. When I was a teenager, my brother would secretly shake up my soda can so that when I opened it, the soda would explode all over my face. That's diffusion—letting the excess emotion escape. A number of actions can help diffuse difficult behavior.

When my daughter has a temper tantrum, attending to her only makes it worse. *Ignoring* her behavior, even moving to another room, tends to take the energy out of her tantrum. Sometimes people persist in acting badly because it gets them what they crave—attention. Ignoring them takes away the reward.

Often people act in a difficult way because they need to be heard and do not know how to ask for this. *Listening* and demonstrating understanding can diffuse anger. Several chapters in this book speak about developing good listening skills.

People who act in difficult ways might believe that no one understands them, so they must act this way in order to get action. We can diffuse the intensity of this behavior by *empathizing* with the speaker. We can say, "I can understand how this might be difficult for you" or "I see how that could cause you to feel hurt and angry." Empathizing with the person does not mean agreeing with their bad behavior.

Sometimes my daughter will respond to me with the words, "Go away. I don't want you." In those moments, seeing her little hand extended like a stop sign, it's hard to remember that I love her deeply. It's even harder to tell her that. But that's exactly when she needs to hear it most. In the midst of her whiny, obstreperous moments, this little girl desperately needs me to *express care* and love for her. Sometimes hearing those words diffuses her anger.

In all of our relationships, even the rockiest ones, the people we connect with need to hear that we care about them. It's especially important to tell people this when they are behaving like three-year-old children who have missed a few naps. Sometimes expressing our care can still stormy waters.

Sometimes people have legitimate complaints but poor methods of communicating them. Taking responsibility for our part in any problem and *apologizing* for it can help.

At times we can work out difficult behavior in a one-on-one session. It's almost always helpful to get distance from a disagreement. Setting aside the conflict for the time being and *offering to work it out* at a later time gives both parties the opportunity to get calm, consider their goal for the conversation, and think through the best ways to approach the situation. In the case of abusive or regularly difficult behavior within a relationship, *always* use the support of a third party. A therapist, mediator, listening team, or coach can support people in connecting with one another in more helpful, meaningful ways.

ANALYZING THE SITUATION

After my colleague attacked me, I knew I had some analyzing to do. Because this was a person I occasionally worked with, we needed to resolve the conflict. I could avoid confronting the issue for a few weeks, but eventually I would need to work it out. I spoke with my coach and a few trusted friends to consider how best to handle the situation. These outsiders were able to approach the relationship with a clarity that I lacked. They asked me questions and offered suggestions that helped me form a useful strategy. Here are some questions to ask yourself when you experience the difficult behavior of another person. You may also use them to support other people in analyzing difficult behavior.

How is this behavior about the other person? We often project our own feelings onto other people. When an attack is bigger than the situation warrants, thinking about the context can be helpful. For example, your coworker feels anxious about problems with her son who has attention deficit disorder. She begins to pick at you and other office members about your lack of organization. Your boss is depressed and lacks passion for her job. She accuses you of lacking passion for your work. A colleague perceives that your work might compete with his goals, so he attempts to discredit you publicly. These situations bear one commonality: the attacker acts out of his or her own life situation.

Ask yourself: In what ways does this behavior reflect the speaker's life situation, concerns, or goals? How can this information help me understand what has happened? Does this information shift the way I might respond?

How is this behavior about me? Toxic behavior is not about us. Nothing we do can control the behavior of another person. We cannot cause or invite nasty words and actions. Still, because this behavior exists within a relationship, which includes more than one person, considering what our part might be in the way the relationship unfolds can be helpful. When we think about our role in difficult situations, we stop being a victim and begin to be an actor in our own life. Some questions we might ask include:

- Is there any truth in what the person is saying? What is it?
- What do I communicate when I allow this behavior?
- In what ways do I participate in this behavior?
- What am I getting out of this behavior or relationship?

What do I need to do to take care of myself in this situation? Difficult behavior can wreak havoc with our personal lives. When I served as the minister of two conflicted congregations, difficult behavior was the norm. Not a day went by that I didn't deal with difficult or toxic behavior. The relentless cycle of conflict left me physically and emotionally exhausted. When I didn't take time to deal with my feelings about the difficult behavior, I would explode at drivers, my spouse, and benign events. I got sick more often than usual. I lost sleep and weight. In time I learned that I needed to care for myself as well as those I was serving. When your life includes regularly dealing with difficult behavior, self-care is essential.

In times of stress, our bodies require more rest and nurturing than usual. Stress may crowd out some of our healthy behaviors (exercise, socializing, prayer) and push us toward our worst behaviors (poor eating habits, alcohol and drug consumption, compulsive spending or gambling). In stressful times more than any other time, we need to be vigilant about caring for ourselves.

Difficult behavior can leave us feeling vulnerable. At times, our physical or emotional safety may be at risk. Think about what you need to feel safe in the situation. This might include not meeting alone with the person who behaves inappropriately, limiting or avoiding contact with this person, or ending the relationship.

When confronting difficult behavior, consulting other people for emotional and spiritual support, for strategizing, and to learn new communication tools can be helpful.

Often when I get into bed for an afternoon read or nap, my daughter will jump in next to me. Because our home is kept fairly chilly in the winter, she'll usually end up crawling on top of me. I'll complain, "Honey, this just isn't comfortable. Can you move?" She'll respond, "But it's comfortable for me!" Each of us has a different comfort level in relationships. We know what works and doesn't work for us. When we consider self-care and what we are comfortable with in relationships, thinking in terms of what we want our relationships to look like can be helpful. When I coach, I often begin by asking about the end: what do you want to happen? In situations of conflict or difficult behavior, the same types of questions are appropriate:

- What do you need from this person?
- What do you need from this relationship?
- What are you no longer willing to tolerate in this relationship?
- What boundaries do you need to set?
- What do you want to do or say about this difficult behavior?
- What do you want to express when you discuss this difficult behavior?
- What do you need to do or not do in order to maintain your integrity?
- What do you need to hear from the other person? How can you ask for that?
- What will be different after the conversation?

How do I act in a way that reflects Jesus's love? Jesus commanded us to love one another. This command is not always easy to follow. As a sign on a friend's wall reads, "Jesus may love you, but the rest of us think you're an ass!" Jesus calls us to love everyone—not just the people who love us back in the ways we appreciate being loved. Jesus expressed this call many times in the course of his ministry. He proclaimed, "Love your enemies and pray for those who persecute you" (Matt. 5:44). He continued by saying, "For if you love those who love you, what reward do you have?" (v. 46). The message could not be more clear: love without regard to reciprocity.

But how? How do we love those who are hard to love? One Transfiguration Sunday at my congregation, Pastor Joe Ellwanger said that Jesus is "transfigured before us again and again." He reminded us that Jesus's death and resurrection do not set us apart from others but calls us to immerse ourselves in the needs of the community. He talked about the ways Jesus is transfigured in our midst, saying that Jesus is transfigured when we pray and when we forgive.

Pray. Forgive. These are good ways to love when we do not know how to love. When we do not know how to make a relationship work, when loving seems to be more than we can do, we can always bring the person we cannot love into the wide embrace of Jesus's love. We cannot love others on our own. We can only love others with the strength of Jesus's transforming love. We do this when we pray for the ones we cannot get along with. We do this when we forgive, letting go of our hate, anger, and need for revenge.

When do I need to let go? Even Jesus, who advocated actively receiving evildoers (see Matt. 5:38-42), set limits to accepting difficult behavior. When Jesus sent out his disciples to preach and teach, he instructed, "If anyone will not welcome you or listen to your words, shake off the dust from your feet as you leave that house or town" (Matt. 10:14). Note that Jesus did not say, "Try and try again." Later, when Jesus spoke about dealing with one who sins against you, he advocated a three-step process of speaking alone to the person, speaking in the presence of one or two others, and speaking in front of the church. He concluded by saying, "If the member refuses to listen even to the church, let such a one be to you as a Gentile and a tax collector" (Matt. 18:17). In other words, when it does not work out, move on. We, too, need to decide when enough is enough, and moving on is healthier than continuing in a sick relationship.

TALKING IT THROUGH

Although I love to analyze my way through a tough situation, sooner or later I'm going to have to actually face that colleague who attacked me. He and the problem won't go away no matter how long I ignore the telephone and e-mail! We will need to have this difficult conversation. When we do, I will try to use all of my coaching skills to communicate (listen and speak) well. Most of those skills (such as listening well, welcoming, and practicing fierce presence) are elaborated in great detail in this section of the book and do not need to be repeated here. The following list of behaviors contains tools specific to the practice of talking through difficult behavior. These will not guarantee a perfect process, but they will help improve the quality of the conversation.

- State your purpose for the meeting. ("I hope that we can resolve . . ." or "I need to talk to you about an experience I had with you.")
- Use "I" language. ("I feel" or "I think.")
- Describe the behavior in terms of your experience. ("I experienced your calling me names as threatening behavior" instead of "You called me bad names! You threatened me!")
- Describe how you felt instead of labeling the person or the behavior. ("I felt talked down to" instead of "You're a pedantic pain in the butt.")
- Express what you need to be different. ("I need you to stop blaming me each time you encounter difficulty.")
- Express any consequences for the person's not changing. ("I cannot tolerate being yelled at; I need this to change or I cannot meet with you alone anymore.")

A Final Word

After the difficult encounter with my colleague, this song kept running through my head: "I pray for you. You pray for me. I love you; I need you to survive."[3] In the face of difficult behavior, we may be tempted to lash out in revenge ("I'll get you for that!") or crawl into bed. ("Wake me when it's over.") I certainly was. This song reminded me of what I had forgotten to do: pray. Aristotle once said that a good story has a beginning, a middle, and an end. Perhaps that's a good prescription for when to pray in the midst of conflict and difficulty— at the beginning, the middle, and the end of the process.

Working out our difficulties with one another can challenge and tire us. Some days it may feel like we encounter more that's falling apart than what is working together for good. In those moments, when we feel like we cannot handle the chaos, we need to hand it over to God. As my pastor prayed one Sunday, "In the midst of things we cannot understand and in the face of forces we cannot face alone, we ask for God's strength." Indeed we do. And we trust that the God who raised Jesus from the dead can also make new our wounded hearts and broken relationships.

Try

1. Practice diffusing difficult behavior. With your partner, take turns being difficult and dealing with difficult behavior, using the first response skills above.
2. Create a strategy for dealing with difficult people. With your partner, take turns presenting a difficult situation. Work through the analyzing questions above and develop a strategy for coping with the behavior.

Talk

1. What biblical, theological, and spiritual resources help you understand and deal with difficult behavior?
2. This chapter has talked about how to diffuse and deal with difficult behavior. Sometimes our words and actions feed difficult behavior, such as when we give an antagonist extra attention to "keep them happy." Make a list of behaviors that feed difficult behaviors. What can you do to avoid these?
3. Talk about ways you can support each other in dealing with difficult behavior.

42 ✸ Apologize

> So to be forgiven is only half the gift. The other half is that *we* also can forgive, restore, and liberate, and therefore we can feel the will of God enacted through us, which is the great restoration of ourselves to ourselves.
>
> Marilynne Robinson, *Gilead*

My daughter was watching television in the family room while I sorted mail on the dining room table. I heard her yell, "I want Jesus. Jesus!!!! *I waaant Jesus.*" Thinking she needed some sort of spiritual help (and who better to give it to her than her spiritual-leader mother), I ran to the back room and asked, "What do you mean you want Jesus?" She looked at me like I imagine she will during her teenaged years and yelled, "Cheez-Its. I said, 'Cheez-Its.' I *waaant* Cheez-Its." Leaving the room, I thought how easy it is to misunderstand one another, even about something so simple as Cheez-Its.

Life is difficult. Relationships are also difficult. In the midst of the same old stuff—hurting each other, apologizing, and hurting again—we hope for something new. Perhaps the next new relationship will be the one where we finally get it right. New relationships—especially professional ones—hold the hope of the tabula rasa, the clean slate. But this tabula rasa is a myth. Like collectors, we bring to every relationship a life stuffed full with the patterns and pains we have gathered from our previous relationships. This collection of difficult and life-giving experiences, beliefs, feelings, needs, and desires drives the ways we relate. Our collection can complicate communication in myriad ways. Perhaps someone we loved turned us away and now we fear rejection. As a result, we do not ask for what we need, and when we don't get it we may feel resentful. Or, our history may make us feel extra sensitive about some issues. When they surface in conversation, our reaction is bigger than may be merited by the context.

In addition to bringing our collection of old stuff, we bring a bunch of hopes and expectations. We may project our needs onto the people we relate with, expecting them to be and do all that we have hoped for. Obviously, all this stuff coming from both parties makes communication enormously difficult. As a result, we mess up. Inadvertently or with intent, we hurt one another. Maybe we say something hurtful. Or we fail to give care in the face of need. Or maybe we simply fail to pay attention to the one we are with. All this seems pretty obvious; we're human, we're imperfect, we fail one another all the time.

Paving the Way

As both a coach and a spiritual leader, I know that misunderstandings happen. While I never set out to hurt those I minister with and to, I know that I do. And as much as I hope that tomorrow will be different, I know that tomorrow I will be the same broken human being I am today. Even though I will try to do my best, I will fail again and again at this job God has called me to do. Kathie Lee Gifford once said that every morning she asked God to prevent her from saying anything stupid or hurtful. Each morning I pray the same prayer. Each night I beg God for forgiveness. (It seems that God can't quite keep up with my tongue!) Because I know that I will hurt and disappoint people, I've learned how to apologize to my clients.

When I was in my first call, I was frequently in trouble for not doing things I didn't know I was supposed to do. I would get a report that someone was mad at me for not visiting them when they were in the hospital. "But I didn't know!" I would say. "You should have known," they would reply. I wondered if they thought psychic powers had been conferred upon me at ordination. We worked together to pave the way for better communication. I repeatedly asked people to tell me when I had hurt or disappointed them. I could not apologize for or repair hurt that I did not know about. I was always thankful when someone approached me privately with his or her anger or pain.

In order to apologize, we need to know how we have hurt other people. We can pave the way for having these kinds of conversations. In the coaching contract I give my clients I say, "If I ever say something that upsets you, that doesn't feel right, or doesn't fit for you, please bring it up. I promise to make you right for it. And I promise to do what is necessary to have you satisfied." I repeat these words verbally to my clients at the outset of the coaching relationship. This conversation sets the stage for talking about misunderstandings and hurts.

A Four-Step Process

Making rules about open communication and apologizing doesn't make it any easier. There's a saying in politics and business, "Never apologize. Never explain. Never concede." Somehow my son learned this at an early age. After he misbehaved, we sent our young son to the timeout step. After a few minutes, we gave him a small lecture about his deeds. "Do you understand?" we would ask him. He would nod his head yes, wanting to be set free. His key to freedom was apologizing. We would prompt him. He would wiggle, looking intently at the floor. We'd encourage. No deal. We'd leave him on the step for another minute. When we came back, he would usually give in, not wanting to lose any more minutes of his precious life to the step. "Sorry," he'd mumble so quickly that it sounded like he'd said, "Sri."

"Excuse me?"

He'd mumble the word again—just a bit louder—and then hearing our "Okay, honey," he'd rush off the steps to freedom.

Repentance is tough. Apologizing, the step in the process that requires us to admit our fault to the person we have hurt, can be even harder. It was tough for my son at age three, and it isn't any easier as an adult.

In my experience, apologizing is a four-step process: hearing our sin, apologizing, making it right, and asking for forgiveness.

HEARING OUR SIN

One of the most important and difficult parts of the apology process is hearing how we have hurt another person. It's not comfortable to hear about our mistakes. We want to defend ourselves. We want to say, "No, you're wrong, I'm not that bad!"

Instead, we need to be still and listen. It's always helpful to the person we have hurt if we can attempt to understand how our words, action, or inaction might have been hurtful. It's important that we hear everything the person needs to say. In my experience, the best way to do this is to listen quietly and then ask, "Is that all?" If not, say, "Tell me more." We can repeat this invitation until the person we have hurt tells us that they are finished speaking. When they are done telling us their story, it is helpful to check that we have understood them. "Is this what you are saying?" we ask, repeating the story they have told us. We do this until we get it right.

APOLOGIZING

We take responsibility for our failure—intended or not. We say, "I'm sorry." We do not qualify our apology by saying

- I'm sorry *if you thought* I was trying to hurt you.
- I'm sorry *if you took* offense at what I said.
- I'm sorry *if you felt* that way.
- I'm sorry *if you heard* me say that.

When we qualify our apology, we avoid taking responsibility, and we demean the other person. It's as if we are saying, "Well I had no hand in this hurt. I'm sorry you're so . . ." Fill in the blank: I'm sorry you . . .

- are so sensitive.
- expect so much.
- misunderstood.
- are confused.
- don't hear well.

Apologies do not need a lot of words. The best apology is a simple, "I'm sorry."

MAKING IT RIGHT

When I was a kid, I heard grown-ups saying, "Forgive and forget." Not bad advice—unless the forgetting comes too quickly. Before the pain of the hurt dulls, taking actions to make the connection right is important. Misunderstandings and mistakes provide us with the opportunity to better the relationship.

Both parties need to discuss what can be done to bring healing to the relationship. That includes asking the questions:

- What do we need to do or say to make the relationship right again?
- What does this situation teach us about needs that have not been met in the relationship?

- What does this situation teach us about the most helpful ways to express these needs?
- What do we need to do or say differently from now on?

Often, the fixes in these situations are quite simple. Perhaps the client needs us to read and respond to his e-mail messages more quickly. Maybe our congregational member needs some verbal indication that we heard and understood her. Perhaps we need to receive clear requests for help—hints are not enough. If we do our work together, we will end the conversation with a better relationship than we began with.

ASKING FOR FORGIVENESS

Before we set aside this chapter in our lives, receiving forgiveness is critical. As a friend of mine was saying the other day, we're not so comfortable with these words, "I forgive you." We're much more likely to say:

- It's okay.
- No big deal.
- Don't worry about it.
- What's done is done.
- All's well that ends well.

But none of these words has the power of "I forgive you." To say "I forgive you" is literally to say we are letting go of any claim for punishment or payment. We are ending our hold on the other person. We are setting them free.

In order to move forward in any relationship, we need to know that our sins are forgiven. It's hard to be content with the no-big-deal phrases when we suspect that this *was* a big deal. The people in the relationship need to move on from a place of freedom, no longer worrying that the sin will plague the relationship. If the wronged person does not offer forgiveness, simply ask, "Do you forgive me?"

Actions to Avoid

My liturgy professor, Gordon Lathrop, told a story about choir members that used to bow during the procession just as each member reached a certain point halfway up the aisle. The practice seemed nonsensical to the new pastor. When he explored the reason behind the bowing, he discovered that there used to be a low arch just at that point in the aisle. In previous times, choir members had to bow to get under the arch.

Like those choir members, we may adopt practices that serve us well at one time and then continue the practices long past their effectiveness. For example, someone may work for an employer who is mistrustful and requires that employees submit long, detailed explanations for every mistake. This worker may believe that every boss needs these long explanations and carry that habit into the next job. Most of us have developed ways of dealing with conflict. Some of these habits may become reflexes, mostly unconscious habits. We often develop these habits as a way of protecting ourselves from being hurt in a relationship. But self-protective habits can also halt communication, keeping relationships from growing. The following actions are self-protective habits that are not helpful in a conflicted situation.

AVOIDANCE

Nobody likes conflict. Some deal with it by practicing avoidance. Instead of treating the complaint seriously, we may make a joke, minimize the situation, leave (physically or emotionally), or brush off the complainer.

DEFENDING

What is it they say in sports? The best offense is a good defense. That may be true in sports, but it can make a mess in a personal relationship. Some of us react to conflict by defending ourselves. This may mean explaining our actions or blaming other people or events for our behavior. We may place our need to be right—and defend our rightness—over our care for the other person or the relationship.

ATTACKING

When an animal feels cornered and sees no escape, it attacks. Humans do too. In response to confrontation, we may avoid taking responsibility by attacking the person who raises the issue.

CONDITIONAL APOLOGIES

As mentioned above, apologies that avoid taking responsibility by shifting the blame to the person who has an issue with us are not apologies. An apology takes full responsibility for hurting another person.

WHEN APOLOGY IS THE ONLY SONG

Sometimes relationships, even professional ones, can develop unhelpful patterns. Kenny Rogers sang, "You got to know when to hold 'em, know when to fold 'em, know when to walk away, and know when to run." Coaching or ministry relationships can become mostly about "how you done me wrong" and less about moving forward. In these times, when apology is the only song you sing, ending the relationship may be healthier than continuing a relationship that is frustrating for both parties.

Repentance

One Advent the pastor spoke about John the Baptist, saying, "The Advent message John the Baptist bears is one we cannot bear" to hear. Facing our sins is like that; hearing how we have failed or disappointed God and one another can be some of the most painful moments of our lives. During that sermon, the pastor reminded us that in order to repent, we must stay in the room with people like John, people who are telling us the truth about ourselves. She concluded by saying, "even the most repentant among us cannot be saved by repentance—the forgiveness we need must come from God's hand."[1]

We need to face the truth of our lives. We need to hear the people who have hard things to say to us no matter how much it hurts. We need to turn toward the relationship, toward the ones we have hurt, be it God, client, spouse, parishioner, child, or friend. We apologize and ask for forgiveness. We do all of this knowing that we rest in God's hands. Our repentance, our work and our words, cannot save either us or the relationship. Only God can.

Try

With your partner, role-play the four-step apology process. If you have time, try some of the unhelpful behaviors with one another. Discuss the difference between the two from both points of view.

Talk

1. What do the Bible and your own theological tradition say about sin, repentance, and forgiveness?

2. Share a story about how someone's apology changed your relationship for the better. What actions or words made the difference?

---

43   ❀   Network

Carol, meet Rochelle.

Rochelle, meet Carol.

Author's personal e-mail

My coaching colleague Tim Pearson excels at networking. The above e-mail came from Tim, connecting me to another coach colleague. One of Tim's gifts is connecting people to people. When he knows two people he thinks might support or encourage one another, he introduces them. Tim's gift has brought many new friends and colleagues into my circle. These people have enriched my life and my coaching practice. As the old saying goes, it's not *what* you know but *who* you know.

In the coaching community, whenever we come up against a new situation or a problem we talk about forming research and development teams. We get people together on the phone to discuss a topic. We glean information from each other on how to coach, market, write, and so forth. In my coach training program, the instructors encouraged us to take this idea one step further and create a list of one hundred people that were part of our "coaching team." The team consists of people from different professions, medicine, real estate, social services, and so forth. The team provides the coach with a list of good people to recommend to their clients who are seeking support and services.

Probably the oldest form of connecting people is the matchmaker. Naomi did it for Ruth and Boaz. A good friend of mine introduced me to my husband—a man living more than one thousand miles away. But there are other reasons to connect people, including

- professional services (dentist, physician, therapist, real estate);
- common interests (art, stamp collecting, sailing);

- common life situations (age, stage of family development, illnesses, loss);
- common goals (create a youth group, earn a degree);
- mentoring (literacy training, career mentoring, Big Brothers Big Sisters);
- organized support groups (grief, trauma recovery, 12-step programs);
- service projects (Habitat for Humanity, shelters, neighborhood ministry programs);
- specific knowledge (about a country you want to visit, an activity you want to learn).

I have seen these networks work in the lives of clients and people I coach. When one of my clients was beginning her ministry, we worked together to connect her to spiritual leaders whose ministry paralleled what she wanted to do. She spent a day shadowing each of these leaders. Another client makes it his habit to connect with people outside his profession, believing that he has something to learn from everyone. Another spiritual leader I know tries to connect the lonely people in her parish with one another, often putting together children with older adults.

Networking at its most superficial level may seem almost utilitarian. A sort of "I'll help you, if you'll help me" arrangement. This type of exchange, while somewhat mechanical and at times lacking depth, can still be quite helpful. When we network, we gain a list of people we can turn to when we need support with specific challenges, such as a broken-down car or birds in the attic. Over time, as our relationships with the people in our networks grow, we become more than mere acquaintances. Our connections deepen and strengthen and a connective web of support emerges around us. Author and consultant Sally Helgesen, in her book *The Female Advantage*, talked about the value of developing webs of inclusion in our leadership. She says, "Webs link people together in unorthodox ways, reaching across traditional hierarchical levels to do so, but also enable them to keep and expand those links once their task is finished."[1] This might mean that as we talk with our car mechanic, we learn that she is also a gifted guitarist. We may invite her to play at our congregation or to teach in a summer arts program for youth. The connection grows deeper and the potential for igniting change is created.

As spiritual leaders, we have seen how superficial connections can deepen. Many of the people who walk through the church doors on Sunday morning do so because someone invited them, connecting an individual to a community of faith. The people who stay are the ones who get connected to other people during the first few visits. People rarely stay at a church just because the music is nice or the paraments are pretty. They stay because people care about them, because they feel the tug of human relationship.

I have watched my young daughter create friends out of acquaintances at the church we attend. At first, church was somewhere she just went with Mom. Now, church is somewhere she goes because, as she says, "I need to see my friends." And she has plenty of friends! Not just the children who flock around her like devoted fans, but also the adults—her beloved pastor, the pastor's aunt, the pianist, and a woman who is ill with AIDS. These people are her safety net, part of the web of people who pray for her and hold her when she feels sad. When Elly learned that one of the little girls at church also suffered from seizure disorder, Elly ran over to hug her, telling me, "We need to pray her better and hug her better." Her connecting does not stop there, though. Elly's new habit is to stand at the front of the communion line, hugging people as they come forward.

At church one Sunday, a woman from Big Brothers Big Sisters came to tell us about a new program called "Amachi," designed for children who have one or both parents incarcerated. *Amachi* is a South African word that means, "Who knows but what God has brought us through this child." That word reminds me that God can make much out of our connecting. When we connect with other people, we get new ideas for changing our lives and the world around us. When we connect the people we minister to and with to others in our circle of influence, we enlarge the potential for change and growth in the world. How does that famous quote attributed to Margaret Mead go? "Never doubt that a small group of thoughtful, committed citizens can change the world. Indeed, it's the only thing that ever has."

Try

1. Who do you know? Put together your list of the people you know in various professions.

2. As you look at your list consider:

   - What types of persons would it be helpful for you to know?
   - How and where might you meet them?
   - Are there people you know of but have not yet met?
   - Who might you connect to whom?

3. Create a "to connect" list of people you want to meet, places you need to connect with (such as a book group, support group, or resource center), and people you want to connect with one another. Connect with one person on your "to connect" list.

Talk

1. Share an inspiring experience around connecting. What happened and why did it work?
2. Share your connection lists with one another. How can you support each other in making connections?

---

44 ✸ Recommend Resources

It is a good plan to have a book with you in all places and at all times. If you are presently without, hurry without delay to the nearest shop and buy one of mine.

Oliver Wendell Holmes

I wanted to comfort Gloria Dump. And I decided that the best way to do that would be to read her a book, read it to her loud enough to keep the ghosts away.

India Opal Buloni in *Because of Winn-Dixie*

In my senior year of seminary, I walked with a friend each evening after dinner. Every time I picked her up at her dorm room, she was reading a different book. "What class is that for?" I'd ask. Invariably she'd answer, "Oh, just for fun." After several weeks of having this same conversation, my friend told me that she tried to read a book a week in addition to reading for class. "It keeps me sane," she said.

During those graduate school years, my professor Tim Lull also talked about reading books. He insisted that we read outside of our profession. He believed that reading mysteries taught spiritual leaders how to think critically. He told us that literature would help us better comprehend the character of individuals. While I was a graduate student, he recommended many authors that have become favorite friends, among them Barbara Pym and W. H. Auden. I would often leave his home or office with a book in my hands and the commission "Read this."

I have been a reader since I learned how at age three. But school nearly robbed me of the pleasure of reading for fun. Largely because of the witness of my friend and the encouragement of Dr. Lull, I began my own personal reading program. Since 1993, I have tried to read at least one book a week—sometimes as many as four. In the years since I began reading regularly, these books have become significant mentors to me. In times when God seemed absent and life was unbearably lonely, books became my spiritual companions. Books keep me up late into the night. Books give comfort in the wee hours when sleep becomes a stranger. They teach me about people I have never met and ideas I have not yet considered. Books take me to places I may never see and times in history that I cannot visit. Their stories create new landscapes in my imagination.

As a coach, I am always recommending books and other resources to my clients. I'm not alone. My current coach suggests a book nearly every week. The women in my coaching group regularly recommend Web sites and other tools. Many of my clients provide the same service to their parishioners and ministry partners. They connect people with tools that can support them. Besides books and Web sites, they connect people to organizations, leadership and other training programs, topical resource groups, and the people who might be able to recommend other resources.

At the beginning of the weekly public radio program "Whad'Ya Know?" the host, Michael Feldman, shouts, "Whad'ya know?" The audience responds, "Not much! You?" In this age of information overload, each of us can know only a small chunk of information. Pointing to books and resources provides additional tools for the people we serve. When someone asks us questions, sometimes the best answer to give is, "I don't know, but I have heard about a resource on the topic."

Try

1. What do you know? Make a list of the topics you might recommend resources about, such as books and resources about 12-step recovery programs, autism spectrum disorders, or communicating well. Write down two or three resources under each topic.
2. What do you want to know? Make a list of topics you are interested in knowing more about.
3. Create a system for storing resource lists. Some leaders I know have stored resource files on computer documents. Others set aside a file drawer for resources. Do what works for you.

Talk

1. Share your lists of resources and expertise with one another. How else might you support one another in recommending resources?
2. Discuss the methods you have found helpful for recommending resources to other people.

45 ❋ Create Records

> I too decided . . . to write an orderly account for you, most excellent Theophilus, so that you may know the truth concerning the things about which you have been instructed.
>
> Luke 1:3-4

I'm a pack rat. I still have the stories I wrote in grade school and some of the clothes and shoes I wore in high school. Shortly after the birth of my second child, faced with an avalanche of stuff, I sorted through the piles of papers I had been accumulating since birth. I discovered a cache of letters from high school and college. A large number belonged to a particularly prolific friend of mine. Not wanting to simply toss this slice of history, I tied them with a ribbon, placed them in a pretty box, and mailed them to her as part of her Christmas present. I received an exuberant thank you. Her note said something like, "These letters provide a record of feelings and events, some long forgotten, but many still vital to me. As I look to new harbors, it is helpful to remember the old ones." I knew what she meant. For years I have kept journals. These records remind me of long-forgotten passions and pains. Looking back, I can measure my progress and connect with the parts of me that got lost in the shuffle of life.

As a coach, I work with clients to create a record of our work together. Although some records such as contracts and receipts are standard, most of the tools we use to mark our time together are individual to each coaching relationship. Below, I have written about some of the tools coaches and clients use to keep records of their work together. Depending on your work setting, some of these tools can also be helpful to you as a spiritual leader. One caution: if your work setting is a congregation or other place where people have fairly open access to your computer or filing cabinet, take steps to protect the confidentiality of the people you work with. For example, some of my colleagues carry confidential files with them. Others keep them on personal laptop computers.

Record-Keeping Tools

Basic records to keep include contracts, receipts, client files, assessments, journals, meeting records, homework assignments, client progress reports, and "extras."

A *contract* or *covenant* sets forth the parameters of the coaching relationship. The contents may include names and contact information for participants; cost, length, and frequency of sessions; a set of policies and practices; and a place for each participant to sign and date the agreement. Spiritual leaders may want to work with their leadership team to develop a covenant for counseling and the other ways spiritual leaders connect with other people (for example, mentoring or small group leadership).

A *receipt* provides a record of the date, time, and nature of the service provided as well as the amount of money paid for the session.

Most coaches keep a *file* for each client. Files include contact information, contracts, receipts, a record of each meeting, and any other recorded material relevant to the work the coach and client do together.

Many spiritual leaders keep some type of record for the people they work with. A parish pastor I know keeps an index card for each member. On it he marks some of the following information: contact information; baptism, membership, and marriage dates; communion, hospital, and counseling visits; pastoral ministries (funerals, weddings); and stewardship information. Other colleagues keep similar records on their personal or handheld computers.

Coaches may choose to use *assessment tools* to help the client evaluate the present or discern steps for the future. Assessment tools exist to appraise just about anything, including one's eating habits, communication style, happiness quotient, emotional intelligence, and learning styles.

I use a wellness assessment with many of my clients. It asks participants to rate their satisfaction with their life in a number of areas, including physical health, relationship health, and job satisfaction. For each item, participants also indicate whether or not they want to improve their score. For example, a client might check that she does not eat well and also check that she is happy with her poor eating habits. This assessment, given at the beginning, middle, and end of my work with clients, is a helpful tool for guiding the content of our work together. It also shows the client the ways in which he or she has made progress.

Assessments can also be helpful tools for spiritual leaders. Gift or asset inventories, leadership sorters, and personality assessments can be particularly useful to support leaders in working together.

I ask each client to keep some sort of *record* of the work we do together. I have noticed that most of my clients set aside a journal specifically for this purpose. In it they make session notes, complete homework assignments, and write down goals for future sessions. They also use the journal to record resources I recommend and to work through some of the questions raised in and between sessions.

When I served as a parish pastor, I kept a personal journal. I recorded both my daily ministry tasks as well as a narrative about my experiences that included my personal reflections. Other colleagues have told me that they use their journals as a record of worship service content, worship attendance, sermon themes, resolutions and goals, and congregational and personal visions.

I keep a written record of each coaching session. In it I list: how the client has done with homework assignments, new events, the topics we discuss, client insights, and any homework I assign. I try to record anything that feels like a significant goal, dream, desire, or insight. I also write down any resources I recommend. I review at least the previous session's notes before each session. Looking back at what the client has said helps me to hold before the clients their life goals and passions. For the most part, I do not share these records with clients. In one case, I had a client who wanted me to keep careful notes of our time together and then send them to her at the end of each session. Because she was a phone client, I typed my session notes into an e-mail while we spoke, then e-mailed them to both of us after the session. This became an easy and helpful way to keep track of our work.

Every session includes *homework*. Sometimes the homework requires that I e-mail instructions or resource suggestions to the client. I do this immediately following the session. Clients always have the option of choosing not to do the assigned homework and choosing to do something that works better for them.

I offer my clients the opportunity to e-mail me a *progress report* before each session. Progress reports include a record of what they have accomplished since the last session, what homework they did, what they did if they did not do the assigned homework, unfinished business, any updates on life events, and a list of questions or goals for the upcoming session. I print copies of each report, as well as any other e-mail communication a client makes, and keep these in the client's file.

Extras are the ways I provide added value to my clients. Between sessions I often will come across a poem, resource, quote, or question that relates to a client. I will put this resource in a card or an e-mail and send it to the client as a way of providing support to the client. I also produce an e-mail newsletter with reflections and exercises in it. All of my clients receive a free subscription, and our work often relates to ideas I raise in the newsletter. Often it is the work I do with clients that suggests the themes and topics for the monthly newsletter.

Spiritual leaders often provide extras for the people they work with as well. These include handwritten cards, inspirational books, devotional tools, written prayers, devotional flyers or brochures, prayer cards, and so forth.

Do What Works

About a year into working with my first coach, I confessed to her that I hated filling out weekly progress reports. "They just don't work for me," I said. She replied, "Then don't do them. Do what works." Her words have become my mantra when it comes to making records. I only do what works and I encourage clients to do the same. Sometimes it takes some time and negotiation to figure out what works for a particular client. That's fine. The result always turns out to be the right thing for the people involved!

Try

1. As you work with people in the next week, try one or more of the above record-keeping practices. Does it work? Is it something you want to add?
2. Make an online search of assessments. Are there any you think might be helpful to use in the work you do? What will it take to get permission or training to use them? How will you go about it?

Talk

1. Talk about the record keeping you do in your ministry situation. What might be helpful practices to add in the work you do with people?
2. What sorts of assessments do you use in your ministry setting? Which assessments have been particularly helpful and why?
3. What sort of "written extras" do you give to the people you minister with and to?

46   ✸   Practice Patience

Are we there yet?
>   Everychild

"But I want to figure it out now!" bemoaned my client. She had recently started a new job. The position was unique to both the congregation and the larger church. She didn't have a job description or a model to follow. She had a big task ahead of her discovering the perimeters of the job and educating both the congregation and the church about it. Like most of us, she wanted to jump ahead through the messy and boring parts.

I often wish that the changes I envision for my life could happen instantly. As a child watching reruns of *Bewitched*, I coveted the powers of Tabitha, the girl-witch who could make almost anything happen with a twitch of her nose. Last Christmas, my dreams came true. Well, sort of. Our son got The Clapper for Christmas. What joy! We scurried home from my parents' house, and almost before we had shed our coats we had installed the device in our son's bedroom, attached to both the light and the radio. Two claps bring light into your darkness, three bring music to your silence. With a little play, we discovered that some carefully toned words, tongue clicking, even the sound of the radio, could turn the light on and off. Too cool.

The Clapper got me thinking: wouldn't it be great if this technology could be applied to the rest of my life? *Clap-clap, clap-on*—the kids are dressed. No morning hassles about what to wear or which pair of my son's underwear, lying side by side on the floor, might be the clean pair. *Clap-clap, clap-off*—the extra poundage around my middle drops off and my tummy is as toned as if I'd had an Extreme Makeover tummy tuck. I'd be like Tabitha! *Clap-clap* and I'd clean up the house! *Clap-clap* and I'd put food on the table! Why stop there? *Clap-clap*, my clients' dreams come true. *Clap-clap*, away with polluted air. *Clap-clap*, food for every hungry soul!

The popular magazines proclaim: DROP FIVE POUNDS IN A WEEK! EXERCISE FOR 20 MINUTES AND LOOK LIKE THIS! TAKE A DAY TO GET ORGANIZED FOR GOOD! We read the titles, buy the magazines, and we try. But real life does not match the immediacy of The Clapper. We do not drop the weight in a week or look like that model or get organized for good. We think, "There must be something wrong—with us." Perhaps we lack commitment or energy or the proper genes. Maybe we're just meant to be unhappy. Maybe we need to get better equipment, a more sophisticated program, a more efficient organizing plan. Or maybe we need to forget about the quick fix.

Quick fixes rarely exist or work. Most changes, at least the kind that are significant and lasting, take time and patience. I have heard that it takes 21 days to change a habit—get rid of a bad one or take on a good one. For most of my clients, the changes they seek take even more time, launching a new career, working toward healthy functioning in a dysfunctional parish, or transforming a dying congregation. When changes involve other people or circumstances outside of our control, transformation can take even longer. These transformations require patience on the part of the dreamer—and heaps of it!

Patience is also required for those of us who support the dreamers, coaches, spiritual leaders, therapists, friends, spouses, parents, and teachers. When our parishioner goes back to abusing drugs and alcohol after six months of being clean and sober, we pray for patience. When our child forgets his homework at school for the umpteenth day in a row, we count to ten. When our friend loses her third job in as many months, we take a deep breath. Patience may be a virtue, but it does not come easily—whether it is our life's dreams we're waiting on or the birth of someone else's new life.

Practicing Patience

These are some of the techniques that support practicing patience.

TELL THE TRUTH ABOUT WHAT IS

Nothing can change or grow if we do not acknowledge what is. Whether you are looking at your own life or supporting another—get honest about what is happening. I once had a client who struggled to lose weight. Although she was a physician, she lied to herself and others about the severity of her situation. She could not make real changes until she told the truth—that continuing her behavior of overeating and not exercising would kill her.

RECOGNIZE THAT WILDERNESS HAPPENS

The space between the now and the not yet can be longer and more harrowing than we imagined or hoped for. We often compare our own situations to those who have already arrived, assuming that they had an easier road or that they simply got to the good place without all the suffering and waiting. They didn't. We don't. Wilderness happens. It's a natural part of the transformation process.

TAKE RESPONSIBILITY

When things don't happen as quickly or perfectly as we desire, we may blame other people or make excuses for ourselves. Own your part in where you are and what is happening. Taking responsibility makes it possible for you to take steps to change the situation. A client of mine had endured two years of interviewing for a variety of positions—and none of the positions had been offered to him. He grew increasingly impatient to get on with his life. He had a list of the reasons things weren't working out, including the bad economy and employers that couldn't see his strengths. When he was challenged to look at his own part in the process, he wondered if he was falling short in the interview process. He took responsibility for the fact that he often didn't make a good first impression. He got some extra coaching around interviewing and was employed within three months.

TAKE STEPS

Patience with the process is easier when we feel that we are making some progress. Nothing is more frustrating than sitting still in a traffic jam. There's an old saying that goes, "Pray as if it all depends on God; work as if it all depends on you." This is the "work as if it all depends on you" part. I've always admired a friend of mine who decided in the midst of one career to embark on a new one. Her first career—ministry—had taken a long time to prepare for. The second one—medicine—took even longer. She had to begin by taking undergraduate courses. I would have gotten impatient with the process. Not my friend. She simply took the steps one at a time until one day she was what she had dreamed of becoming, a physician.

LET GO OF WHAT YOU CANNOT CONTROL

Part of our impatience is due to worrying over or working on the things and people that are out of our control. We cannot fix the lives of our parishioners. We cannot make the congregation see it our way. We cannot get our spouse to stop drinking. When we take responsibility for our part, we also need to commend to God the part that does not belong to us.

PRAY

Which brings us to the "pray as if it all depends on God" part of the process. Anne Lamott has suggested making a "God box" for the things in our lives that we are impatiently waiting on and praying for. The box gives us a place to put the things and people we are impatient to change—letting them rest in God's in-box for a change. I have a small box in the corner of my office. In it are the names of people I love, my own hurriedly scribbled frustrations, the challenging situations of clients and friends. Leaving it there reminds me in moments of restless wandering that God is somehow still watching over my impatient moments.

LAMENT

When impatience gets the best of us, we sometimes need to say that. I recently spoke with a client who was feeling discouraged about her work. She said to me, "I know it's not productive, but sometimes I just need to say that this job is discouraging." I agree. This goes back to telling the truth. The psalmists and the prophets lamented their own difficult and tragic moments. We can, too. Sometimes we cannot move on until we properly express the despair of the moment.

A Final Word

When I think about patience, the best image for me is Jesus's parable of the barren fig tree. The owner of the fig tree saw that in three years it had born no fruit. He wanted it cut down. The wise gardener suggested that the owner let it alone for another year, "until I dig around it and put manure on it" (Luke 13:8). So this is the patience of God— giving the tree one more chance and a little more help. The tree gets a year, the tender care of the gardener, and the benefit of nourishment.

In the midst of life's wildernesses and in the age of the quick fix, we need the same.

Try

This week, think about your growing edge; is it being patient with others or yourself? Choose one situation that you seek patience for and apply the tools above to it. At the end of the week, reflect on: What worked? What didn't? Why?

Talk

1. What are the benefits of patience? When is patience a problem? What are some ways of telling the difference?
2. Share with one another the techniques you use when you are feeling impatient with someone you minister to or with.
3. What biblical, theological, or other metaphors for patience have helped you in difficult times?

---

47 ⊛ Bear Light

I am about to do a new thing;
now it springs forth, do you not perceive it?
I will make a way in the wilderness
and rivers in the desert.

                                                        Isaiah 43:19

[God] has been a way for me.
[God] has done great things for me.

                              Jessy Dixon, *Songs to Get You Through*

We all encounter times when we cannot see the way God is making in the wilderness, when refreshment seems no more than mirage. I didn't go to church much for five years. For the last two of those years, I did not belong to a congregation. I now do. The shift from outsider to member happened for me because of the people who shined their lights on the path, showing me that God had made a way through the wilderness. These lights were not great big balls of fire. They were more often the dimly burning wicks Isaiah spoke about (Isa. 42:3). I saw a client creatively leading her church, providing a home for those who had never found the church to be a place of welcome. A friend shared her own struggle with the church and how she was gradually experiencing healing through the kind acts of loving friends. Another friend gently prodded me to go to a church near my home, "You might love this church." Once inside the doors of that church, a stranger turned around and said, "Welcome." A young boy led my then-three-year-old daughter back to me after the children's sermon. A woman hugged me and said, "I'm glad you're with us." Little lights. But like headlights on a dark night, each light illuminated the next step of the path. Each reminds me that God is at work in my life. And that's all I need; that's all any of us need.

As a coach, I am called to bear light for others. I did not make the path; God did. In this light-bearing business, I have two jobs. First, I shine my light around the edges of the path, reminding clients that God is the one working in and on their lives. Second, I hold up the light, so that the client can see the next part of the path.

We cannot always see God at work in our lives. In times of wilderness, we may feel that God has abandoned us. We might even blame God for the absence of blessing we desire or the presence of illness, hardship, or death. In moments of plenty, we barely have time to breathe let alone notice God. We might even take credit for our hard work, believing that the blessings come from what we do instead of what God has done. Many of my clients are spiritual leaders, busy bearing light into the lives of other people. Always the light bearers, they rarely have anyone to remind them that God is at work in their lives as well. They forget—or get uncomfortable with—their own need to be comforted. As the old minister says in the novel *Gilead*, "I've spent a good share of my life comforting the afflicted, but I could never endure the thought that anyone should try to comfort me."[1]

As coach, I gently ask clients to consider how and where God is present to them in their lives and work. I might ask questions like, "Where is God in this?" I wonder aloud about where and how I see God working in the story of their lives. If a story they tell reminds me of words from a hymn, the worship service, or the Bible, I quote it to them. Then I will ask, "What do you think?" If their story suggests a biblical story or metaphor, I ask them to think about that. I often ask clients to tell me what sustains them in the midst of whatever it is they are experiencing. These are usually signs of God at work in their lives—even if what sustains them is Eminem's music and a steaming latte. Finally, I might share how God has been present to me. Always I want the client to tell me how God is present to them. I do not want to force upon them my view of God or God's work in their lives.

The second task I have as light bearer is to illuminate the path. My clients know that God is the one who opens up the way in and through this life. But that does not mean seeing the path is always easy. All of us reach times when we feel confused about where God is calling us to be and to serve. We might be overwhelmed by the myriad voices telling us what we are good at and where we *should* work. Our own yearnings may pull us in directions that seem impractical and even difficult. Our present life might cloud our ability to see the path. We might be too content to move forward. Or we may be feeling insecure, depressed, or anxious. We do not believe that God could be asking us to serve. As a coach, I remind clients that God is calling them to use their lives. I am like the proverbial pebble in the shoe, repeatedly asking, "Where is God calling you?" or "What is God calling you to do?" It does not matter if the next step is enriching a current relationship or starting a new career. Each of us needs to have people who are shining the light onto the path, showing us where the path may go. Again, the path I illuminate is not my own but another's. I am hesitant to point to specific paths. My light might be misdirected by my own desires or needs. Instead, I persistently hold up the light and ask the client, "Where do you see God directing your path?"

In the fall, my son's school celebrates *Laternennacht*, a German festival of lights based on the legend of St. Martin. The children raise their homemade lanterns and lead their parents and friends on a journey around the neighboring park. Last year we were some of the last people in the line. We witnessed this amazing path of light, lanterns bobbing up and down in darkness, weaving around the park pathway. This image reminds me of how we serve one another. Each of us walks through our own life's path, holding up our lights. And those who wander with us see these lights and the path God is making for us.

Try

1. As you encounter people this week, look for how they are lights to you. How do they remind you that God is at work in your life? How do they light the way for you?
2. Look for ways you can be light for other people, either to remind them of God's presence in their life or to help illuminate the path. In what ways does seeing yourself as a "light bearer" change how you think about your roles?

Talk

1. Share the story of someone who has been a "path lighter" for you, reminding you of God's presence and abiding love. How does that person's work continue to support and guide you?
2. Discuss ways you either point to God's work in the lives of others or shine light on their path.
3. What biblical stories or other resources (songs, poems, favorite quotes) encourage you to be a light bearer?

 # PART 3

THE COACHING CORE

Acting for Change

⊛ Introduction

Like good stewards of the manifold grace of God, serve one another
with whatever gift each of you has received.

1 Peter 4:10

At a prayer breakfast I attended on health and poverty in the inner
city, one of the speakers talked about the troubling statistics in my
city. In 2003 and 2004 poverty in Wisconsin grew faster than in any
other state. Milwaukee became the seventh poorest city in the country. More than 41 percent of those living in poverty are children.[1] The
speaker urged the people present to take action, saying something
like, "Nothing ever happens from a passive stance."

How true. Recently my pastor spoke to the congregation about
the dangers of passivity. "What happens when you don't take care of
something?" she asked. "It withers and dies," she said. "Just look at
my plants." She went on to speak about the children God has entrusted
to us. She urged us to pray for them, to care for them, to wrap them up
in our love and attention.

My church is a place where children gather. They show up—with
parents and neighbors, alone and with friends, sometimes along with
their baby brothers and sisters to be baptized. At church, these children find arms that will hold and rock them. Those of us who attend
this church know that God gave us these children to care for. They are
our responsibility, our work, as surely as if the doctor or judge had
placed them in our arms and called us "parents."

The pastor regularly reminds us of this purpose—to love these
children and teach them about Jesus. Nobody needs to guess how to
do this. Programs and ministries exist to give the children a place to
be welcomed, fed, and taught after school. Every Sunday morning, we
are encouraged to sit with and help the children who do not come

with parents or guardians. On Sundays adults can also connect with young people during Sunday school or at the free lunch after church. These ministry programs and weekly conversation about our purpose as the people of God makes it possible for our congregation to do more than dream about loving these children. This is the work God has called us to and we do it.

In this world, God has work for all of us to do. Big jobs, too: seeking justice for the disenfranchised, making poverty history, welcoming strangers, and praying for lonely people. We often respond to this call the way my children respond to my call to work:

"It's hard!"
"What am I supposed to do about it?"
"I'm too little."
"It's not my mess."

But the stuff of this world is our mess, our responsibility, our work. The coaching conversation is intended to get people to inventory their lives, define their work, and then do it. Coaching is a catalyst for action, not postmodern naval gazing. As the Indigo Girls sing, "Now I know a refuge never grows / From a chin in a hand in a thoughtful pose / Gotta tend the earth if you want a rose."[2]

Coaching moves people from thought to action, getting them to dig in the dirt of their own lives, planting and nurturing the seeds of change. This change happens through a magical mixture of conversation and programs. This section looks at these programs—what I call the core work of coaching—completing unfinished business, strengthening foundations, assessing assets, and visioning. It's this work that gets us all off our keisters and into the world. As the Indigo Girls put it, "But my life is more than a vision / The sweetest part is acting after making a decision. . . . / If I have a care in the world I have a gift to bring."[3] The world has many cares. We bring a multitude of gifts. This section helps us bridge that gap.

48 ❀ Accepting the Past

The past is a guidepost, not a hitching post.

L. Thomas Holcroft, English dramatist and translator

On one of my first days in the office at my new parish, a woman came in to talk. She was beside herself with grief and anger. I immediately became involved with her story of betrayal. It seemed that a former pastor had, while explaining a commandment, taught her daughter every swear word he knew. The mother showed me the handout. "That must have been very hard," I empathized. "When did this happen?" Her anger was so raw—I thought this must have been an experience with either the last pastor or the interim minister. She told me that it had happened more than twenty years before.

With clients one of the first things I do is to support them in accepting and forgiving the past. Most of us, like the woman in the story above, have had difficult experiences. We have struggled with health and relationship difficulties, encountered work problems, and faced disappointments. Some of us have experienced great tragedy and trauma in our pasts. The experiences that haunt us and prevent us from moving forward in healthy ways need to be dealt with in therapy. Not everyone will need to do such work. But all of us need to come to terms with our pasts, to unhitch our lives from the difficult past experiences that bind them. As novelist Gina Berriault said, "Forgiveness means giving up all hope for a better past."[1]

As I work with clients to accept and forgive their pasts, we work in three areas:

1. Avoiding three traps that keep us stuck in our past stories: the why trap, the blame trap, and the role trap
2. Completing unfinished business
3. Grieving the past

This chapter will consider the first point, avoiding the three traps. The second and third points will be discussed in the next two chapters. Although these chapters are presented in order, this work can be done in any order that is helpful.

The Why Trap

In thinking about the past, and the hold the past has over our present day, we can get stuck in the question of why: trying to understand why we experienced what we did. As spiritual leaders, we have certainly mastered the school game. We have successfully completed at least a bachelor's degree and many of us have earned additional degrees. We are used to understanding things—complicated concepts and texts. We look for answers and find them. Moreover, we try to support people in understanding the difficulties in their own lives. We may try to offer solutions to their problems. It makes sense that when bad things happen, we want to know why. At some level, we may think that if we knew why things went wrong we could somehow fix it. We could, as my son says, "rewind." We could get a do over and make it happen differently. In novelist Joan Didion's book about the death of her husband, *The Year of Magical Thinking*, she speaks about her need to understand why he died, "I still wanted [an autopsy]. I needed to know how and why and when [death] had happened."[2] A few pages later she writes, "Whatever else had been in my mind when I so determinedly authorized an autopsy, there was also a level of derangement in which I reasoned that an autopsy could show that what had gone wrong was something simple. It could have been no more than a transitory blockage or arrhythmia. It could have required only a minor adjustment—a change in medication, say, or the resetting of a pacemaker. In this case, the reasoning went, they might still be able to fix it."[3]

Asking why isn't always a fruitless endeavor. Two good things can happen. First, we can learn things that might be useful for the future. One of my artist friends tells me that mistakes are a normal part of the creative process. Her mistakes point her to the better solution. Second, understanding why can absolve our guilt or inappropriate sense of responsibility. When Didion finally learned the cause of her husband's death, the answer did one of the best things that knowing why can do—it absolved her of guilt. She realized that nothing she could have done and nothing the paramedics could have done would have saved her husband from this death. As Didion learned, understanding the past can never change it. Thinking it can is what gets us stuck. We get stuck amassing clues to our own or another's behavior. We forsake the day at hand, losing the present moment in favor of reliving a past we cannot fix.

To move forward we need to forgive ourselves for not being God. We did the best we could at the time. Had we known better, we would have done it. In the end, we may need to accept that some things exist beyond our ability to understand them. Like a puzzle with missing pieces, we may never see the full picture. The whys and hows of some events will remain a mystery. It happened. It hurt—sometimes more than we can articulate. We move on to do better today and tomorrow, to follow God and to serve one another as best we can.

The Blame Trap

"Not me" has become a regular figure around our house.

"Who left the front door open?" I call.

"Not me."

"Who left the television on?" I ask.

"Not me."

"Who ate my Rice Krispies Treats?" I wonder.

"Not me."

My daughter points to her brother. My son points to his dad. On it goes around the house. I take responsibility for asking questions that have only one purpose: finding the culpable party. As a family, we have discovered the best defense is to blame someone else—or, at the very least, to absolve ourselves. Not me!

One way that we stay stuck in the past is by blaming our current situations on the people and events of our pasts. We would be a success if only our parents had cared enough to send us to first class schools instead of making us pay our own way through state college. We wouldn't be working at small failing churches if only our bishop had believed in us. We could be married by now if only our church wasn't so demanding of our time. You get the point. We have developed a formula for understanding our lives. The formula depends on blaming some one or some thing outside our control or power. We say, "If only [name] hadn't [action] us, we'd be [result]. There's a multitude of ways to complete the sentence, but it all ends up the same: we blame others for the mess of our present circumstances. Life coach Debbie Ford says,

> Many of us will go to our graves blaming others for the conditions of our lives. We will do anything to avoid taking responsibility for our part in our dramas. But making others wrong and holding on to the pain of our past means committing ourselves to a lifetime of limitation and misery. And as long as we are blaming others for our circumstances we have no freedom, because our resentment keeps us bound to the very people—and the very circumstances—we dislike. As long as we carry that seed of resentment in our hearts we will have to create some kind of pain, drama, or discontent in our lives in order to keep our blame alive.[4]

Ford believes the only way out of this trap is to take responsibility for ourselves. We give up any excuses (we may call them reasons) for our life situation that point to other people or events. We ask ourselves, "How am I responsible for that choice?"

Then we move forward. We forgive ourselves. We forgive other people. We forgive everyone for being human, for making mistakes, for screwing up—sometimes so royally that people were deeply hurt. We look at our pasts and say that whatever we did with our lives, whatever we didn't do with our lives, whatever was done or not done to us—God forgives us. God forgives the others. God gives us the grace and mercy to live a new day, to follow God.

The Role Trap

I noticed that within weeks of the start of school, many of the children in my daughter's four-year-old kindergarten class had a role. Clown. Caretaker. Troublemaker. Cheerleader. Brainiac. Each child acted his or her part perfectly. I wondered if these roles would stick, if these would be the labels assigned to these children in their high school yearbooks.

Like the children in my daughter's class, many of us are assigned, or take on, roles when we are very young. Victim. Bully. Savior. We don't know how to be or act outside of this role. In addition, our family, friends, and colleagues may only know how to relate to us in terms of this role. We may want our lives to be different, but we are used to playing this part. We have a story about how our lives go, and it serves as a template for each of our experiences. So the kid who was beaten up on the playground in grade school and hung out with the outsiders in high school becomes a spiritual leader. When she doesn't get asked to be on any of the presbytery's committees, she feels left out. When a group at her church meets without her, she fears that they want to kick her out. She understands the events of her life in terms of the "victim" or "outsider" role she played as a child. As the Indigo Girls sing, "I know how this goes. The plot a predictable showing."[5]

Our lives can quickly become stuck when we need to prove that the stories about our lives are true. I once knew an organist who had learned to play in only one tempo—fast and bouncy. It worked well on hymns like "Battle Hymn of the Republic." But her tempo nearly ruined the contemplative nature of hymns like "Silent Night." When we view our lives through one story or role, we become like this organist—making every song fit the tempo we know. If our stories about ourselves and others emphasize the bad, the half-empty side of life, we may begin to feel despair.

We need to learn to tell a new story about who we are and how we engage with the world. To begin to tell a new story, we first need to name the old one. What role or story have we clung to throughout our lives? Many of us have more than one role or story that defines (or confines) our lives. Once we have named these stories, we need to ask what they have given us. How has living these stories benefited us? For example, the person who lived her life as a victim realized that the role always gave her a story to tell that got her the care and attention of others. Finally, we need to ask what sort of stories we want to tell about ourselves in the future. How do we want to be and act in the world?

Here, as with the other two traps, we need to practice forgiveness. Perhaps we need to forgive the people who cast us in these roles in the first place. Maybe we need to forgive ourselves for using these roles as an excuse for not living the life God has called us to. We forgive. We move on. We live into the new roles and stories God has called us to.

Forgiving

The common theme in resolving all of these traps is forgiveness. I once heard forgiveness defined as, "giving up what is rightfully ours." When we forgive a debt, we release the other person from paying us the money that is rightfully ours. When we forgive someone who has hurt us, we let go of our right to blame him or her. When we forgive ourselves, we let go of the regret and self-punishment we feel we deserve.

On Sunday the pastor asked the children, "What do we do when someone does something wrong to us?" The children's hands went up.

"Don't do something wrong back," said one.

"Pray," said another.

"Forgive them," said a third young person.

The pastor asked, "What if this person does something wrong to you *again*?"

A young girl in the front said, "Pray some more."

The pastor quoted that day's text from Isaiah, "But you have burdened me with your sins; you have wearied me with your iniquities. I, I am [the One] who blots out your transgressions for my own sake, and I will not remember your sins" (Isa. 43:24b-25). She said, "If dragging someone's sin around with us is a burden for God, it must be a burden for us."

God lets go of our sins. We need to let go of the sins we carry, too. We need to forgive other people as well as ourselves. Jesus is our model in this practice of forgiving, of letting go of the pain and blame and anger that rightfully belongs to us. In the middle of Jesus's dying, after he had been condemned to death on the cross seemingly by the whim of the crowd, Jesus prayed to God, "forgive them; for they do not know what they are doing" (Luke 23:34a). Jesus could have been angry and vindictive. Who would not understand that? Jesus was an innocent man being put to death by a society that feared his message of God's welcome and love for all people. Instead, Jesus prayed for the forgiveness of those who had sent him to his death. Jesus gives us the same benefit, forgiving us the behaviors and words that he could easily hold against us. Knowing this gives us the courage to accept the pains and sorrows of the past and move on to a better future, lived in service and praise of God.

Try

1. Make a list of the failures you remind yourself of regularly. Ask God for forgiveness. Do you need to ask anyone else for forgiveness? If so, do it.

   Remind yourself that you did the best you could at the time. Burn the list, asking God to give you the grace you need to move forward in faith.
2. Make a list of the people and institutions you still feel anger or resentment toward. What do you need to do to let go of your anger and forgive them? Do it.
3. Make a list of all of the achievements and successes in your life. Organize your list with categories that fit for you. For example: professional, relational, health, creative, and spiritual. What does this tell you about who you are now? How can you celebrate these achievements?

Talk

1. How does holding onto past struggles and successes benefit you?
2. How does holding onto past struggles and successes keep you stuck?
3. What practices do you use to let go of and forgive the past?
4. How might you use the tools in this chapter to support those you minister with and to in accepting the past?

---

49 ❊ Completing Unfinished Business

Remind yourself that when you die, your "in basket" won't be empty.

Richard Carlson, *Don't Sweat the Small Stuff . . . and It's All Small Stuff*

Recently I discovered that one of my clients finds delight in finished products. She used to clean houses professionally. She spoke longingly of the satisfaction that comes from a job with a clear beginning, middle, and end. "When I was done, I was done!" she said. "And I had this beautiful product."

"You made order from chaos." I added.

"Yes," she said, with a sparkle of light in her eyes.

I could relate. I shared her joy of completion. We talked excitedly about how much we loved activities that produced clear results—dishes, laundry, or cookies. "Ministry isn't like that," I said.

"No. Not often." she replied.

My seminary professor Timothy Lull used to tell us that people who go into the ministry have to get used to living with a full in-box. He reminded us that we would always go to sleep at night with some of our work unfinished. Part of achieving success in life and work is learning to live with this incompletion. As Richard Carlson said, we will die with work in our in-basket.

Unfinished business falls into two categories. The first is the regular stuff in our in-baskets, the cycle of tasks that pass through our life and work with varying degrees of urgency. The second category of unfinished business is the stuff we need to complete in order to make peace with the past and connect to the present. This second category of unfinished business is the stuff that holds us back from living the lives we were meant to live. It's the stuff we worry over at three o'clock in the morning. It's the duties and tasks that nag at us when we're supposed to be paying attention to the sermon.

Defining Unfinished Business

We each have our own special cache of unfinished business as unique as we are. Still, unfinished business usually falls into predictable categories: deferred self-care, deferred responsibilities, making amends, offering forgiveness, and communicating gratitude.

Deferred self-care goes something like this: "Forgive me, doc, for I have sinned. It's been many years since my last appointment!" When life gets busy, we tend to let go of the things that aren't hollering at us. So we ignore our teeth, eyes, and bodies until they start to hurt.

Deferred responsibilities is the "enjoy now, pay later" category. It might include amassing credit card or other debts, forgetting to get the car serviced, ignoring the little leak in the ceiling, or neglecting to create a will. It's stuff that doesn't always look urgent but over time can become a huge problem.

In every 12-step program, participants are required to make a list of people they have hurt and then *make amends*, unless doing so would injure them or others. When we commit to clean up our unfinished business, we look to make it right with those we have harmed in our lives.

The other side of making amends is forgiving those who have hurt us. Until we do, our anger about the past can damage our present.[1] Jesus invited his followers to make forgiveness a part of one's prayers, "Whenever you stand praying, forgive, if you have anything against anyone; so that your Father in heaven may also forgive you your trespasses" (Mark. 11:25).

When we become aware of the people who have made it possible for us to be here, we express our *gratitude* to them. As the Yoruba proverb goes, "If we stand tall, it is because we stand on the shoulders of many ancestors." In his book *Authentic Happiness*, positive psychologist Martin Seligman suggests that in order to be authentically happy we need to say thank you to the people who have changed our lives. In the past few years, I have made it my practice to write thank you notes to people who have made a difference in my life. Seligman pushes the assignment further, asking readers to not only write a thank-you letter but to read it in person to the one we are thanking.[2]

Unfinished business leaves its mark on the present in many ways. Deferred care for ourselves can result in ill health or even death. Deferred care for our possessions can lead to expensive emergency repairs. We might feel guilt or sadness about the people we have hurt or the work we have left incomplete. We may experience explosive anger over situations that remind us of those who have wounded us in the past. We might hesitate to enter into new relationships or jobs because the pain of past wrongs is still present and our fear of repeated hurts overwhelms us. When we take time to complete the unfinished business, we can move forward. We get a sense of what it means to have a "tabula rasa," a clean slate.

A New Way

We are human. We fail. We sin. We will always have unfinished business. But, we can take steps to reduce the amount of unfinished business we have to "catch up" on at any given time. We need to define our unique stack of unfinished work and create systems that avoid the trap of unfinished business. When I work with clients on completing unfinished business, I invite them to first create a chart or list of unfinished work. The list of categories above can be a helpful tool in creating that list. Next, I encourage them to take the following steps to address unfinished business:

- Create regular times to have the check-ups necessary for good self-care.
- Create a system (or systems) for keeping up with your responsibilities. This might include creating a system to sort incoming mail, deal with children's school papers, and respond to incoming phone calls.
- Practice daily gratitude. At the end of each day, record three people or events that you are thankful for. Once a month or once a quarter, write notes to the people you need to thank. Or speak your thanks to people in person.
- Practice forgiveness. Regularly look at your life and forgive those whom you hold grudges against.

A Final Prayer

I like the way we confess our sins. In the faith tradition I practice, we use these words to describe our sin: "We have sinned against you in thought, word, and deed, by what we have done and by what we have left undone."[3]

God knows about unfinished business. And God forgives us. Yes, we have work to do. And yes, we get that clean slate whether we do it or not. That's grace.

Try

1. How will you live with the unfinished business of your life and work? Some of my clients have created a prayer or a ritual to

use when they leave work each day or lay down to rest each night. What might you do?

2. Look at the categories of unfinished business above. Make a list for each category and do it!

3. What systems do you need to create to keep unfinished business to a minimum?

Talk

1. Talk about how you have learned to cope with the reality of unfinished business in your work and life. What helps? What doesn't?

2. Share with each other the systems that you use to manage unfinished business. You may want to take some time to support each other in finding solutions to particularly difficult situations.

---

50 ❁ Grieving Our Losses

Every great loss demands that we choose life again. We need to grieve in order to do this. The pain we have not grieved over will always stand between us and life.

Rachel Naomi Remen, *My Grandfather's Blessings*

A friend had just celebrated a year of sobriety when her sister died. Standing with my friend after church, she said, "I don't know how to get out of this." Another friend, a woman who has lost many of her loved ones, replied, "You can't get out. You can only go through it."

Our conversation reminded me of a hike I took in my twenties. I'm terrified of heights, so I don't know how I thought climbing up a huge mountain would be a good idea. I guess I thought we'd be in it and not clinging to the side of it. But there we were, walking around the edge of this tall mountain. To my right the mountain shot straight up. To my left it dropped down more feet than I wanted to imagine. I wished I could cling to the side, cast the perfect spell, and magically transport myself to the bottom and safety.

"The only way off is through," said my leader.

"Thanks for sharing," I said, white knuckling the comforting pillar of stone. I thought, "Now help me get off the damn mountain in a way that does not involve spiraling to my death."

He did. He said, "Don't look down—just focus on the next step ahead. Focus on me—hold onto my jacket if you need to."

That's how I got off that mountain: one step at a time, looking forward, holding onto the jacket of a kind man.

Most of us have our mountains of grief to get up, down, over, or through. We do not move through this life without collecting losses. Elizabeth Bishop put it this way in the opening line of her poem *One Art*, "The art of losing isn't hard to master."[1] And it isn't. On some days it seems that *to live* is *to lose*. Just about everything we hold precious can be lost—friends, loved ones, the promise of a new life, a job, good health, hopes, dreams, relationships, and one's possessions. Loss rarely happens on our schedule (when we're prepared for it) or with the things we could stand to lose (like that extra holiday weight). Loss is random and wounding. It breaks apart our souls and the rhythm of our lives. Healing comes much more slowly than we imagine or expect. This is how novelist Joan Didion expressed it in her memoir about the death of her husband:

> Grief turns out to be a place none of us know until we reach it. We anticipate (we know) that someone close to us could die, but we do not look beyond the few days or weeks that immediately follow such an imagined death. We misconstrue the nature of even those few days or weeks. We might expect if the death is sudden to feel shock. We do not expect this shock to be obliterative, dislocating to both body and mind. . . . In the version of grief we imagine, the model will be "healing." A certain forward movement will prevail. The worst days will be the earliest days. . . . [We cannot] know ahead of the fact (and here lies the heart of the difference between grief as we imagine it and grief as it is) the unending absence that follows, the void, the very opposite of meaning, the relentless succession of moments during which we will confront the experience of meaninglessness itself.[2]

Didion is writing about the grief that follows death. Other losses leave us grasping for meaning, too—the loss of health, relationships, and jobs, to name a few. Loss destroys our normal, the daily routines that we have depended upon to frame the shape of our days. We need to grieve this loss, moving slowly into a place of healing. A friend of mine who has experienced great losses calls this "living into a new normal." The old normal is gone forever and we mourn that. In time we cross the mountain and find the village of the new normal. Didion's words remind us that there is no one path of healing, no right way to travel to the other side of the mountain. All we know is that grieving allows us to choose life again. When we do not grieve, we cannot be fully engaged with life. We may hide behind or within our sadness, fearing that engaging again will only lead to more loss. Our grief becomes like a shell, protecting us from both hurt and love. The loss stands between us and living our lives.

Most of my clients, like most people spiritual leaders relate to, have losses to grieve. When these griefs come up, we talk together about how they might create a path to the other side of the mountain. Making the path must be the griever's work. I cannot do this for them. I cannot give them a magic ritual or prayer that will fix their griefs. No coaching or pastoral care agenda exists that will erase the crevices that loss has left in their lives. I can only listen to their stories and encourage them to keep walking over that mountain, one step at a time.

Telling the Story

The first step in crossing grief's mountain is often telling the stories of our losses. We need people to bear witness to our griefs. No matter what it was that happened, if we are still affected by a loss, we need to talk about it. When my husband and I lost a baby through miscarriage, we found it immensely helpful to talk together and with others about what could have been. We grieved the due date, the names we had chosen, the clothes we had purchased, the plans we had made to laugh and play together. When people could hear our story and empathize with us, we began to experience healing. We all need people to witness our stories and understand that our losses have changed us. We are no longer the people we once were. We are different.

Unhelpful Responses to Grief

As a coach and a spiritual leader, I have often borne witness to these stories of loss. From my experience in these roles and in my life experience as a griever I have discovered that certain "helpful" behaviors rarely help people. These include

- providing a recipe or fix for the person who is grieving;
- labeling the stage of grief the person is in;
- offering superficial comfort;
- comparing losses;
- pretending the future can be the same as the past.

Providing a recipe or fix for the person who is grieving is not helpful. Nothing I say or do can take away someone's pain. I can only be present to it, no matter how large or loud or uncomfortable the grief might be for me.

Because no path, no normal way to grieve, exists, labeling the stage of grief for the griever is not helpful. I have heard many grief counselors say that no one moves through the stages of grief in order or even just once. We skip around, sometimes landing in more than one stage at a time. I have found it helpful to support those who grieve in being okay with what is instead of beating themselves up for not experiencing grief the "right" way. There is no right way. There is only the way that works for the grieving person at the moment.

Offering superficial comfort to someone, such as, "Look on the bright side" or "Stop feeling sorry for yourself" is not helpful. Comments like these usually reflect our impatience with another's grief process, our discomfort with another expressing difficult feelings, and our own unresolved grief. Phrases like these are a marginally more polite way of saying, "Would you please shut up about that already?"

The process of grief is less a straight highway than a meandering path. According to Didion and others who have written about grief, grief comes in waves not stages. One might experience good days or even months and then suddenly have a very difficult stretch. As leaders, we are simply called to walk beside those who grieve—as companions on their journey. We do not need to dictate the path or the speed by which it should be taken. (Some losses become disabling for the person who is grieving. In these cases, it is essential that they consult their doctor and a psychotherapist.)

We cannot compare our losses. Many times, people will speak of their griefs and then say, "But it's not really that bad. I know people who have had it much worse." They may think that their loss is too small or too long ago. No one should diminish the effect a loss can have on a person. The fact of another's suffering does not erase our own.

Pretending the future can be the same as the past is not helpful. The future cannot be. It would be nice if it could. Replacing what we lost with something new, like finding a new umbrella, would be great. We cannot. Sure, we may love again. We may have another child, marry again, befriend new people. But it will not be the same. It will be a *new* normal. It will not be normal in the old, familiar way. It will be normal in a new way.

Grieving Well

We all collect our losses as we move through life. We all need to make that grief journey to what my friend calls the new normal. Over the years, many of the people I have worked with have found it helpful to create a ritual or series of rituals to help them mourn their losses. One client wrote a letter to a congregation that had hurt him. When he finished it, he burned it and asked God to heal his anger over the good relationship that had been lost. A friend of mine spends the anniversary of her mother's death remembering her mom, looking at old pictures, playing her favorite movies and songs, reading through old letters and cards. There are other ways to remember: special meals, prayers, social gatherings, cemetery visits, and journaling.

Never Alone

None of us grieve alone. God grieves with us. As a friend reminds me, "The mountain of grief . . . cannot be handled by mere humans. God is the one who handles our grief and God handles our grief by entering the grief of death on the cross. The hope of the resurrection is ours because the God of grief is also the God of life."[3] Sometimes I forget about Easter. I forget that God did not let Jesus stay dead. God freed

Jesus from death. God brought Jesus to new life. This same God stands with us in our sorrows and eventually frees us from them, too. This is good news—for me, for you, for us all. As Bono sings, "You don't have to go it alone."[4]

Try

What griefs stand between you and life? What steps do you need to take to begin moving through them?

Talk

1. What has sustained you and those you work with in times of grief?
2. What prayers, songs, books, biblical verses, and other resources do you find helpful in the midst of grief? Share these with each other.

51   ❈   Creating a Healthy Foundation

> Do you not know that you are God's temple and that God's spirit dwells in you? . . . For God's temple is holy, and you are that temple.
>
> 1 Corinthians 3:16-17

On Monday morning I dragged myself out of bed at 5:30, ate two pieces of cinnamon toast, swallowed a few cups of coffee, and sat down at the computer to work. But I was tired, yawning so hard that my eyes filled with tears and the words melted before me. By nine I could not keep my eyes open. I put the computer to sleep and shuffled off to do the same. The next day I managed to get through the morning writing and my afternoon client sessions on caffeine and a prayer. I knew something had to change. My life had become a slave to circumstance. During weeks of caring for a sick spouse and children as well as racing to finish too many projects, I had been ignoring my foundation.

When I talk to clients about their life foundation, I like to use the image of a house. Load-bearing posts and footings support a house's weight. Load-bearing posts that are rotting or have a crumbling or sinking concrete footing can cause sagging floors and cracked walls. A house needs healthy load-bearing posts and footings to endure constant use and difficult weather. As Jesus said, "I will show you what someone is like who comes to me, hears my words, and acts on them. That one is like a man building a house, who dug deeply and laid the foundation on rock; when a flood arose, the river burst against that house but could not shake it, because it had been well built" (Luke 6:47-48; see also Matt.7:24-27).

Defining and strengthening one's foundation is a recurrent topic in the coaching conversation. In my coach training program, students were required to take a 12-week class on personal foundation. As I mentioned in part one, the instructors stressed that healthy coaches needed to have strong foundations, too. We were trained to support clients in strengthening their own foundations. Here are some tools I use to support clients in creating a healthy foundation.

Guiding Metaphor

I find metaphors to be a helpful way of diagnosing and discussing a problem. Like seeing one's home from an airplane, talking about one's life metaphorically allows clients to get distance from the issues. They see their life in a unique way. In addition, as people play with the metaphor, they discover new ideas about themselves and their lives. When I'm feeling unsettled and beaten down, I will often say that my load-bearing posts are rotting. My coach knows what this means—and is able to support me in diagnosing the problem and solving it. A client of mine who crochets will often say that her foundation chain is unraveling. Another client talks about her life as a journey and will speak about having a path that needs repair.

Here are metaphors that I have found work well for conversations about foundations:

- Garden or farm (Discuss soil. Use Jesus's parable of the sower.)
- Baking bread (Discuss ingredients and process for making good bread. Use Jesus's words about yeast.)
- Buildings (Discuss Jesus's parable of the house built on rock versus the house built on sand.)

- Knitting (Discuss casting on. Use the image of God knitting us together in Ps. 139:13.)
- Path (Discuss the materials needed for a safe and secure path.)
- School images (Every skill builds on another.)
- Athletic images (Use the image of how training programs work to build a strong foundation for athletes. Look at Hebrews 12:1.)
- Spokes on a bicycle wheel (Think about how spokes support the work of the wheel.)

Defining Foundation

Although I have been trained to support people in strengthening their life's foundation, the content of coaching must be client focused and not coach driven. For that reason, I believe it is essential for clients to define what it means for them to have a strong foundation.

The tool I often use for defining foundation is the wheel of life. The wheel of life is a circle divided into six or eight pieces, like a pie. Each piece is labeled to represent a portion of the client's life. I usually provide clients with a blank wheel of life and invite them to complete it. When they finish, we discuss their choices. I might invite them to consider expanding their definition of personal foundation, pointing out areas that appear to be weak or missing. But in the end, the client decides how foundation is defined.

Assessing Foundational Health

When I spoke with my doctor about my exhaustion, he asked if I had any idea why I was so tired. I had an idea—getting up too early, going to bed late, working too many hours, not exercising, drinking too much caffeine and overdoing the sugar, and not seeing friends. I had hoped he would have a magic pill. Getting back my energy the old-fashioned way—through healthy diet, exercise, and a better lifestyle—sounded exhausting.

Like me, most clients know what areas of their foundation need work. When we look at their wheel of life, I ask clients to rate each slice of their wheel. We begin by creating a scale that makes sense to the client. This is a tool I learned in a seminar with coach Martha Beck and have adapted for my own use. I ask clients to think of one of the worst moments in their life, when they felt that everything was a com-

The Wheel of Life

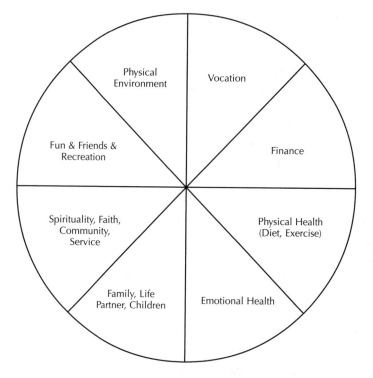

plete mess and they had handled the stress poorly. That situation is
the measuring stick for the minus ten rating. I then ask clients to think
about one of the best moments in their life, a time when they felt strong,
healthy, spiritually content, and connected to the community. This
memory becomes the measuring tool for a plus ten rating. After developing the scale, clients rate their current life foundation using the
scale. For example, in my own situation of feeling exhausted, I might
rate my physical health at a minus one—because it's not nearly as
bad as it used to be, but it isn't so great either. On the other hand, I
would rate my vocational health at a plus seven, because I am feeling
good about my work. My only challenge is to moderate the amount of
time I spend working.

Developing a Plan

Once clients have assessed their foundation, they will need to decide
what they want to do to strengthen it. Here are some brief tips for
developing a plan to make foundational changes.

SET PRIORITIES

On New Year's Day I took time to consider how I wanted my life to be different in the new year. As I pondered the past months and sketched out ideas for the next ones, I noticed that a cardinal had paused on the forsythia shrub outside my front window. I stopped writing and watched him for nearly 30 minutes. I have read that seeing a cardinal in one's dreams means vitality and happiness. I imagined that seeing one in person *while writing one's New Year resolutions* must be way better. Or not. I made three resolutions that day. I have broken the first (more times than I can count) and forgotten the other two. The problem? Too many resolutions.

You might have fifty things you want to change in your life. Fine. Rate them. What would be best to change first? In my own life, I use two rules to set priorities.

Do the easiest thing first. When you do something easy, you succeed. Success brings a feeling of euphoria and gives us the energy for achieving something new.

Focus on the change that will bring the most rewards. Some changes—like giving up chocolate—just leave us feeling deprived. There's no big payoff to letting go of little treats. Other changes, like beginning to exercise, provide immediate rewards. Within days we feel more energetic. This energy allows us to tackle the next item on our list.

REMEMBER TO KISS: KEEP IT SIMPLE SHERLOCK

If, like me, you have so many resolutions that you can't remember even one, that's a problem. Choose one thing to change—just one. Changes tend to breed more changes. In therapist Michele Weiner-Davis's book *Change Your Life and Everyone in It*, she says, "a single change, no matter how small, leads to other changes. If you take one small step to change your life, the positive changes start to snowball, taking on a life of their own."[1] In presenting this idea, Weiner-Davis points to the meteorologist Edward Lorenz's idea that: "small, almost imperceptible changes in weather could affect global weather patterns—a phenomenon he called the 'butterfly effect' because, as he put it, a butterfly flapping its wings in Brazil might create a tornado in Texas."[2]

TAKE SMALL STEPS

A companion idea to choosing one action is the idea of taking small steps, a technique I have mentioned often in this book. Plenty of new athletes have been felled by injury when they try to do too much too soon. In the writing of this book, when I thought, "I am writing a book," I panicked, got very tired, and felt the need to sleep or eat donuts. That doesn't work so well. Instead, I wake up each day thinking, "I am writing an essay today." I can manage a twelve-hundred-word chapter.

This reminds me of my friends who are in recovery. They tell me all the time that the only way anything can be accomplished is one day at a time. None of them think about the whole rest of their sober life. No, that would be deadly. Instead, each focuses on getting through this day, this hour, this minute. The small step makes the goal doable. Break your one change into small steps and focus on taking one step at a time.

DO WHAT WORKS

This year I asked everyone I know, under the guise of research for the book, about their resolution-making practices. People were remarkably uncomfortable with my questions. A few even refused to answer me. One friend said with great honesty, "I have ideas for the new year, not resolutions. I am afraid that if I make a resolution, I will break it."

Resolutions work for some people, not for everyone. Other people like to declare a life theme that corresponds to the part of the life wheel they want to strengthen, such as friendship or health. You could also try the following:

- Set goals. (I will exercise three times a week.)
- Choose a question. (What is my life's passion?)
- Select a value. (Honesty)
- Choose an asset to strengthen. (I will listen even more attentively.)

Figure out what part you are good at and get help with the rest. I love starting things. I like to come up with the idea, buy all the stuff, and then begin! Unfortunately, I get bored pretty easily. So my collection of pilates tapes is gathering dust next to my leg weights and home weight-lifting book. My stack of cookbooks stay pretty much closed-up on the shelf while I eat Pop-Tarts and cheese sandwiches. Clearly I need help with follow-through.

If, like me, you need help with follow-up, get a buddy to support you or even accompany you on the journey. If you get overwhelmed by beginning something new but embrace routines, you may want to get a trainer or take a class to support you while you turn a new skill into habit. In many ways, coaches can support people in seeking help with the hardest parts.

TELL PEOPLE ABOUT IT

About a year after I began writing my memoir, I started talking about it. Once people knew, they began to bug the heck out of me about it. It's a good thing, too! Without that constant reminder, I wouldn't feel obligated to finish the book. Tell other people your goals and encourage them to bug you about them.

REEVALUATE

When I started walking ten thousand steps a day, spring had just sprung. It was no problem to hop outside at 4:00 PM each day and take a three-mile walk. But at the end of November, as the days grew shorter and the temperature plunged below freezing, I couldn't get the energy to walk around the block, let alone three miles! Plus, I could never get going soon enough to make it home before dark. So I joined the gym. Still, crawling into my car when it was dark and cold—even at 4:00 PM—was hard. And I was usually too tired by then to think that anything but a glass of wine and a book was a good thing. In reevaluating the situation with my coach, she suggested I exercise first thing in the morning. "Pay yourself first," is how I put it to my own clients. I tried it, and it worked for me. Reevaluating my plan gave me the opportunity to save it.

So let's say you set the goal of getting in shape and a month from now you're still the inveterate couch potato you have always been. It might be time to revaluate your goal. Sometimes just changing the wording of the goal or making the steps smaller can change everything.

Seek Inspiration

On the path to a new thing, you can easily get discouraged. Here are some ways to seek inspiration:

- Read about people who have accomplished their goals.
- Watch movies about people who make a difference in the world.
- Put up inspirational signs in your home. Buy them, cut them out of magazines, or make reminders to fit your own goals.
- Choose a talisman. I have turtles all over the house to remind me that nearly everything can be done one step at a time. What mascot would remind you to achieve your goals?
- Send yourself cards. I love cards, and I love getting mail. When I need a lift, I send myself an inspirational card. Corny but fun.
- Listen to music that makes a difference. I've put together a compact disc of songs that both kick me in the keister and encourage me.

Have Faith!

The 12th step in any recovery program is service—to carry the message to other people. At my church this past New Year's Eve, two women gave testimonies about their life before and after entering treatment and recovery. They used Psalm 90 as their text. One woman spoke about this verse, "The days of our life are seventy years, or perhaps eighty, if we are strong" (Ps. 90:10). She talked about how she had probably wasted 20 of those God-given years to using drugs. Then she spoke about her recovery and her dependence on God, the one true foundation. I know the speaker from church. I see that she works hard to keep her foundation strong. She attends church every week, serves in the community, and regularly attends recovery meetings. She was one of the first persons to welcome me to the church and never fails to take an opportunity to hug me and let me know that she prays for me and my family.

The pastor encouraged us to take time that evening to reflect on our own lives using Psalm 90. I did. The psalm opens with the words, "Lord, you have been our dwelling place in all generations" (v. 1). When it comes to strong foundations, the first and most significant ingredient is God. We dwell in God. When our own foundations crumble and we waste our days, we can know that our foundations are set inside a footing that nothing can destroy—God. As the sign over psychiatrist Carl Jung's door is reported to have said, "Bidden or not bidden, God is present."

Try

Create your own wheel of life, rate each slice, and choose one area to strengthen.

Talk

1. What biblical or spiritual images or texts deal with the concept of foundation?
2. In what ways is it helpful to talk about foundations with a congregation or organization as well as with individuals?
3. What are the foundational practices for people of faith? In what ways can these be communicated to your congregation or the people you work with?

---

52   ❀   Giving Permission

Make time for play each day. . . . We're asses if we don't! Nobody is going to force you—no one says go out and play. It's a shame there is no philosophy of life anywhere that insists on play.

Joan Anderson, *A Walk on the Beach*

When I was a kid, my mom liked us to ask permission before we took or ate or did something. This prevented us from doing things like drinking out of a soda can filled with hot kitchen grease. But sometimes—no doubt to save herself the grief of our constant pestering—she would give us a sort of blanket permission slip. Like on Halloween. After mom made the initial check of our loot for razor blades and poison, she gave us permission to just eat it all—whenever and however we wanted. I was always really good about making my stash last. I was telling a friend about this.

"I was good at that, too," she said.

"How good?" I persisted.

"Oh, it would take at least a week to finish it."

"A week!" I exclaimed. "Try 52. By the time I got to the last of my Halloween candy it was so hard and rotten not even the dog wanted it."

Now that's delaying gratification! Studies say that children who can delay gratification—wait for their reward—will be more successful than their peers. Psychologists at Stanford University put preschool children alone in a room with a marshmallow. The children were told that they could either eat the one marshmallow in front of them or wait and receive two marshmallows to eat. One-third of the children were able to wait the full 15 to 20 minutes for the second marshmallow. The researchers followed up with the students 14 years later. The students who were able to wait the full 15 to 20 minutes scored higher on their SAT tests and were more emotionally stable than their peers. Clearly, we need to know how to delay gratification. Without that skill, most of us would sit in bed all day watching television, reading trashy magazines, and feasting on homemade sugar cookies. (Okay, I would do that. You might have other vices.)

Still, most of my clients and colleagues are pretty good at delaying gratification. Perhaps we have taken the Protestant work ethic to heart. Maybe we believe we need to work to earn our salvation. Whatever the reason, we could afford to indulge in a little immediate gratification or even some immediate self-care. I recently heard of a clergy person who nearly missed her sibling's funeral because she didn't feel she could take off an extra Sunday! Instead of practicing joy or even good self-care, we work ourselves crazy. We work our way through our to-do lists promising that if we finish working on the tough stuff, we will reward ourselves with a dose of pleasure. When we do come home, we are so exhausted by our work that we only have energy for mindless pleasures: endless television and empty calories. Sometimes we need someone to give us permission to take pleasure first.

As part of her four-year-old curriculum, my daughter had to take a nap at school every day. If she rests well, the teacher awards her a "resting star"—a sheet of paper with a star and the words "resting star" written boldly across the top. As a coach, I regularly give my clients permission slips for pleasures and passions. Because we have dozens of these resting star slips lying around the house, I have started to bring them to clients and friends as reminders to spend time nurturing themselves with the gift of rest. I remind them that the more they do and the better they do it, the higher their pile of work is going to be. They will never get to the bottom of it—so why not do what brings them pleasure and stirs their passions *now* rather than later?

Recently a client said to me, "Thanks to you I never take my work home with me anymore. I spend my evenings listening to music and working on my scrapbooking." Another client gave me credit for the daily progress she is making toward a speaking career. A third thanked me for encouraging him to pursue his PhD while in the parish. "*Stop!*" I said to every one of these clients. I continued, "I did nothing but give you a permission slip to follow your passions. *You* are the one who chose to use it."

A friend recently gave me my own permission slip. On a sheet of paper she wrote: "Be a *lazy slug!*" I keep that paper on my desk, reminding me to do just that. Another friend, who I will call Lydia, is a veteran napper. She will often ask me: have you napped today? When I get to a point in my day when life seems overwhelming, I look at my lazy-slug sheet and think, "What Would Lydia Do?" The answer is always the same: nap! And so I do. Oh, and I'm eating my Halloween candy this year before it hardens and molds. Now it's your turn: go play!

Try

Write yourself a permission slip to do something you love and never take time for. Now do it!

Talk

1. How might permission giving or withholding affect the work of the people in your congregation or ministry organization?
2. What biblical or theological images come to mind when you think about

    • delayed gratification?
    • permission giving?

    How might these affect your ability to give and receive permission?
3. Share an example of how receiving permission from someone enabled you to do something important or meaningful. Or talk about a time when you desired but did not receive permission and it affected you negatively.
4. Who might need to receive permission from you? Give it.

5. How can you make permission giving a regular part of your interactions with people?

---

53 ✸ Assessing Assets

Only after I stopped looking at others did I finally see myself. Only after I stopped looking to see where I fit in my age group as a runner and where I fit in some elaborate demographic as a person did I see that I am no more than who and what I am.

John Bingham, *The Courage to Start*

At a retreat for spiritual leaders, I invited participants to create a mind map of their assets. After nearly thirty minutes of work, I wandered around to check on their progress. I noticed that one of the participants had a completely blank page.

"Can I help?" I asked.

"I just don't think this way!" she wailed. "I don't know my assets."

Her comment wasn't unusual. Many of my clients have struggled to identify their assets. I often say that most of us wouldn't know our assets from a hole in the ground! And why should we? We live in a deficit-driven culture. In fact, our economy is built on helping people feel dissatisfied with who they are and what they possess. Just turn on the TV or open a magazine; the content will feature advice-based stories that are designed to help you improve your life. In addition, it will be filled with advertisers telling you that you could be richer, look younger, lose weight, and live a more interesting life if you would only purchase, read, watch, or use their product. In other words, without their help, you are poor, old, ugly, chubby, and boring. This culture teaches us to assess our deficits.

In my college and seminary training, most of the work we did was also deficit based. The job of the professor or supervisor was to look at where we were lacking and try to "fix us." My son's first grade teacher had the same philosophy—find the problems and fix them. Show the kids where they had gone off the road, and in that way get them back on the road. It was the school psychologist who finally suggested to her, "What about catching them doing it right? What about reinforcing the good behavior?"

I have noticed the pastor modeling this tool at my congregation. She frequently acknowledges the good people do. She points out the people who are like yeast, silently working to change the world. Miss Charlotte gathers children from her block and brings them to Tuesday communion. One of the young people, Gabrielle, collects my daughter Elly each week for the children's sermon time, holding her with gentle care. Thirteen-year-old Timothy escorts an elderly woman to her pew at church. Nine-year-old Jackson invites my son Sam to go to Sunday school with him. Eight-year-old Ebony and her ten-year-old brother Mark watch over Mahalia while the little girl's mother sings in the choir. Without the pastor's words, these small acts might go unnoticed, perhaps even by the people doing them. I've noticed that when I call attention to my daughter's assets, she becomes more of who I name her to be. I see the same phenomenon at church. Those who the pastor recognizes as hospitable seem to open their arms even wider, embracing the ones others might ignore. The ones she names as helpful seek those in need of assistance. And the ones she points to as loving seem to grow even bigger hearts right before our eyes. When we recognize the assets of other people, these assets grow.

In my coach training program, I learned to focus on client strengths. Our curriculum encouraged us to do the following:

- Point out client strengths.
- Invite the client to assess his or her strengths.
- Ask the client, "Where have you gone right?"
- Make the client right—even when the client had messed up.
- Support the client in acting out of her or his strengths.

In part 1, the chapter on assets discusses why coaching focuses on strengths instead of weaknesses. This chapter discusses the tools coaches use to support clients in assessing their strengths. Like many of the core actions of coaching—completing unfinished business, strengthening foundations, and visioning—assessing assets is a tool that can be used repeatedly. In fact, every coaching conversation contains some asset-based work, be it an exercise, a question, or simply an observation. The exercises below can be used individually or in combination. People who are new to asset-based work may need to try more than one approach before they find a tool that works for them.

Understanding Asset Types

I often begin retreats by asking participants to share their name and a wisdom or gift they bring to the gathering, such as creativity or organizational skills. Many participants come up with their wisdom quite easily. For those who struggle to think of something, I have created a list of wisdoms. Sometimes it is easier to assess our assets based on a list of descriptive terms or categories. Luther Snow, relying on the work of asset-building pioneers John McKnight and Jody Kretzmann, suggests these five types of assets: physical, individual, associational, institutional, economic.[1]

Physical assets are objects that you can walk on, touch, see, or taste like land, a tree, an ocean, or the tomatoes in your garden. This includes the stuff you own—buildings, kitchen equipment, books, DVDs, and your Beanie Baby collection.

Individual assets are your talents, experiences, skills, and preferences, such as your ability to ski, your experience as a foreign exchange student in Argentina, your ability to build bookshelves, and your interest in cooking Asian food.

Associational assets include the people you connect with, such as family members, friends, voluntary associations, and formal networks of people. This might include a book group or service club, the acquaintances you have made running through the city trails, the people you connect with online around common interests or issues (for example, writing for children or children with Autism Spectrum Disorder), or a formal national network (The Society for Children's Book Writers and Illustrators).

Institutional assets are businesses, public agencies, and nonprofit institutions like a neighborhood arts cooperative, your congregation, the YMCA, or the public library.

Economic assets encompass your spending and investing power and your ability to provide valuable goods and services. These assets might include the vast amounts of wealth you stow in a Swiss bank or your ability to knit scarves and sell them at a neighborhood street fair.

Understanding the categories of assets is the first step in claiming assets. When I review this list with people, I invite them to add their own examples to each category. Once they grasp the sense of each category, I send them off to create their own personal asset inventory.

Asset Inventory

When I was in high school and college, I worked at area stores taking inventory. Armed with clipboard, paper, and pens, my job was to move through the store counting and recording the inventory by type. Because the success of these businesses depended in part upon our accuracy, we used a strict system developed by each store to take inventory. Inventorying personal assets is a much less precise practice. The methods listed below offer some basic ways to create a list of one's personal assets. People will connect to the method that works for them. Individuals may also choose to combine methods. These methods may be used to take inventory of a whole life or simply a portion of one's life. For example, an individual who is contemplating a move might want to make an asset inventory of each possible location.

ASSET CHART
An asset chart lists asset categories across the top or down the side of a piece of paper, providing room to list specific assets. Asset categories usually include the ones listed above but can shift to fit the specific needs of the person completing the inventory. The following asset inventory chart was created for a group of spiritual leaders.

Asset Inventory Chart

Physical					
Individual					
Relational					
Institutional					
Economic					
Vocational					
Spiritual					
Educational					
Other					

MIND MAPPING

A mind map takes the same categories—again, modified for the individual's situation—and represents a person's assets graphically. In a mind map, the central theme (for example, assets) is written in the center of the paper inside a circle. In asset mapping, the main categories radiate from the center like the rays of the sun or branches on a tree. Each ray or branch leads to an explosion of assets that fit each category. An asset map might look like this:

Sample Mind Map

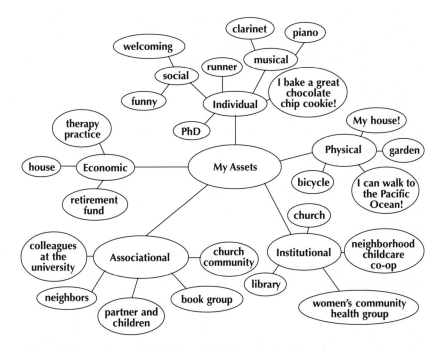

PLAYING CARDS

Assets can also be captured individually on some form of a card: an index card, vocabulary card, notepaper, or sticky note. One can distinguish categories by using different colored cards or markers. This technique is helpful for clients who want to play with shifting their assets around—how combining this or that resource might create a new opportunity. For example, imagine that Bob has a list of individual assets that include cycling, organizational skills, public speaking, connecting well with children, and mechanical skills. Bob's institutional assets include the elementary school his children attend, his congregation, and the public library. When Bob shuffles his cards and begins arranging them, what emerges is a plan that connects many of these assets together: a bicycle clinic for children.

ASSET NOTEBOOK

People who want to add to their asset inventory over time or want to create an inventory that they can return to repeatedly might make an asset notebook. An asset notebook can be a journal or a three ring binder that is split into asset categories or types. An asset notebook has room to hold additional information such as lists of achievements, stories that demonstrate personal strengths, brochures and clippings that describe institutional or associational assets, photos of one's relational assets, and statements that reflect economic assets. Asset notebooks can be helpful in preparing for job interviews or even in beginning to envision one's next phase of life.

Digging Deeper

Some people do well with an asset inventory tool and a little free time. Other people require more tools to help them dig deeper. This section offers a few tools for discovering more assets.

PROMPTING QUESTIONS

As I thought about interviewing for my first call, I realized that I had no idea what the situation would be like. I had already been taken by surprise in the approval interview held by a regional committee in my denomination. They had asked questions I hadn't expected and wasn't prepared to answer. I didn't want to repeat that experience. When I presented my dilemma to my mentor, he offered to coach me through the interview process. One of the ways he did that was by asking me questions about myself—my experiences, beliefs, and strengths. His questions helped me to access strengths and stories I did not know I had. The following questions are designed to support people in accessing their assets. They can be used individually or with one of the inventory tools above.

- What are you passionate about?
- What do you know a lot about?

- What can you do with your hands or body?
- What unique experiences have you had?
- What skills or strengths do you use at home?
- What skills or strengths do you use at work?
- What skills or strengths got you through school?
- What skills or strengths do you use in relating with other people?
- What do people say you are good at?
- What types of skills do people ask you to help them with?
- What are some of the crazy things you are good at?
- What are some ordinary things you are good at (things that don't even seem like skills)?
- What were you good at doing when you were younger?
- What skills or strengths do you use in your hobbies or interests?
- What skills or strengths do you use in a crisis?
- What do you see as your greatest personal achievements? How do these reveal your assets?

HIDDEN ASSETS

We call our daughter St. Anthony after the patron saint of lost things because she can find anything in the house. Remote control, car keys, shoes, mittens, socks—you name it, she'll find it. If I knew how to bottle this skill I would. Many of us could use this trait when seeking to locate our assets. Sometimes I wonder if buying each of my clients a St. Anthony medallion might help. Instead, I have developed a few tools to help clients find hidden assets.

Uncover weaknesses. Our assets often hide inside traits other people understand to be our weaknesses. One of my clients likes to take tangents in everything she does—work, conversations, and, of course, while traveling. For those she works with who are goal centered, this trait is seen as both annoying and disruptive. Yet, when this woman looked more deeply at herself, she saw that this weakness hid gifts. Because she took tangents, she often saw things on side streets that could never be found on a main road. She was open to wildly creative ideas that came from wandering.

Explore needs. Assets also hide inside our desires and needs. Looking at our needs as just another thing that is wrong with us and should be fixed can be tempting. One of my clients needed more intellectual stimulation than she was getting from her normal duties at work. She was especially interested in feminist issues and felt frustrated by her colleagues' lack of interest. She saw this need as a problem until it occurred to her to start her own feminist reading group. Her need for intellectual stimulation became an asset that was able to organize and lead a group of like-minded women. A similar thing happened in my neighborhood. Because we live near a university, the homeowners share the neighborhood with college students who are simply renting. Several years ago it became increasingly clear that something needed to be done about the trash, late-night noise, and speeding cars. Out of this need grew an active neighborhood association.

Narratives. "Tell me a story about when you were four," my daughter asks. She finds great joy in hearing about the trials and tribulations—and sometimes the successes—of my youth. She's too young to tell me why she likes these stories so much, but I suspect that in these stories she finds courage to face her own challenges. People who have trouble coming up with lists of assets can sometimes tell personal stories that are overflowing with assets. Stories of personal achievements and good moments always uncover assets. But don't stop there. Funny stories, embarrassing moments, tales of frustration, terror, or failure, all of these reveal the incredible array of assets people carry around with them. I recently talked about college with a friend from that era of my life. We were talking about the diverse groups of people I hung out with—the guys who played Dungeons and Dragons, the people at the theater, and the professors in the religion department. As we told these stories, my friend said, "I always thought you were gifted at getting along with all sorts of people, even those the rest of the world would be scared of." It was a trait I hadn't recognized in myself and wouldn't have been able to find without the stories we told.

Getting help. As I mentioned above, my daughter can find anything much quicker than the rest of us bumbling fools. It can often be the same with assets. Our friends, family members, and even acquaintances can often see assets that we cannot. As a coach, I frequently am able to point out assets that clients cannot see. I also encourage people to interview friends and family to discover their assets. Gathering with colleagues and holding an asset brainstorm can also be helpful. Some ministry teams find that this is an effective way to build community and discover new ministry ideas.

Making Asset Inventories Practical

One spring when I was feeling particularly antsy, I went out and bought a bunch of art supplies. It was so much fun to choose watercolors and brushes—I felt incredibly creative and just knew I would be a wonderful artist. Unfortunately, when I got home, life crept in and I never got around to actually using the art supplies. Sitting in my closet, unused, they were pretty much useless to me. It's the same with assets and these asset inventories. Putting together the inventory may give you a boost, but they need to be put to better use than that, otherwise they are mostly useless. Here are some ways to use your lists of assets.

Daily reminders. I sometimes wonder if putting my watercolor supplies on my desk would have reminded me to use them. I keep my bead supplies out all the time and find myself stopping for a moment or several to play with the beads, sometimes staying long enough to make a bracelet or necklace. Asset inventories can be like these beads—daily reminders to use the skills and strengths God has given us. One of my clients made an artistic mind map of her assets, using many colors. She keeps it on her desk where she can see it as she plans and works through her day. Other clients have kept their asset inventories in their date book, on their computer desktop, and in their journals.

Good soil. I love the parable about the sower and the seeds. It reminds me that sometimes the challenges we encounter are not because we aren't sowing seeds—or getting sowed upon—but that the soil isn't quite ready to receive the seeds. Asset inventories can be like good soil—they enrich our lives, making us more receptive to the seeds we encounter. In my work with clients, asset inventories become the good soil we work with as we sow seeds. The asset inventory becomes part of our discussion each session. As we look at this experience or that problem, we also consider how assets are revealed, used, or enriched. When a client gets stuck, we might pull out the asset inventory and spend time reviewing it, thinking of wacky ways their assets might enrich their life. As we look at the assets, stirring them up, moving them around, we are planting seeds in this good soil.

Connecting assets. Asset-builder Luther Snow recommends that people connect their assets to find new assets and projects. This can be done in two ways. First, as mentioned above, people can connect their own assets to see new ways they might put their strengths into service. Our combined assets can inform every area of our life: forming new relationships, new hobbies, vocational opportunities, and physical challenges. Second, people can gather to connect resources and find new ways to work together. Perhaps one person's computer skills with another person's writing ability could become an e-mail devotional for the Advent season. Creative solutions come when we combine assets. People can join their assets to create just about anything, including support systems, service projects, and work programs.

Giving It Time

About a week after we moved into our new house, the dishwasher overflowed, dumping water into the kitchen and below onto boxes piled in the laundry room. At the same time, the sink drain stopped draining. The trouble? A badly connected dishwasher and a pipe clogged with mold and debris. "It's the worst pipe I've seen," grunted the plumber. "How did that happen?" I queried, suspecting that one of the kids had inadvertently stuffed a meatloaf or a sneaker down the tiny drain. "This drain hasn't been used enough. When you don't use a pipe, it grows moldy and rusty and eventually gets like this."

Under use! I'd never have guessed that! And, it got me thinking about life. That's how the parts of our lives that we fail to use become—moldy, rusted, and clogged. It takes time to clear out a clogged pipe. If we haven't been using our assets, claiming them, trusting them, and putting them to work may take time. We will make many false starts, working around our assets or ignoring them. That's okay. Keep at it. Use those assets a little at a time, and in time they will become like second nature to you.

Try

Make an inventory of your assets. Underline assets you use regularly. Circle assets you rarely use but would like to develop. Using the list of your assets, reflect on the following questions:

- In what ways do you make use of your assets in your work and personal life?

- What actions might you take to make better use of your assets?
- What assets would you like to use more in the coming year?
- Who and what might be resources to you as you work on building and using your assets?

Talk

1. With your partner, take turns complaining to each other for 45 seconds. Next, take turns naming your assets to your partner for 45 seconds. Reflect on the following questions:

   - Which felt better?
   - Which went faster?
   - Why do you think that's so?

2. Share your lists or maps of your assets.

   - Do you see additional assets your partner might have overlooked? Share them with each other.
   - Brainstorm together ways you might use your assets in the coming year, including connecting more than one asset to create new opportunities.
   - How might you combine your assets in a project or adventure? For example, one of you might like to fish while the other works in an inner-city parish. Perhaps you could plan a fishing expedition with the children of the inner-city parish.

---

54 ❁ Identifying and Nurturing Passion

But don't be satisfied with stories, how things
have gone with others. Unfold
your own myth, without complicated explanation,
so everyone will understand the passage,
We have opened you.

Rumi, 13th century Sufi mystic and poet

"I've been asking other pastors if they're passionate about their work," my client said. "I want to know if they get excited about going to work each day."

"And? What did you find out?" I asked.

"The people I spoke with said that they don't feel excited."

"What do they feel?"

"Tired, mostly. Some said it was okay but not great."

That's sad, I thought. Not surprising, but not welcome news.

Common wisdom often says that having a job we feel passionate about is just too much to ask of God and the universe. I disagree. I ask each of my clients both to discover and then to develop their passions at work and in their personal lives. This chapter will look at the work I do to support clients in discovering their passions. The next chapter will explore how I "midwife" the dreams into reality.

Discovering One's Passion

I recently saw a television show in which one of the protagonists bemoaned the fact that he had lived his life to please other people. All of his choices—school, career, marriage—were made to make someone else happy. I am sure that many people, especially women, resonate with that. We have made our life decisions in the company of other people, parents, siblings, spouses, friends, and church acquaintances, hoping for their approval and blessing. The people who make decisions in reaction to others or to spite others are just as tied to the rumble of the crowd (though they might be wooing jeers instead of applause). Either way, to win approval or to gain disdain, the choices do not come from passion.

At some point in life, we wake up and notice that we are not content with the way things are. We wonder when we stopped enjoying our job or our marriage. We have trouble getting out of bed in the morning and drink too much at night. We try to remember the last time we really laughed—and cannot. We may seek help. We read books; talk to a friend, therapist, or life coach; revisit old interests and connections. We are seeking the thing that seems elusive—the passion that makes us forget the time, feel amazingly intelligent, and so excited we cannot stop thinking or talking about it. Many of my clients come to me because they want to rekindle this feeling, something that many of them haven't felt since childhood.

Finding one's passion is about more than surviving a midlife crisis, overcoming depression, or even developing an interesting hobby. Our passion is a clue to our life's mission—what God has put us on this planet to accomplish. Detecting one's passion is holy and important work because it is the work of discovering how God wants us to use our lives to serve one another and the world. Frederick Buechner has said, "The place God calls you to is the place where your deep gladness and the world's deep hunger meet."[1] When people come to me feeling lackadaisical about their lives and ask me to help them find out what's next, I take them—and the work—very seriously. Although the clients are the ones playing detective, I'm often responsible for giving them the tools they need to solve the case.

Remembering Ten

When I was 10 years old, I loved to put on plays in my backyard. Write, direct, act—I did it all. Although I majored in theater in college, I left it behind to pursue a more "respectable" career. A few years ago, I volunteered to usher at our local repertory theater company. The training began with a tour of the belly of the theater. As we wandered through the set design and creation area, past the props, and then up to the main stage, my eyes began to tear. The smell of paint and sawdust stirred deep memories of a place I had loved since before I could talk. Ordinary people make magic here! I used to be a part of that. Suddenly I knew that my life needed to change some—I needed to be creating magic. I needed to regularly smell the comforting theater odors. I wanted to walk the boards, conjuring stories for people. I had reconnected with my 10-year-old self and understood the passion that drove me then.

Ten seems to be a magic age for most of us. We have lived long enough for our passions to have grown and developed. Yet we are too young to be socialized out of them. Though our parents may believe that dainty girls do not play basketball or real boys don't do art, we're given a little freedom because we are, after all, still children. When clients come to me seeking to connect with their passions, I begin by asking them to look at themselves when they were 10 years old. I encourage them to revisit childhood diaries, mementoes, and friends; to talk with parents and siblings; and to consider the following questions:

- How did you spend your free time?
- What did you collect?
- What could you lose hours doing?
- What sort of make-believe games did you create?
- Who were your friends?
- What did you read?
- What subjects did you love in school?
- Which ones did you despise?
- What did you get into trouble for?
- What did you keep secrets about?

Sometimes clients need to look beyond 10 to their earlier years. That's fine. The point is always to seek the clues that lead them to the ideas, people, and activities that stirred their souls.

Getting the Essential Self to Talk

In Martha Beck's book, *Finding Your Own North Star*, she makes a distinction between the "social" and "essential" selves. According to Beck, the essential self is that part of ourselves in our genes. It is our "characteristic desires, preferences, emotional reactions, and involuntary physiological responses, bound together by an overall sense of identity."[2] The social self is the part of us "that developed in response to pressures from the people around" us.[3] Our social self is shaped by "cultural norms and expectations."[4] While the essential self acts to please itself, the social self acts to please the people and culture around it. Both selves are necessary for healthy formation. Without our social self we would be psychopaths, without conscience, totally addicted to following the whims of the id. Without our essential selves, we would become responsible robots, doing our work but disconnected from our souls. Unfortunately, most of us do not cultivate both selves in equal measure. People who are searching for their passion usually need to work on waking up their essential self.

In my own experience, our work-a-day world often requires us to silence our essential self. And for good reason. The essential self often disrupts cultural norms. It's the part of ourselves that wants to dance down the aisle at church, lick the bottom of the ice cream bowl, or curl up on the floor of the bookstore to read a story we love. But the essential self cannot live shut up inside of us forever. It needs air.

Usually it speaks to us through our bodies. When we are doing things our essential self despises, we lose sleep, watch the clock, forget things, get anxious or depressed, eat too much or too little, get sick, make blunders, lose energy, pick fights, or retreat from life. When we do things our essential self loves, we lose track of time, sleep well, remember even minor details, feel unreasonably healthy, experience energy boosts, become social wunderkinds, and practice healthy habits. People looking for clues to their passions need only to examine their lives in conjunction with this list.[5] One of my clients examined her life in light of the characteristics of the essential social self's behavior and discovered she always felt most energetic and healthy when preparing and preaching her sermons. Her low-energy weeks always coincided with making shut-in visits. In those weeks, she would ruin her diet by devouring buckets of chocolate in the car between visits. She sought a job that would use more of her essential self's passions. Another client experienced much angst over completing papers for her PhD program. She experienced stomach viruses and low energy levels that kept her from doing the assigned work. After months of beating herself up, she noticed that she experienced an energy boost every time she read to her daughter's preschool class. After much debate, she decided that her essential self was telling her that she needed to be working with kids instead of adults. She quit her PhD program and became a children's librarian.

I have found that my essential self never lies. When I say yes when I mean no, I get sick, lose sleep, and end up feeling angry at everyone. As Anne Lamott wrote, "My therapist, Rita, has convinced me that every time I say yes when I mean no, I am abandoning myself, and I end up feeling used or resentful or frantic. But when I say no when I mean no, it's so sane and healthy that it creates a little glade around me in which I can get the nourishment I need. Then I help and serve people from a place of real abundance and health, instead of from this martyred mentally ill position."[6]

Magnetism

Often my clients give me the best coaching tools. One of my clients is a student of the simple living movement. She had been reading a newsletter from simple living guru Janet Luhrs. Luhrs had invited readers to look at their life and the stuff in it with one question in mind, "Does it inspire or drain you?" My client had applied that question to everything from the people she encountered to the books she read. She found the question to be a good measuring stick for her energy level.

I thought the question was simply magical. Sometimes finding our passions is a matter of basic magnetic science: what draws and what repels us? What inspires and what drains us? I ask my clients to use these questions first as an evaluation tool for their current life. This helps them get more information about what is working and what needs to be changed. Then I invite them to turn outward, toward the activities, ideas, and places they do not know or have forgotten about.

I encourage my clients to take psychogeography tours.[7] Psychogeography is the study of how the environment affects human behavior and emotions. One method that psychogeographers use is called *dérive*, which literally means drifting. In *dérive* the traveler sets aside time to wander in a location without his or her usual agenda—work, leisure, shopping, or relationships. Instead, the traveler lets what attracts and engages him or her in the terrain determine the agenda. This technique allows travelers to gather information about what inspires them.

The easiest psychogeographic experiment is to simply choose a starting point—your front door, city hall, the Eiffel tower—and make a journey by alternately turning right and left until you get to a dead end. Carry paper and make note of the places that stir your imagination. What are they? You can also take field trips to interesting places: art museums, libraries, junk shops, rummage sales, flea markets, sporting events, small villages, urban areas, film festivals, and conferences for other disciplines. Wander through these places, letting your desires set the agenda. Dwell in the places that draw you and ditch the ones that don't. Consider:

- What tugs at your heart?
- What gives you energy?
- What places excite you?
- What makes you feel young and in love?

These are clues to your life's passions. I think Rumi said it well:

Be patient.
Respond to every call
that excites your spirit.

Ignore those that make you fearful

and sad, that degrade you

back toward disease and death.

Rumi, 13th century Sufi mystic and poet[8]

WHERE HAVE YOU BEEN BROKEN AND HEALED?

The coaching profession tends to be strength focused. As a coach, I encourage clients to build their lives around their assets and strengths instead of shoring up or dwelling on their weaknesses. Even so, our brokenness can also teach us about who we are and what God has called us to do with our lives. An article in *Spirituality and Health* magazine recounted how the experience of illness moved people to become healers.[9] Chiropractor Mark Halpern's bout with a connective tissue disorder led him to study Ayurvedic medicine. He eventually founded a college of Ayurvedic medicine. Physician Rachel Naomi Remen used her own experience battling Crohn's disease to develop a new philosophy about working with people who have chronic illnesses: get them to connect with their strengths. She has used this philosophy in her work counseling chronic and terminally ill patients and instructing other physicians about how to relate better with their patients. For me, it was my own encounter with a difficult parish that inspired me to create resources for spiritual leaders.

I tell my clients to take stock of their own lives, their own beautiful imperfections. I ask them to consider their struggles, failures, mistakes, illnesses, and the places in their lives where they have been broken. I invite them to think about what these experiences taught them about who they are and who they might support. I want to know what strengths they developed to face this adversity. These, too, are clues to the passions that stir within them.

Start Now!

When I speak, I meet many people who have great passions that they are waiting to get around to doing. One woman I met had always dreamed of living by the ocean. Unfortunately, her husband hated the water and so she hadn't been to the ocean in twenty years. A man I met loved his children and wanted to spend more time with them. He said, "I always think I will get to them when the work is done, but it is never done." I've always wanted to write a novel. But, my family needs to eat. No one will pay me to write a story—yet. But, if I never write that novel, they never will pay me to create stories.

I remind my clients that their in-box is always going to be full. The more we do and the better we do it, the higher the pile of work will be. So, once you find your passion, do not delay or deny it! Take a break and do what *you* need to do. For my part, I've started that novel. I try to write a page each day. I figure that in a year, I will at least have something longish enough to edit!

Try

Choose one or more of the exercises above and do it. Then reflect with your partner on the questions below.

Talk

1. What are the biblical and theological foundations for seeking to live life based on what we are passionate about?
2. Share the exercise you tried. What happened? What did you learn?
3. Talk about your relationship to passion. Are you passionate about your work and life? What needs to change? Brainstorm with each other about how that might happen.

---

55 ❀ Midwifing Dreams

You must harbor chaos if you wish to give birth to a dancing star.
                                                    Friedrich Nietzsche

In the early stages of a caterpillar's transformation into a butterfly, the inside of a chrysalis looks like "an undifferentiated lump."[1] The lump contains everything necessary for the butterfly to emerge. The chrysalis offers protection to the creature during metamorphosis. If the chrysalis were opened, there would be no hope of a butterfly. When we experience life changes, we have moments when we are like that undifferentiated lump inside the chrysalis. Our new self is emerging but not quite formed. We are fragile—not quite formed—and cannot live well without the sanctuary our cocoon provides. If we share our new dreams and passions too soon or with the wrong people, they may dash our determination or our desires. Discouraged, we might lose hope of becoming what we had dreamed of.

One of the roles of coaching is to provide the safe place from which a person's passions can be transformed into some form of reality. The coach works as a sort of midwife, supporting the client in birthing a dream or a project or a whole new way of living. When I gave birth to my children, I learned some lessons that I now apply to coaching.

It's Called "Birth *Process*" for a Reason

A baby needs both to gestate and "get born." So do dreams. Birthing dreams is a natural process with built-in steps—a beginning, a middle, and an end (which is also another new beginning). Still, waiting is hard. Once the destination of our journey is in sight, it's difficult not to echo the gazillions of children who have bellowed to their parents, "When will we *get there*?" We need faith as the writer of Hebrews defined it: "the assurance of things hoped for, the conviction of things not seen" (Heb. 11:1). The coach tries to provide some of this assurance, reminding the client that the journey is as important as the destination.

When I was pregnant with my second child, I had a long to-do list. I was in the middle of a rigorous coach-training program, building two new Web sites, writing a book, parenting a young son, and working as an editor. My coach encouraged me to set daily, weekly, and monthly goals. The practice of setting regular goals eased my anxiety. Though there were many things outside my control, I knew I was taking daily steps toward my goals.

When I work with clients who want to turn their passions into life changes, I ask them to write down the steps they need to take to get to their goal. Once they have set those steps in writing, I ask them to break each step into many smaller ones. How small depends on the client's time constraints and personal readiness. I encourage clients to take the size and number of steps that make sense for them at the moment. For example, a client who wants to turn her passion for art into a career might have set as her first step, "Explore art careers." I would invite the client to break that goal into several smaller goals such as:

- Make a list of questions, such as, "How do they make a living?" and "What sort of training did they do?"
- Research artists online and at libraries, museums, and bookstores.
- Talk to local artists about their work.
- Research art schools online.
- Tour local art schools.

After a client has a small set of goals to accomplish, I encourage her or him to do just that—get it done! It does not matter what the client does first; just choose a goal and do it. This process is repeated over and over again until the client finds the path or process that is going to work for them.

Get Good Support

Most expectant mothers who are in the process of gestating or birthing babies are offered oodles of good support. Books tell them what to expect when they are expecting and birthing; physicians and midwives check on their progress regularly; classes teach them how to give birth; vitamins and healthy food support the growing baby; and, hopefully, partners and friends give them encouragement and a helping hand with the nesting.

People who are birthing dreams also need support. The coach is obviously one support for the client. But, like most stools or chairs, people birthing dreams need more than one leg to support them properly. I encourage clients to seek people who can encourage and assist them in the midst of their transition. Usually people who are happy with their lives or content with where they are in the process of their own transformation offer the best support. I invite clients to first look to the people who have sustained them in the past. Who was present to them during earlier crises? Were there church or community groups that cared for them? Did certain friends exhibit an ability to provide fearless and sturdy assistance? Next, I invite clients to connect with friends and acquaintances who are also in transition. People in transition understand other people in transition and can usually be helpful to them. Third, I ask clients to seek out other people who share their interests or dreams. People with similar goals can recognize one another's specific needs for support.

Once clients have identified their support system, I encourage them to set up regular meetings with the people in their circle. In the past years, as I have transitioned out of parish ministry and into full-time writing, editing, and coaching, I have worked to develop a network of support. Because what I am doing keeps me out of ministry's mainstream, away from professional meetings and gatherings, this network provides valuable social and professional services. I meet with my coach and the other people who support me at least twice a month. These meetings keep me connected with people who remind me of where I have set my professional and personal sights. When I lose focus or get discouraged, I need people to remind me of my goals, cheer me on, and offer their prayers on my behalf. My network does that for me.

One final note: avoid the people who cannot support you in the way you need. Unfortunately, not all support will be the right kind of support. People will give you unsolicited (and unhelpful) advice. People will criticize. Their response to your dream will be about them (and not you or your dream). Ignore them. Or as Jesus said, "If anyone will not welcome you or listen to your words, shake off the dust from your feet as you leave that house or town" (Matt. 10:14).

Beware of Bearers of Horror

Everyone has a horror story. Each time I was pregnant, people told me about moms who died in childbirth. "Great story," I would growl. Just what a pregnant hypochondriac needs to hear! It's no different when you're birthing a dream. If you are job hunting, you'll hear about the nasty market. If you are starting a business, someone will tell you how her neighbor's business failed. People will say, "It'll never work, you can't do it, it's doomed." I encourage my clients to eschew prophets of doom. If anyone should surprise them with a horror story, I invite them to say, "Thanks for thinking of me, but I am trying to focus on the positive. I'd prefer not to hear that story."

Instead, I encourage my clients to collect stories of people who have faced tremendous challenges and succeeded. I have begun to collect these stories in a box I call my "All Temperature Cheer" file, so that I can pull them out whenever life gets a little messy. In it sits the story of 78-year-old Verna J. Willis who divorced in her late forties while five of her seven children were still living at home. She managed to finish her PhD program and get a tenure-track position at age 62.[2] I love the story of Mandi Caruso, who has lived five years beyond the three-to-six months she was given when she was diagnosed with cancer. After having a double mastectomy, she had her chest tattooed with a painting by her daughter, and which covered her scars like a shirt, so that she could surf topless.[3] Then there's the story of Helen Hooven Santmyer who started her epic novel, *And Ladies of the Club* when she was 69-years-old. In 1982, when Santmyer was 87, the novel was published. Two years later, when Santmyer was in a nursing home, the book became a bestseller. I pull out these stories to remind myself and my clients that dreams take time and many detours but can eventually come true.

Stay Present Focused

In the middle of labor with my first child, hungry and tired and wanting to be done, I told the nurse that I didn't think I could do it anymore. She said, "Do you think you can do one more contraction?"

"Just one?" I asked.

"Just one."

"I can do that."

"That's all you have to do. One contraction at a time," she said.

Her wisdom got me through the next several hours and has been passed on to many people since. Birthing happens one contraction at a time. When you birth a dream, focus on the step you are on. Do not think ahead about the next step or the hardest step. You will get it done, one step at a time.

Trust in God

My daughter was born quickly, in three pushes. I am a small woman and she was a big baby, more than nine pounds. She was turned the wrong way, "sunny side up," as the doctor said. In the middle of the pushing, I had to go deep inside myself to a profoundly centered place and tap into energy I didn't think I had. And I probably didn't. In that moment I had a sense of something greater than myself stepping in to make this happen. I believe that center was God.

In the midst of difficult transitions, we need to trust that we have the wisdom to do our best. But often our best isn't nearly enough. That's why we always live life depending on God. As my pastor said, "It is not impossible for God Almighty to use you just as you are and also to make you into something new. God does it all the time—God does the impossible all the time. Believe in God and have courage. Do not fear, because God is at work . . . in you."[4]

Her statement was a helpful reminder to me. God accomplishes what is impossible for us. We might look at our lives and see only a scattering of broken pieces. God pieces together these slivers and shards, making us both beautiful and useful. In a sense, God is the true midwife here. As a coach, I can only do so much. It's the same for spiritual leaders. We can't move people from point A to point B, away from a place of abuse, toward drug and alcohol treatment, into a regular school schedule. We can't make people parent well, tithe, or speak kindly. We can only trust that God is working to help the people we care about and care for birth the best things for their lives.

Try

Coaches and spiritual leaders need support, too! This week, your task is to make a visual representation of your network and identify people who can be "midwives" to you. Set up an initial meeting with at least one of the people on your list. Ask the person if they would be willing to meet with you regularly to support you in achieving your goals.

Talk

1. What are some biblical or historical models for midwifery?
2. Share a story about someone who has been a midwife to you. How did that person support you in birthing something new?

56 ❈ Nurturing Creativity

One night I hung out with a friend at the campus art studio as she and her colleagues prepared for a jewelry sale. Only this jewelry was nothing like I'd seen before. No beaded necklaces or bejeweled earrings. One woman had used electrical heat shrink tubing and tiny gems to make rings. Another had used artificial nails to form rings that looked like small chrysanthemums. My friend had combined wire screen and hand-dyed velvet to create stunning cuff bracelets. Doilies, soda-can tops, bicycle spokes, buttons, rose petals, wax—anything could be salvaged and shaped to create works of beauty. None of these people had read the warning tags (this product only to be used as intended under threat of law). And thank goodness! This work was innovative, original, outside the proverbial box.

One challenge in coaching is getting clients to think and act creatively—to move outside the box. Most of our training as spiritual leaders taught us the form and contents of the box. We learned the shape of what is not what could be. The box is the realm of the right answer. When the professor asks, "How did John the Baptist die?" or "How do you define repentance?" we know that there is only one right answer for each question. Our training gave us a system (hence systematic theology) or a way of viewing the world. We have learned to formulate our questions, thoughts, and dreams limited to the worldview inside the box. Anything that would threaten the status quo of the box might be too frightening to think about. Because many people we connect to are also inside the box, they affirm us for keeping our thinking and dreaming inside the structures we know.

Here's an example from my own life. During my first parish call, I knew that parish ministry was not what I wanted to do for the rest of my life. But I also didn't know what else I could do. I saw my choices as limited to the paths I could see—I could shift to a different type of church, get a PhD and become a professor, move into an administrative or executive position within the church (bishop's assistant or church executive), work for a parallel organization (church publishing house or insurance agency), or write books for the church. I went to my mentors for advice. Of course, my mentors were all inside the church, so they laid out options that were inside the box. I studied the paths of other people, trying to find a trail that I could follow. None of these trails excited me. I knew I *could* do them, I just didn't know that I *wanted* to. I interviewed at several PhD programs. Each time I left with a ghastly headache and the desire to take a long nap. It took several years for me to discover that I would need to create my own path and that my path may not be one of the acceptable routes inside the church's box. My path might begin at the place where the sidewalk ends.

I needed someone who could push me to think outside the box—or at least to turn me around so I could get a different view of the inside of the box! The woman who did this for Jesus was a Gentile, a Syrophoenician (Mark 7:24–30). When she approached Jesus to ask him to heal her daughter, Jesus said, "Let the children be fed first, for it is not fair to take the children's food and throw it out to the dogs" (Mark 7:27). Jesus was thinking inside the box—inside his mission and culture. In that world, the people who were Jewish were the children. The Gentiles were the dogs. Jesus came to feed the children. Then the woman did the extraordinary; she spoke words that pushed Jesus to take a different view of the box: "Sir, even the dogs under the table eat the children's crumbs" (Mark 7:28). Something shifted. Jesus healed the woman's daughter.

According to theologian James Alison, Jesus ultimately *broke* the box. If our worldview says that life is a game with winners and losers, and the ultimate loss is death, then when Jesus died he lost the game. Or not. When God raised Jesus from the dead, God showed us that the game does not matter. Death does not matter. According to Alison, we are no longer inside this box on the moral path from birth to death, trying to live right so we get to heaven. Instead, we are set free to share in God's life. We no longer have something to lose (that is, life—eternal or temporal). There is no box. There is only a God who *likes* us and wants to work with us to recreate the world.

This Jesus who broke the box becomes the ground of creativity coaching. Knowing that we have nothing to lose frees us to risk everything. Believing that there is no one right answer or perfect path can give us the confidence to step forward in faith. Most clients "get" this intellectually. Many of us preach it. Still, we are quick to remind ourselves, we live in the real world. Despite having been set free from the box, we may still see ourselves as living inside the box. We may believe the box still matters. My first tack with clients is to get them to think about the possibility that the box does not matter. Not only that, but the people who say that the box matters may not need to matter that much to the client. I invite clients to tap into this no-box world by asking questions like:

- What would you do if you had nothing to lose?
- What would you do if money were no object?
- What would you do if you didn't care what people thought?
- What would you do if you knew you would not fail?
- What would you do if you knew you had one year to live?

This exercise encourages people to go to the places inside themselves where boxes do not matter. The next step is to begin to take day trips outside of the box to see what paths need to be explored—or created—outside the box. This does not necessarily mean career paths, though it can. One client of mine discovered a yearning to work with his technical side. He ended up using his technical savvy to create audio files for his church's Web site. A colleague of mine saw that the traditional way that most pastors did ministry was not going to work for her as she struggled to raise three young children. She worked out a call that was not only part time during the week but enabled her to worship with her family at her husband's congregation every other Sunday.

I once received a hand-painted card that said, "The most visible creators I know of are those artists whose medium is life itself." We create our lives. Perhaps like the artists I spoke of at the beginning of this chapter, we grow when we explore new materials, new tools, new ways of looking at and thinking about the art we make.

Try

Take a day trip outside your "box."

Talk

1. Discuss the ways your training or experience as a spiritual leader keeps you inside the box.
2. Share what you did on your day trip outside the box. Reflect together on:

- What did your day trip teach you about yourself? About the box?
- What support do you have for venturing outside the box?

3. How might "outside the box" thinking change the way you relate to others?
4. In what ways do you encourage yourself and others to live and think outside the box?

57 ❀ Visioning

In darkness and in light, God beckons us to keep vigil and to companion one another in this and every season. In giving voice to our visions, we find strength in the shadows and a presence that guides the way.

Jan L. Richardson, *Night Visions*

The Sunday after the Martin Luther King Jr. holiday, the pastor spoke to the children about aiming high. They had spent the last Tuesday Praise time articulating their own dreams—for their lives, for their community, for their country. She read some of those dreams to us during worship, visions of becoming educated as nurses and teachers, dreams of a community where black and white and beige and red work together without hatred, a hope that every child will know his or her father and mother, a vision of a community where all children and adults are enveloped by God's love and no one will be left behind. As the pastor put her hand up into the air she said, "Aim high." "Aim high," repeated the children. "Aim high," echoed the adults. Aim high.

The Indigo Girls have a song called, "Perfect World." In it they say, "We get to be a ripple in the water."[1] The point of this song is that we have a purpose. God calls each of us to use our wisdom to make a difference in the world. What we do with our daily lives matters. Living this life is a privilege. It's not, "We *have* to be a ripple in the water," but "We *get* to be a ripple in the water." The question I invite all of my clients to consider—and the question I believe every person of faith needs to ponder—is this: "How does God call us to be a ripple in the water?"

We are often too busy dealing with the dregs of daily life to dream. As Rev. Clare Ferguson, the main character in the mystery *Out of the Deep I Cry*, says "When I became a priest, I surely didn't think I was going to spend so much time thinking about leaking roofs and the price of oil and water heaters."[2] Still, even in the midst of the mundane, even when our futures seem unclear, God does have a dream for our lives. In the midst of the transitions in my own life, of learning about God's vision for my life, keeping these words from Isaiah in my mind has helped me: "I am about to do a new thing; now it springs forth, do you not perceive it? I will make a way in the wilderness, and rivers in the desert" (Isa. 43:19).

The question of course is always how—how will God do this, how will we recognize God's plan for our lives, when will it unfold? In the television show, *Joan of Arcadia*, a teenaged girl heard from God quite a bit. God appeared to Joan as an attractive teenaged boy, an overweight garbage collector, a girl on the playground, a lunch lady, an old man on the bus, an older woman seeking a large-print book. Each time, God had a bit of wisdom to offer and a plan. Work at a bookstore. Build a boat. Have a garage sale. Each tiny action moved against and with other characters' actions and in some small way brought movement and peace into the lives of others.

So I have been looking around my neighborhood, listening carefully and paying attention to the garbage collectors and girls on the playground. So far, God isn't talking to me. I have been looking for some neon signs from God about what to do next with my own life. When I go to the grocery store, I stare at the security guard, hoping he might have a proverb to share. I faithfully read my horoscope. I read those change-your-life books. I pray. The only things I see showing up in multiples are those e-mail messages about topics that would turn most of our faces red. I'm pretty sure that those are not messages from God. God isn't showing up at my door or in my car to tell me what to do. I am guessing it's the same for you. I know my clients and friends have the same problem. So how do we know where God is leading?

In Gail Godwin's novel *Evensong*, Margaret, a 20-something seminary student, writes to her 40-year-old friend Adrian. She asks about God and her vocation, "Where is God in all this?" Adrian says,

> Your question may be the only one that matters. Despite all the convoluted guesswork of theologians ever since Job's friends hunched beside him on the dung heap, "Where is God in all this?" (just the question itself alone, I mean) may be enough to keep us busy down here. Maybe the thing we're required to do is simply keep asking the question, as Job did—asking it faithfully over and over, whatever ghastly think is happening around us at the time—until God begins to reveal himself through the ways we are changed by the answering silence. . . . How can you be sure ministry is your vocation? I can only offer this conjecture. Something's your vocation if it keeps making more of you. Neither I nor anyone can tell you whether the ministry will ultimately do that for you.[3]

According to Adrian, God leads us into the places that make more of us, that grow us into being the people God has intended us to be. When clients come to me dissatisfied with their lives, I want them to begin to consider where God might be leading them. Most clients have a sense of what isn't working. They also have some ideas about what they love to do. But they may not have considered the destination: their life vision. I encourage them to take Stephen Covey's words to heart: begin with the end in mind. In order to move forward, we need a sense of where we might be going. These are some of the techniques I use to help clients envision their ideal life.

What Dreamers Do

In Ephesians, Paul invited his readers to put on the armor of God:

> Therefore take up the whole armor of God, so that you may be able to withstand on that evil day, and having done everything, to stand firm. Stand therefore, and fasten the belt of truth around your waist, and put on the breastplate of righteousness. As shoes for your feet put on whatever will make you ready to proclaim the gospel of peace.

> With all of these, take the shield of faith, with which you will be able
> to quench all the flaming arrows of the evil one. Take the helmet of
> salvation, and the sword of the Spirit, which is the word of God (Eph.
> 6:13-17).

I love this passage despite its violent battle imagery. It provides
the helpful image of making ourselves ready to be followers and
proclaimers of Jesus, much like we make ourselves ready for the day
by putting on clothing. People who want to seek God's vision for their
life need to get ready to dream. I encourage clients to adopt the practices that will help them to be open to detecting the vision God has for
them. It's what dreamers do! These practices include:

- making time to be
- walking
- prayer

MAKE TIME TO BE

I recently encouraged a client to pay attention to the objects, actions,
emotions, and people who inspired her. "Take time," I said, "An hour a
day. Thirty minutes a day. Just wander, be, see what draws you."

"Can't do it," she said.

"Because?" I asked.

"I'm too busy."

Aren't we all? But rushing from one project to another only leaves
us overwhelmed and confused. Our brains and hearts are so jam-
packed with tasks to complete and stuff to remember that we couldn't
recognize a dream if it grabbed us and pulled us into the action.

In the midst of writing this book I also finished writing an article
on a different topic, coaching another writer about her book, editing
a periodical, writing a monthly column, and seeing clients. Not to
mention caring for two children who have a gazillion things for me
to remember. I don't need an espresso to feel like my head is spinning: it is.

While I was madly dashing from one idea to another, often stuck
on how to put this book together, my whole family started puking.
Talk about a forced break. But the break did wonders for this book.
Ideas appeared. "Being time" freed up the mouse-on-the-wheel of my

brain enough to find some new paths to explore. It allowed me to listen. As Madeleine L'Engle said, "When I am constantly running, there is no time for being. When there is no time for being there is no time for listening."[4] Being time is never wasted time. In fact, being time is absolutely essential for those who want to aim high. Being time helps us see where we might aim.

WALK

I have read that walking is an especially good exercise for our brains because it isn't too strenuous. The movement increases blood circulation and, because the legs don't take up a whole lot of extra oxygen, that oxygen can go to the brain. Studies have shown that walking improves memory and increases cognitive function.[5]

In her book *Walking in This World*, creativity guru Julia Cameron talks about how walking helped her move through a difficult period in her life: "A day at a time, a walk at a time, even a simple step at a time, my sad and tangled life began to sort itself. I say sort itself because all I did was 'walk through it.'"[6] Cameron quotes Augustine, who she says was a walker. Augustine declared, "'Solvitar ambilando': It is solved by walking."[7]

PRAY

In Luke's account of Jesus's baptism, Jesus was baptized by John and then he prayed. It was while he was praying that the Holy Spirit descended upon him, and God said, "You are my Son, the Beloved; with you I am well pleased" (Luke 3:22). Later in Luke's Gospel, Jesus taught his hearers to pray the Lord's Prayer. Afterwards he reminded them, "Ask, and it will be given you; search and you will find; knock, and the door will be opened for you. For everyone who asks receives, and everyone who searches finds, and for everyone who knocks, the door will be opened" (Luke 11:9-10). These texts remind me that God seeks our presence and prayers.

A client recently told me about meeting some famous writers. I wondered aloud, "How did you get to do that?"

"I asked them. Called them up and invited them to breakfast."

My jaw dropped. Eternally shy, I'd never have the guts to do that. Still, I did. When I attended a conference featuring one of my favorite musicians, I very much wanted to have a conversation with her. So I steeled myself for rejection, marched right up to her, and asked if we could have a meal together during the conference. We did.

It seems to me that prayer is not much different than this. It's simply the practice of regularly placing ourselves in God's presence for a conversation—one in which we both speak and listen.

Research!

Inventors amaze me. So do explorers. They imagine something, an object or a place, that exists beyond the realm of what most of us think is possible. Somehow these individuals get past the "but we've never done it that way before" thinkers to the place where anything is possible. This is a difficult task. Most of us simply live our lives doing what we know, and if we do not have models that push us outside the status quo, we may have difficulty moving beyond what we know. Anthropology professor Mary Catherine Bateson wrote, "It is good to have a wealth of models, for sometimes local ways of thinking about lives interfere with the ability to live them well, turning those that do not conform into perceived failures."[8] Many of us don't have the wealth of models that Bateson talks about. Instead we have models that are simply at different points down the one or two paths we happen to know about. This is where research comes in. Those of us who do not have models of the extraordinary lives we want to create must find them.

Don't imagine this research as the kind of stuff you did for those terminally boring papers you had to write in graduate school. No, this research is fun. I encourage clients to create a life-vision binder or journal to hold the information they uncover. Research might include:

Reading. Internet sites, periodicals, and books contain a wealth of information about how people are constructing their lives. The best finds happen when researchers move out of the space they know and start reading and learning about fields vastly different from their own. Though the teacher may never want to be an astrophysicist, he might learn something new about his life dreams from reading about their life dreams.

Networking. It's not so much who *you* know but who *the people you know* know. Start asking about the friends of friends and acquaintances. Maybe they know someone who has an incredible life story.

Just learning about the different ways people have composed their lives can be helpful. If that's not enough, move on to the next phase.

Interviewing. Call up these interesting people you have heard about from the friends of your friends and ask them if you can interview them about their lives. People like to talk about themselves. Arrive with a list of questions and let them wax eloquently about how they got where they are and why they chose this path.

Field trips. When we first moved to Milwaukee, we toured one of the local breweries. It reminded me of all those great field trips we took as kids, giving us a detailed view of how things were made and how other people lived. I often encourage clients to create field trips that will help them to imagine what might be. One of my clients who longs to live outside the country decided to take a test trip to Montreal. Traveling alone, she visited the usual tourist sites but also spent time in various neighborhoods, trying to see if this was the type of culture that interested her. A colleague was intrigued by the idea of becoming a nursing home chaplain. In order to test his interest, he arranged to shadow a nursing home chaplain for a day. In my own search for the ideal life, I took a series of field trips to feminist bookstores. Besides wandering through the shelves, looking for stories of other women's lives, I spoke with the owners and women who worked in the stores. I was curious about how they got interested in starting such a venture. Also, I asked them to suggest books, music, and periodicals that might help me formulate my own life vision.

Classes. If all else fails, go to school! One doesn't have to commit to a PhD to try out a new field. Many stores offer classes related to the products they sell. Where I live, a local bead shop offers classes on jewelry making while one of the computer stores will teach people how to make home movies. Local community recreation departments, nonprofit agencies, and school continuing education departments also offer classes at reasonable prices. For people who do not live in a city, the Internet offers a wonderful array of free and for fee classes. In addition, some local public television stations broadcast shows related to community college distance learning classes. When I was pregnant with my son and rising each day at 5:00 AM, I watched a whole series of programs on how to open and operate home day care. For those who have more money to spend, it's always possible to find institutes around the country and abroad where you can get a taste of how the professionals do it. A friend of mine who was contemplating a career in baking attended a master baking class with a world-renowned baker. Short classes like these can provide the learner with enough information to decide whether or not the field could become a life-long passion or career.

Guiding Metaphor

As I mentioned in "Creating a Healthy Foundation," metaphors can enrich a client's approach to an activity. When I work with clients around life vision, I invite them to choose a guiding metaphor for their vision that will be meaningful to them. Here are some metaphors that work nicely for life visioning:

> What sort of race are you running?
> What kind of journey are you on?
> What type of structure are you building?
> What does your life quilt look like?
> What is in your life collage?
> What type of a garden are you planting?

Piece by Piece

When I make prayer beads for someone, I usually have some ideas about what colors I want to use but no idea how the beads will fit together in a congruous whole. I dump all the potential beads on an old cloth diaper and then I play. I move the beads around until a pattern emerges out of the chaos.

I encourage clients to do a similar thing with their lives. Many times we can see the pieces of our lives even when we cannot see the whole. I invite clients to consider the pieces they want to include in their vision of the ideal life. Life pieces might include things like personal character traits, activities to participate in, people to connect with, places to live and visit, ideas to consider, and vocational dreams. Clients who know themselves well can often simply make a list of the things they want in their life collage. I encourage these clients to do this on index cards (one life dream per card). One client had a list similar to this:

- Live in a warm place.
- Create something beautiful and colorful with my hands.
- Connect with artists and other free spirits.
- Be my own boss.
- Learn one new idea each day.
- Work with children.

With these dreams listed on her index cards, she then spent time playing with the cards. She thought about different ways each could take form. "Creating something beautiful and colorful with her hands" might include baking cakes (she loves to bake), creating wearable art (she is a gifted weaver and knows how to dye yarn and fabrics), or learning a new skill such as jewelry making. She added another stack of cards with these possibilities sketched out on them, each category written with a different color marker. Then she played cards. She laid out the cards and arranged and rearranged until she got a vision that felt right.

I encouraged this client to find a way to summarize this vision on a piece of paper, so that she could keep it before her as she went about her life and as we worked together. She took the ideas articulated on the cards and made a drawing of a wheel with spokes. Each spoke had the words of one piece of her vision articulated on it in colorful letters. In the center of the wheel she had written, "God." Inside the circular shape of the wheel, where the tire would be, she wrote her theme verse, "For mortals it is impossible, but not for God; for God all things are possible" (Mark 10:27).

Clients who are not so self-directed often need prompts to help them articulate the pieces of their dreams. At the end of the book, *The Lion, the Witch and the Wardrobe*, the Professor warns the children not to speak of their adventures except to those people who have been to Narnia themselves. When the children wonder how they will know who has been, he says, "Oh, you'll *know* all right. Odd things, they say—even their looks—will let the secret out. Keep your eyes open."[9] My job as the coach is to work with clients to help them keep their eyes open. One way to encourage this process is to invite the client to set aside time to open their eyes and begin to gather pieces of the vision. I ask clients to gather magazines, old books, pictures of themselves that reveal who they are, and anything else that might inspire them in visioning their ideal life. I invite them to page through the magazines and books they have collected and cut out anything that they feel drawn to—words, pictures, even just colors. In addition, they can gather from the other items they have collected the pieces they feel most connected to. When they have collected a good stack of pictures and objects, I instruct them to begin arranging them on a piece of poster board or in a tray. If they are working with mostly flat objects, they can then glue their final product to the poster board, perhaps giving it a name. If they are working with more three-dimensional objects, then they might choose to decorate a box to keep the objects in. The clients then take this collage or object box and articulate to me or to a trusted friend how it reflects their vision.

At a workshop I led on creating one's life vision through collage, one woman put together an interesting portrait of her hoped-for new life. The collage was titled, "The trouble with being good." It included some quotes about telling the truth. Brightly colored kites flew at the top while rainbow boots stood in the bottom left corner. The centerpiece of the collage was a lush beach scene with deep blue waters and verdant palm trees blowing in the wind. In the bottom right corner was a baby crab, crawling steadily through the sand. Above the tiny crab's picture she had pasted the words, "Take Comfort in Your Strength."

"So how does this articulate your vision?" I asked her.

"It tells where I will live—by the ocean. It speaks about me listening to my own truth instead of trying to please others—that's a problem for me. It reminds me of my strength. Finally, the crab teaches me that I only have to take one step at a time."

The details of her vision would need to be spun out, perhaps in coaching sessions or with a friend. But she had the big pieces—she knew what she wanted to be like in this new life of hers.

The Whole Story

I once read about an author who dreamed a whole novel in one night. It took her some years to get it all down on paper—but when she did, it sold and later became a bestseller. For clients who think in big pictures, life visions often emerge like this—as complete stories. For these clients, I offer several techniques for capturing their life visions.

WRITE YOUR OBITUARY FEATURE STORY

Every day our local newspaper carries a few obituary feature stories. These stories capture the life stories of interesting people in our community who have recently died. I encourage clients to write one of their own. What would they want to be said about them at the end of their lives? What would they have done with their time and money? Where did they live and whom did they love? What values would they have communicated with their words and actions? What would their legacy be?

WRITE A BRIEF BIOGRAPHY

I was talking with a client about how daunted we both felt at a book reading after hearing the introduction of an author younger and more accomplished than we perceived ourselves to be. "So how would you like to be introduced 10 years from now?" I asked her. She thought about it and decided to use the question as her assignment. This assignment has many variations—write book jacket copy, a newspaper release, a curriculum vita, a holiday letter, a Web site biography page, a magazine feature article, or even a transcript of a television program.

CREATE A PICTURE

Clients who are visual learners and thinkers often like to put their life visions into pictures instead of words. They can do this through any artistic medium including collage, painting, drawing, sculpture, or fabric arts. At a workshop I led, one of the participants visioned her perfect life as a great big bunch of colorful flowers. Another created a vista—a house on the beach with one of the walls opened up so that we could see the contents of her home. Each piece in the house reflected something about her dream for her future life. A third made a shadow box, filling it with images and objects of her ideal life. This woman wanted to move to the mountains, so her shadow box was papered with mountain scenes. Inside it she placed miniature objects that reflected her dream of a more simple, rural life—a log cabin, skis, freshly baked bread, and the pieces of a home office.

CREATE OPTIONS

I used to love those books with variant endings. At set points in the story, the reader gets to make choices about what happened next, shifting the outcome of the story. Of course, none of the options were limitless. Each choice narrowed the field of future choices. Many of my clients balk at the idea of creating just one life vision. Although they know that every choice they have made and will make limits their future options, they want to have some variety as they consider the next steps. I invite people to create three life-vision scenarios. With scenarios in hand, I ask them to tell me about each of them. I also want clients to seriously consider each scenario, perhaps taking a day to imagine what living each vision would be like. Afterwards, I ask them how they felt talking about each scenario. Here are some of the questions we consider:

- Did one vision feel more authentic than another?
- What are the similarities or patterns that emerge in all three of the visions?
- In what ways are they different?
- After talking about the visions and living them, do you want to let go of aspects of any of the visions?
- Do you feel tied to aspects of the visions? Which ones and why?
- What do these visions tell you about the values you need to have in your ideal life? (This question can be altered and repeated by changing the word values. Options include: relationships, living arrangements, work, leisure, activities, and so forth.)

Choose a Talisman

When I first started working as a professional freelance writer, I found inertia to be a powerful force. Because I hadn't been used to creating a life without consulting the outside world, I did what I knew. I let the schedules of my interim position churches, husband's job, and my friend's lives determine when I would write. I was too willing to fill up the calendar with everyone else's desires but my own. Desiring a change, I tentatively began to set boundaries around my time. I told everyone that I couldn't meet or work in the morning because that was my writing time. At first, I felt like a fraud. I spent those hours doing more worrying than writing. I needed a talisman to encourage me. I had loved turtles for years, and they became the perfect symbol of the new life I was creating. Much later I found this description of why the turtle makes a good mascot for the writer: "turtles have everything I think a writer needs. They have tough shells to deal with criticism; soft sensitive insides; the need to stick their necks out if they want to move forward; and the steady patience to keep slogging away, day after day."[10] My turtles have led me through the writing of nine books and the pain of two childbirths. They line the shelves in my office, hang around my neck and wrist, and sit upon my children's beds. We name them, talk to them, and let them remind us that we can do anything we want to do, one small step at a time.

Each of us needs to choose a talisman that speaks to our own needs. A client of mine carries with her a small square silver medallion in an orange pouch. The medallion says: "Wish it. Dream it. Do it." A friend of mine has found inspiration from the butterfly. Another friend surrounds herself with red cardinals.

A Caution

Being who God has called us to be is difficult work both for us and for the ones who love us. Visioning what might be sets us on a path that requires that we

- take a break from our busy lives and dream about what is possible;
- articulate that dream to ourselves;
- talk to the people we love about our vision of how we want to spend our days;
- set goals that will move us from here to there;
- make changes in the way we are living each day, so that we can begin living a little more of our vision each day;
- cope with the questions and challenges of people who do not understand or who feel threatened by our vision.

At some level, articulating and then living our vision means that we make choices that may upset other people—even people we love dearly. We may be used to living another way, doing the things that we believe everyone else wants us to do with our lives or what we think will bring happiness to the congregation, the bishop, our spouse, our parents, our siblings, our colleagues, our professors, and a long line of other people we consult in our mind's eye. We do things because that's the way we have always done them. We do things because we want people to like us. Or because that's what good Christians do. We go along to get along. We wonder:

- What would they think if I really did what I want?
- Would people still like me if I told the truth?
- What would they think if I bucked the system?
- What would happen if I followed my bliss?

In our anxiety about other people, which is mostly good-hearted and done out of love, we are like airplane passengers who have forgotten the rule: put the oxygen mask on yourself before attempting to assist others. We cannot help those around us if we are dying. The question we need to ask ourselves is Mary Oliver's question: "Tell me, what is it you plan to do/with your one wild and precious life?"[11] We only have this one life to live. We need to do so out of our own vision—not the vision of another person!

Try

Choose one of the visioning exercises that inspires you and do it!

Talk

1. What biblical passages do you connect with visioning?
2. How do you distinguish vision and mission?
3. How do you think people can tell the difference between something being God's call and human desire?

---

58   ◉   Setting Goals

I used to work at The International House of Pancakes. It was a dream, and I made it happen.

Paula Poundstone

My parents have been dropping off a box or two of my old stuff every few weeks. Mostly I just stick it in the attic. But one day, lacking anything better to do (or avoiding my writing), I sorted through a box of old papers. Mixed in with my second grade math papers and eight-year-old attempts at fiction writing, I found several of my New Year's letters to myself. In high school I had the habit of spending a portion of New Year's Eve alone, reflecting on the past year and setting goals for the next one. I wrote my reflections in the form of a letter to myself, to be opened on the next New Year's Eve.

I chuckle at my goals. Written in the bold hand of a teenager, each one is peppered with capital letters, multiple underlines, and a gazillion exclamation points. Rounder then than I am now, I always entered the New Year wanting to drop a few pounds and get in better shape: LOSE WEIGHT!!!!!!! STOP EATING SO MANY OF GRANDMA'S DONUTS ☺ !!!! NO MORE POP TARTS AFTER SCHOOL!!!!!! Then there were the "boyfriend goals." Usually I had two or three centered on some crush I had: GET A BOYFRIEND. ASK X (☺) TO TURNABOUT. GO TO PROM!!!! Finally, I had a category of personal achievement goals—practice my clarinet more, do my homework *right* after school, and start college shopping.

I wish I could travel back in time and talk to my teenage self about having more fun. In addition to that, I would probably teach myself how to set better goals. Most of my New Year's resolutions lasted a minute and a half—at least the ones I controlled. The ones I didn't hold complete control over (like "get a boyfriend") just depressed me. When it comes to making resolutions or getting things accomplished, the difference between success and failure might be as simple as how one sets goals.

SMARTS Goals

When I work with clients, I always encourage them to set goals. It's common knowledge that people who set goals accomplish more than those who don't. Goal setting works. Of course, how we set goals matters. I teach the SMARTS system of setting goals. SMARTS is an acronym: Specific, Measurable, Achievable, Reasonable, Time bound, and Self-designed. I encourage clients to keep this acronym in front of them as they create and measure their goals. Let's look at each step.

SPECIFIC

Every December and January, I talk to my clients about their New Year goals. One client told me that her goal was to be a better leader. "Too vague!" I said. Specific goals help us achieve the desired result. I encouraged my client to get specific. In what ways did she want to be a better leader? What might that look like? I wanted her goal to define what she wanted to accomplish. My client took my questions home and returned the following month with a more specific goal. She knew she wanted to do better at asset-based leading. This meant that she would speak and preach about biblical and congregational assets. In addition, she would call attention to the assets of congregational members every time she could. Her goal statement said, "In my leadership this year, I will daily speak about and call attention to the congregation's assets."

In checking for specificity, ask:

- What exactly do I want to accomplish?
- Does this goal reflect that vision?

MEASURABLE

We need to be able to measure our performance against our goals. We need to be able to see that we have accomplished our goal. Goals that have to do with feelings, such as "I will feel happier at work," are difficult to measure. A better goal for the happiness seeker might be, "At work this week, I will spend five minutes each day speaking with someone I enjoy."

Goals that require someone other than ourselves to drive them are also difficult to measure. Put yourself in charge of achieving your goal. One of my clients said, "I will get published by a major company this year." I encouraged her to shift her goal from an outcome goal to a performance goal, something she could control. Her new goal was, "I will submit my book proposal to five agents this year." This was something she could measure.

In checking for measurability, ask:

- How will I be able to measure my progress?
- Who is driving this goal?

ACTION ORIENTED

I read somewhere that the people who can sustain long-term relationships are the ones who see love as an action instead of a feeling. While that insane first-love feeling is intoxicating, long-term love is fed by what we do for one another. In that sense, the song "What have you done for me lately?" is pretty wise.

When it comes to goals, the ones that describe a feeling, idea, or state of being can be inspiring, but they are not practical. Practical goals are action oriented. They use action words that describe what we will do to achieve the goal. So we say, "I will walk 30 minutes a day" instead of "I will get in touch with my body's capacity this year." Or we say, "I will write and send a card to my spouse once a month." instead of "My spouse will know my love for her."

In checking for action, ask:

- Did I use action words in this goal?
- Does this goal illustrate the actions I need to take to achieve it?

REALISTIC

In the movie *St. Ralph*, the 14-year-old protagonist Ralph sets the goal of winning the Boston Marathon. Everyone tells him his goal is ridiculous—the boy can't even run a block without panting like a dog in July. As the movie progresses, we see the boy training hard. A few weeks before the Boston Marathon, Ralph wins a local marathon race. After that, his coach changes his tune. Suddenly winning the Boston Marathon is a realistic goal for Ralph.

In setting goals, it's important to create a goal we can accomplish. For example, setting the goal of working for a major celebrity when you live in Nowheresville, Pennsylvania, might be a pipe dream. However, setting a goal like, "This year I will spend three hours each week researching the possibility of working for a celebrity" might get you closer to your dream.

In checking to see if your goal is realistic, ask:

- Is this goal challenging enough to motivate me?
- Is it possible for me to succeed at this goal?
- Do I know other people who have succeeded at similar goals?

TIME BOUND

I have always found it easier to write with a deadline. Whether external or internal, deadlines motivate us to get moving. Without a deadline or some sort of time limit, goals can become daydreams. Without a deadline, we might set the goal of learning to lift weights and then spend several years vegging out on our sofa, lifting nothing heavier than a can of beer.

Besides needing deadlines, goals also require time to complete. I could set a deadline to finish writing a book in a week, but it won't get done unless I have also carved out the time to write the book. As you set your goal, consider:

- When will I do this?
- When is my deadline?

SELF-DETERMINED

A plethora of stories exist about people who have lived their lives to please someone else, only to reach midlife (or the end of life) feeling resentful and rebellious. Most of us are social beings, and we want to earn social capital. We want the people we love to be proud of us, of who we are and what we do. Sometimes we seek to earn that love by setting goals that are more about pleasing others than ourselves. Even so, we are usually more motivated to achieve goals that we determine to be central to our life and consistent with our passions. Consider:

- Do I want to achieve this goal?
- Am I trying to please someone by setting this goal?

Achieving Goals

Once a client has created a SMARTS goal, the next step is achieving it! I've noticed that the most successful clients use the following practices:

POST REMINDERS

The other day over coffee, I questioned a friend about her New Year's resolutions. Then she asked me about mine. Here's the rub: I couldn't remember them all! Too many, too vague, too new—whatever the issue, I had no clue. We cannot achieve what we cannot remember! I encourage clients to post goals in their office, bedroom, kitchen, date book, computer wallpaper, and anywhere else that might support them in remembering their goals.

In addition, it helps to create brief reminders of their goals. Some clients have done this by creating a theme for the year. Use a song title, a line from a favorite poem, a piece of art, or anything that inspires you to direct your year. One of my clients who wanted to be more assertive in her life chose Martin Luther's famous quote, "Sin boldly."

VISUALIZING SUCCESS

I once read that visualization is an important part of an athlete's training. Successful athletes envision good workouts and victorious events. Athletes increase their odds of victory through visualization. Visualization trainers teach people to use all five senses. So a marathon runner might picture the starting line, hear the nervous chatter of the other runners, smell the spring flowers, or taste the sweat running down her face.

I encourage my clients to use visualization to help them achieve their goal. I encourage writers who experience fear around the blank page to end and begin each day visualizing their next writing period as successful. I invite those who are hoping to add exercise to their schedules to begin by visualizing themselves getting up, dressing, doing their walk, and finally completing their exercise routine. Visualization is also a helpful tool to use before difficult meetings, prior to public speaking, and to prepare for frightening medical procedures. In my experience, visualization is one way of practicing achieving one's goals, making it easier to actually do the work to meet goals!

RECORD YOUR VISION

Another way of envisioning success is by recording a vision of yourself achieving your goal. In the book *Write It Down, Make It Happen*, author Henriette Anne Klauser offers numerous ways in which writing down one's life intentions can help us achieve them. She encourages readers to make lists, create stories, and write letters to God.

One of my clients made a mind map of her goals, using multiple colors of markers on plain paper, and kept it with her wherever she went. She believed that this written record of her goals helped remind her to organize her daily priorities around these goals. Another client decided to write down an affirmation each day that echoed the work she had planned toward achieving her goals. She said that this work encouraged her to keep working toward her goal of getting a graduate degree. About once a year, I set aside an hour to write down fifty things that I want to do before I die. I write fast and allow for repetition. This tool is a helpful way for me to evaluate my goals. It also reminds me of some things that I need to put on my goal list!

PRACTICE GRATITUDE

I tend to be the kind of person that wails a lot going into a big project, complains a bit in the middle, but when I accomplish it—I simply move on to the next thing! I forget to celebrate, to thank the people who have helped me achieve my goals, and to thank God for being with me on the sometimes rocky road to achieving these goals. One of the best ways to avoid this is to practice gratitude. Our family has made it a practice to talk each night about what we are grateful for. I also keep a personal gratitude journal, recording my gratitude for each step I take toward achieving my goals.

In addition, I encourage my clients to reward themselves with small treats in the midst of their work to achieve their goals. I have them make a list of things that they love to do, taste, touch, smell, feel, and see. Then I ask them to create a list of rewards that are simple and cheap (and that do not sabotage their goals). These rewards are good ways of nourishing ourselves along the way.

GET SUPPORT

Finally, I have noticed that the clients who have at least one other person who knows their goal and will support them (and cajole them) into achieving it have a higher success rate. When I started coaching professionally, hardly any of my friends even knew what coaching was. My coaching classmates became my lifeline. We would talk regularly to share current and emerging goals. I counted on these coaching colleagues to hold me accountable.

A Final Word

You would expect a coach to set goals, right? Of course! And I do. But I still struggle with the concept of actually voicing my desires for life.

Where I grew up, the cultural messages were: don't be greedy, don't ask for too much, and just be grateful for what you've got. Last spring I had the opportunity to take a course with one of the artists I admire. Falling back on my cultural norm, I would have been happy to be in the same room with this woman. But my friends encouraged me to set goals for the meeting. "What do you want to happen?" they asked. I began to articulate my hopes and dreams for the class: I wanted to have a one-to-one conversation with this artist. Because I had a goal, I entered the sessions prepared to ask the speaker for what I needed rather than sitting quietly, hoping that I might be noticed or that she might know by osmosis that I hoped to have a conversation with her. It worked. The conversations happened. I don't think they would have if my friends hadn't pushed me to articulate my desires.

Try

Set a goal and use one or more of the techniques above to try and achieve it. If possible, use a technique that is new to you.

Talk

1. Discuss how articulating one's desires fits in with biblical thought and your theological tradition.
2. Share a story that illustrates how goal setting has been helpful to you in your ministry setting either personally or as a group. In what ways did goal setting affect you or the dynamics of the group? How did it influence the outcome?
3. What tools have you found helpful in setting and achieving goals? Share a story to illustrate your point.

59 ❀ Transforming Messes and Mistakes

> "You can't create without making messes and generating chaos and
> blundering down blind alleys and crawling back up again—you can't
> create without those efforts which end in disaster, because it's the
> disasters which show you how to get things right."
>
> Eric Tucker in *The High Flyer*

"Rewind!" screams my son every time he does something that he would
rather not have done. Like the apostle Paul, my son is plagued by the
fact that he often behaves outside his will: "For I do not do the good I
want, but the evil I do not want is what I do" (Rom. 7:19). I know what
he means. I promised myself I would exercise every day this year. I
haven't—unless you count walking from the car to the donut shop
(three steps), repeatedly lifting mugs of coffee, and crumpling up the
discarded chapters of this book. I've had a few "Rewind!" moments
myself this year!

When I first started writing, I had the hardest time with the idea of
first drafts. In my mind's eye, the article, story, or poem I envisioned
was perfect. That perfection never carried over from mind to page.
Instead, the words on the page seemed trite and boring. I learned to
love rewriting because I knew the work could only get better. When I
read Anne Lamott's advice in her book *Bird by Bird* to write "shitty
first drafts," I finally found a goal I could keep.[1]

Staying Connected to the Process

No matter what we are working on, life is bloody difficult. We get stuck
and discouraged. We make messes and mistakes. We fear failure. In
the face of these experiences, we may be tempted to give up. Or at
least *rewind!* According to Eric Tucker in Susan Howatch's novel *The
High Flyer*, however, it's the mistakes that teach us. Whether you are
creating new life choices or the perfect room, it's the disasters that
deliver the greatest lessons and, eventually, propel you to success.
Okay! So we can jump into our goals with both feet because we know
we cannot lose, right? Yeah, right! For most of us, *knowing* that mistakes teach is all well and good, but not enough to keep us engaged.

Here are some practices I use with my clients to keep them connected to any creative process in the midst of messes and mistakes.

BREATHE DEEPLY

I have read that when we get anxious, we tend to take frequent short, shallow breaths. Deep breathing brings oxygen into our brains and gives us the power to solve problems. Before you do, say, or think anything, take a deep breath.

TAKE A BREAK

In the evenings, I listen to music and crochet. Last fall, I made a poncho. Each row had a different pattern. I would finish a row and struggle to understand the next. Read the pattern. Crochet. Rip. Read again. Crochet and rip. Stop. Twenty-one rows into the project and I (finally) learned that sometimes the best way to continue is to stop for a time.

On the verge or in the midst of a mess, stop and walk away. Sometimes a bit of rest and refreshment (always refreshment!) can make the mess seem less daunting.

FACE THE TRUTH

It does no one any good to pretend that things are working when they aren't. The first time I lead a participant-driven Bible study, no one talked. Actually, the first three times I led that Bible study with the same group no one talked. One of the members came up to me after the third session and said, "That really bombed." Though I wouldn't have used the same language, I had to admit he was right. Until I could see the truth, I couldn't learn from it.

Ask yourself what happened—and tell the truth when you answer the question! Sometimes it helps to review a difficult situation with a friend or colleague who can help you face the truth.

INTERROGATE REALITY

Like a relentless lawyer, question the situation. We learn from our mistakes and messes only when we question them. Once we see the truth of a situation, we need to question it.

Once I admitted that the Bible study bombed, I had several choices. I could hang my head in shame and walk away from the experiment or I could figure out what happened. I talked with the member who had complained, and we looked at why the new Bible study method wasn't working. We looked at my leadership, the materials we had chosen, the participants, and even the arrangement of the furniture in the room. To the outsider it might have looked like we were seeking a scapegoat, someone or something to blame. In fact, we were more like car mechanics, discerning the problem that had felled the engine. In the end, we decided that it was too early to make an assessment. What looked like a failure might just be growing pains. We decided to try two more sessions. At the fourth session, something clicked and the participants actually participated. By interrogating reality, we prevented ourselves from making a too-quick decision.

TAKE RESPONSIBILITY

Part of discovering why a mess is a mess is taking responsibility for your part in the mess. Figuring out what you did wrong—and doing it differently—can help you to avoid future mistakes and further pinpoint the cause of the problem.

In reviewing the "bombed" Bible study, I realized that part of the problem might be my willingness to step in and give the answers. The participant I worked with to evaluate the program suggested that I be even more hands-off than I had been. At the next Bible study, I asked questions and practiced silence. I sat on my hands and bit my cheek through the awkward moments (when I used to jump in) until finally someone answered. Afterwards we wondered if that small tweak opened up enough space for people to participate.

GET HELP FROM THE EXPERTS

Sometimes our mistakes cannot be fixed alone. We need help. I went through a season of baking yeast bread that did not rise properly. Interrogating reality gave me a list of possible problems: kneading time, yeast freshness, flour quality, house temperature. I changed what I could and when the bread still turned out like a doorstop, I sought help from the experts. I read my bread book, talked to baking friends, even surfed the Net. I finally discovered the problem was probably a mixture of two issues: poor quality flour and a drafty house. Without the experts, though, I couldn't have solved this one.

LEARN

Part of examining our messes is just thinking about what they have to teach us. Use your journal to reflect on these prompts.

* What does this disaster, mistake, or mess have to teach me?
* What about this process do I need to let go of?
* If I were to coach a friend about this situation, I would say...
* If I could try something wild and off the wall, not caring about the result, I would do ...

RELISH THE MESS

The messy stuff is part of what makes the whole of life so amazingly rich. When my daughter was two, we spent many days rolling in the mess of our lives. One day we baked cookies (but burned the first pan). We exercised (mostly she climbed on me while I *tried* to exercise). We set up a fort in the dining room, dragging our chairs and blankets until we had a twisting cave-like space to eat our cookies in. We made messes and cleaned them up. I'm sure that most of what I did that day could have been done faster and more efficiently had I been alone. But, it would not have been much fun. I would have mised the messy, difficult parts. After all, every good story has difficult parts, missteps, and messes. That's what makes them delicious. Part of enjoying life is enjoying the messiness of the journey and not only the clean goal of the destination. As novelist and poet May Sarton said, "Without anxiety life would have very little savor."[2]

Try

Do something you have never done before. A creative endeavor would be best. Take a dance class, learn an instrument, make a clay pot, bead a necklace, paint with real watercolors, or learn to knit. Choose a small project and dig in. When you are finished, reflect on the following questions:

* What was your attitude toward making mistakes? Did this attitude change the way you participated in the project?

- What mistakes happened? In what ways did you overcome them to finish the project?
- What did this experiment teach you about how you deal with mistakes?

Talk

1. What biblical or theological themes (such as confession and forgiveness) may help someone deal with making mistakes?
2. What tools do you use to support the people you serve in overcoming mistakes?
3. Share an experience that showed you the value of making mistakes. What happened? How did the mistake or mess-making lead you to a better product?

60   ❁   Overcoming Blocks

So we must daily keep things wound: that is, we must pray when prayer seems dry as dust; we must write when we are physically tired, when our hearts are heavy, when our bodies are in pain.

We may not always be able to make our "clock" run correctly, but at least we can keep it wound, so that it will not forget.

Madeleine L'Engle, *Walking on Water*

I used to think writer's block was just another word for procrastination. When someone whined about being blocked, I assumed it was because they had ignored the cardinal rule of writing—in order to get anything done, you have got to put your butt in the chair and do the time. Aside from a couple of weeks when I struggled to dig a sermon out of a collection of impossible texts, I had never really experienced writer's block. Then I started writing this book. The first few chapters came easily. Then nothing came. I would have weeks where I wrote and weeks where I beat my head on the desk. A friend e-mailed me, "*Do not*, I repeat, *do not* pound your head against the table. It does not dislodge thoughts, as one might think. It only leaves a lump." I laughed and then continued to beat myself up! I was stuck—hopelessly, impossibly, undeniably stuck.

It happens to all of us. We reach a standstill in a significant relationship. We know we are unhappy with our jobs but we cannot figure out what else we might do. We do not understand how we can solve the interpersonal issues with the staff at our congregation. Whatever the circumstances, we need help. Being stuck is one of the situations that comes up with some frequency in coaching. Here are some tools I give to clients to support them in getting unstuck—without having to resort to beating their heads against their desks!

Get Some Distance

In the middle of one of my first editing projects, I became stuck. I had reached a point where the book didn't seem to work and I had no idea how to fix it. It didn't help that I was working under a tight deadline. Pregnant with my first child, the book and the baby were due at about the same time. The pressure was on! I had to get this book done! I called my boss, the supervising editor, and asked for advice. "What do I do?" I whined.

"Go to a movie," she said.

"A movie?" I repeated, a bit confused by her response.

"Yes. You won't solve the problem by staring at it. Get away. It will look better tomorrow. I promise."

I was suspicious. My work style had always been that of a bulldozer—plow through until the work is finished. Tired, stuck, hungry—none of that mattered! Here was an experienced, respected editor telling me to go see a movie! Crazy! What was the world coming to? But because I liked and respected her, I tried it. The next day, when I sat down to look at the book, I saw the solution within minutes. Maybe she wasn't so crazy after all.

Now I encourage all of my clients to step away from the issue. Get space, get perspective, get a massage! We cannot solve problems when we are tired or burned out. I encourage them to take a break and do something totally different. I want them to allow their subconscious mind time to work out a solution while they work or play at something less sticky. In the book *The Breakout Principle* by Herbert Benson and William Proctor, the authors suggest that breakout solutions appear when we leave a big problem behind and do something repetitive like needlepoint, tennis, or walking. Often in the midst of these repetitive exercises, the solution will magically appear! Amazing!

Take Small Steps

As I have mentioned other places in this book, small steps make big tasks doable. Usually by the time we get to cleaning up my kids' room, the mess is so enormous that we all feel like crawling into bed and taking a nap! We have discovered the best way to attack the problem is to break it into less daunting steps. I give each child a small task, like picking up all of the Barbie dolls or blocks. Like stepping on stones across a river, we get to the other side one small step at a time.

When a client is stuck with a project, I will encourage them to divide it into as many small steps as possible. After they have a list of small steps, I ask them to set a goal of achieving a certain number of small steps a day. When author and coach Martha Beck was trying to finish her dissertation, she did the same thing. Some days all she did was make one phone call. Still, one phone call was some progress forward and that was all that was necessary.[1] Remember, the turtle beat the hare one small step at a time!

Work around the Block

I once worked with a student who was having a difficult time completing papers. When she got stuck, she would abandon the project and take a nap or surf the Net. We worked out a strategy that supported her in making progress toward finishing the paper when she couldn't write. She looked over her list of small steps that needed to happen before the project could be completed and highlighted all of the steps that were different from writing: research, creating a bibliography, completing an interview and fact checking. She agreed that the next time she got stuck with writing, she would work on one of these other tasks. Doing that gave her the comfort of knowing she was still working on getting the project done. It also relieved her writing anxiety, and when she came back to the writing several hours later, she was able to do the work.

Get a Better Tool

When I was first learning to make lefse, a Scandinavian flatbread that is cooked like a tortilla, I couldn't get the dough to roll out like my grandmother's had. No matter how hard I tried, it didn't come out right. Then I enlisted a friend's help. When we met at her house, I saw my problem and her solution: I had been using the wrong kind of rolling pin. My grandmother (and my friend) used the traditional lefse rolling pin covered with a sock. Who knew?

When a client is stuck it is often because they are approaching the problem with the wrong tool. A hammer is a very good and helpful tool but, no matter how hard you try, it just will not saw through a two-by-four. I've found it helpful to spend time with clients brainstorming possible new tools and approaches—no matter how crazy they may sound. It's often the craziest ideas that lead to the solutions that work.

Get Help

"I can do it myself!" I must hear that phrase a hundred times a day from my young daughter. It doesn't matter what the chore—putting on shoes, getting a drink, washing her hands—she wants to remind me that she is capable of more than I give her credit for. Still, she still yells, "I need help!" from time to time. No matter how big we get, we all need help.

When we are stuck we can't always see why we are stuck; we just know we are stuck. Another person's point of view can move us toward solving the situation. Clients who have engaged a coach or people who have sought out a spiritual leader are often pretty open to this step. They have already sought professional help. I give my clients several other ideas for getting outside help:

- Research. Often the solution to one's crisis can be found in a book, periodical, or online. When in doubt, look it up!
- Seek the advice of experts. Interview the people who seem to know stuff. When I got stuck on this book, I turned to friends, colleagues, and clients and interviewed them around some of the questions I was asking in the book.

- Create a research and development team. My colleague Susan Lang and I wrote the book *Welcome Forward: A Field Guide for Global Travelers* in less than two weeks. We were able to meet that crazy schedule because we spent the first three days of the process with a group of experts. Our research and development team gave us all of the information and anecdotes we needed to create a good product. Since then, I have used research and development teams to write this book, create a new business, and navigate difficult life changes. I have seen my clients make use of them to solve congregational budget crises, confront church conflict, and practice visioning.

Finish Anything!

When we get stuck, we can begin to believe that we are unable to finish anything. Often we need the experience of finishing something else to gain back some confidence. When I get embroiled in a process that isn't working, and yet I am committed to the project, I do something creative that I know I can finish and that will not fail. I bake cookies, plant flowers, even do laundry! The simple joy of finishing a creative project boosts our energy and gets us back in the rhythm of finishing the task we have started.

The *Kairotic* Moment

A friend of mine writes her sermons on Saturday nights. At lunch the other day, I asked her about her writing process. I'm always curious about how other people, especially those who do not make their living writing, put together ideas into a written piece. At one point I asked her, "So could you write Sunday's sermon on, say, Tuesday?" She said no, she couldn't. "Why?" I queried. She answered, "Because I can't write until it's time to write."

As I thought about our conversation, it occurred to me that my friend was talking about kairotic time. In Greek, two words define time: *chronos* and *kairos*. Chronos refers to chronological or clock time. Kairos refers to the right, proper, or opportune time. Madeleine L'Engle calls kairos God's time.[2] She says, "Kairos. Real time. God's time. That time which breaks through chronos with a shock of joy, that time we do not recognize while we are experiencing it, but only afterwards, because kairos had nothing to do with chronological time. In kairos we are completely unselfconscious, and yet paradoxically far more real."[3]

Often we look at being stuck as a problem in chronological time. We view life as linear and know that the only way through is through. Like the kids going on a bear hunt, we logically know that we cannot go over or under or around the river, we need to go through it. Like me on my bulldozer, we keep trying to plow through, even when the blocks are sturdy and unmoving. When we shift our thinking to kairotic time, we trust that the muddy water will clear. We believe that the right action will arise on it's own. We see that at the right and opportune moment, we will be able to understand the way around, over, under, or through. Like my friend who writes her sermons on Saturday night, we will find that God will open the way for us.

A Spirituality of Stuckness

When the tech at the computer store lost everything on my hard drive, I would have become violent with anyone who told me that I could learn something from the experience. But I did. (Besides the obvious, always back up your work.) I lost pretty much everything I had—including my vast collection of e-mail contacts. In addition, I was leading a retreat the following weekend, had lost everything I'd prepared, and wouldn't have my computer back in time to recreate it. Stuck at home with no e-mail and no computer, I had to get creative. My neighbor, a management consultant, lent me both her computer and her expertise. With her help, I was able to prepare for the retreat. Without my computer, I had very little to do for two weeks. I spent more time with my family, went on walks with friends, and wandered around the house. Not having so much pressing work gave me the opportunity to narrow my focus. Suddenly I had the opportunity to pay attention to the many joys God had put within arm's reach. That small gift blessed me beyond measure.

When a client gets stuck, I ask them to consider the spiritual lessons of being stuck. I ask them:

- What can this particular situation teach me about the whole?
- How can I learn about my approach to problems?
- What is the life lesson in this mess?
- In what ways does being stuck offer an opportunity for growth?

- What can this experience teach me about God?
- How does "being stuck" inform me about my own spiritual journey?

A Final Word

The only thing I remember about my first sermon is the title: "Caught between a Rock and a Hard Place." It seems to be a fitting phrase for this chapter on being stuck. In hearing that phrase, I remember the biblical characters that were in just those kinds of situations. Abraham and Sarah after Abraham lied about Sarah being his wife. Ruth, after her husband, father-in-law, and brother-in-law had died. Mary, after she'd become pregnant with Jesus and before Joseph decided to stick by her. Mary and Martha, after their brother Lazarus had died and before Jesus reached them. Peter, after he denied Jesus. These are not just tough spots—these are times when people feel pressed up against the edge of life and death, sanity and craziness. Some people look at these situations and say, "There but for the grace of God go I." But that's not quite right, is it? God does not grace some of us with smooth paths while throwing stumbling blocks in front of other people like boulders. No, the truer statement is that only by God's grace do any of us survive the many large and small challenges that confront us in this life. We all suffer. We all get blocked. And we all move through the "rock and hard place" moments by God's grace.

Try

Most of us have one thing that we have been blocked about for some time—a piece of unfinished business, a difficult relationship, even a messy attic! Choose one area in your life that you currently are feeling stuck about and use one or more of the tools above to get unstuck.

Talk

1. Who are your examples or mentors in overcoming being stuck? Are there biblical or historical characters that inspire and sustain you? If so, who and what have they taught you?

2. Share your experience of getting unstuck (see "Try" above). What happened? What tools did you try? What worked and what did not work? What would you do differently next time?

3. If you didn't do the above exercise, share a past experience of being stuck. What worked then? What might you do differently now?

4. What other tools help you when you experience a block?

61 ❀ Making Meaning

Finding meaning does not require us to live differently; it requires us to see our lives differently.

Rachel Naomi Remen, *My Grandfather's Blessings*

I often tell my friends, "Life sucks and then you write a book about it." At least I do. Writing helps me make meaning out of misery. According to social psychologist James W. Pennebaker, writing about life's difficult events can help people heal from trauma. Pennebaker asked his subjects to write for fifteen minutes a day on four consecutive days. Half of the group members wrote about a difficult or traumatic event in their lives. The other half of the group, the control group, was asked to write about their day or to describe their living environment. A year later, Pennebaker examined the subject's medical records. The people who wrote about their difficult experiences were healthier than the others. What made the difference? According to Pennebaker, it was the meaning making that mattered. The people who showed increased insight into their difficult situation during the four days stayed healthier than those who simply wrote about their feelings or the color of their carpet.[1]

When we make sense of our lives—especially the suffering—we get healthier. We *need* to examine our suffering. We also need to discover the greater purpose behind the suffering we encounter. According to Pennebaker, we would be healthier if we processed our tough times through writing.

Many clients enter coaching because they are experiencing a difficult time. Our work together often includes the search for meaning in the midst of difficulty. The conversation may begin with complaint-focused stories about people and events that stand at the heart of the painful experiences. The clients are looking outward—at the difficulties they face, at the wrong done to them, at the people who hurt them, and at the obstacles they must overcome. As a coach, my job is always over time to support clients in shifting the camera's focus. I want them to pan the camera onto their own life and process, asking, "What does this teach you about you?"

At the beginning of coaching, the "this" we're talking about is almost always a difficult experience. Over time, I encourage clients to examine all kinds of life experiences (joyous, challenging, inspiring, boring, moving) from the question, "What can you learn about yourself from this?" I have developed a series of questions to support clients in examining their lives. The process usually works best if the client reflects on these questions alone and we discuss them in a follow-up session.

- What happened?
- Why do you think it happened?
- What effects did this event have on your life?
- What do you know now that you didn't know before this event happened?
- What meaning might you derive from this event?

I have been struck by how life shifting this exercise can be. A friend reported that her best and worst experiences of the year were the same events. She discovered that it wasn't so much what happened in her life that mattered but how she responded to it. A client offered a similar story, saying that her experience of bad events shifted when she changed the story she had created about them. For example, she felt more content when she viewed the loss of her job as an opportunity to find a better job instead of as a personal failure.

I did this exercise for the first time last Mother's Day. My schedule took me out of town that afternoon and, in a fit of loneliness that threatened to become despair, I listed the three things I was grateful for and why they had happened. In my reflections I saw the too-often invisible chain of events that lead to the good things that happen in my life: small kindnesses, loving gestures, blessings that I would ordinarily dismiss as random. I counted the evidence of grace and love in my life. Yes, I was alone. But on the plane with me I had cards from family members and friends and a whole pan of Rice Krispies Treats a friend had made for me. Another friend would meet me at the airport, leaving her own Mother's Day celebration to welcome me. Asking what the events meant, and how they had come to be, forced me to look at the choices I was making in my life and the grace that followed and met me, even when I could not see it.

For us to find meaning in the hopeless and happy events of our lives, we need to examine them from more than one direction. As Remen said, we need to see the events differently. When we do this, we have the opportunity to change the way we think about and live our lives. In connections that seemed random and fleeting, we find the people who love us back to life. Instead of seeing despair and emptiness, we may see the places where we have found warm welcome. We see that God has not abandoned us but in fact has led us to this place, guiding us each step of the way.

Try

Choose three different events from your life and reflect on them using the questions above. When you have finished, consider the following questions:

- How did this exercise shift the way you think about or experience your life?
- What might you do differently as a result of doing this exercise?
- Did this exercise raise any unfinished business—people you need to thank or acknowledge? If so, do it!

Talk

1. What biblical stories or theological ideas relate to the practice of meaning making?
2. How is your work in ministry about helping people make meaning?
3. How do you answer or deal with the trite and commonplace truisms related to suffering and tragedy?

✸ Frequently Asked Questions

It happens all the time—on the airplane, at church, at my children's schools. Someone asks what I do and I answer.

"You do what?"

"I coach."

"Ahh," they say, thinking they've got it. "What sport?"

"Life."

"Life? What do you mean?"

"I support people in rhyming their lives with their dreams."

"Uh-huh. And that means?"

And we're off. Questions follow at a rapid pace.

This appendix is intended to address frequently asked questions in the following areas:

How do I find a coach?

What does being coached look like?

How do I end a coaching relationship well?

If I want to become a coach, what do I do?

Finding a Coach

HOW DO I FIND A COACH?

First, ask yourself, "What type of support do I need?" Here are some possibilities.

1. Do I need support for professional growth? Common issues include identifying assets, developing leadership skills, setting priorities, managing time, visioning and goal setting, managing conflict, and strategizing.

2. Do I need support for personal growth? Common issues include assessing strengths, achieving balance, seeking clarity, growing spiritually, navigating life transitions, and enhancing wellness issues.

3. Do I need support for my relational health? Common issues might include improving communication skills, managing conflict, healing established relationships and beginning new ones.

4. Do I need emotional support? Common issues include healing from childhood or adult abuse, recovering from addiction, working through grief, managing anxiety and depression, and dealing with complex emotional and social issues.

5. Are there special issues or situations I need help with? These might include managing a specific diagnosis, such as attention deficit disorder (ADD), attention deficit hyperactivity disorder (ADHD), or anxiety; support through a specialized situation such as a job search or living with a chronic illness; or working on a unique goal, such as writing a book or starting a business.

HOW DO I DECIDE WHAT TYPE OF PROFESSIONAL CAN BEST SUPPORT ME?
In the helping professions, no "one-size-fits-all" solutions exist. Every situation requires unique care. A variety of helping professionals offer support and work around strength assessment, visioning, goal setting, and so forth. But each of these professionals has trained differently, holds different objectives, and offers unique types of support.

The differences between some of the various helping professions can be best illustrated with the following "person in the hole" joke. Please note that this joke is a stereotypical characterization meant to give you a quick idea of the differences between helping professions. Each of the professions characterized below offers a rich array of services that overlap with the other helping professions.

A man walks down the street. He falls in a hole. He uses his cell phone to call for help.

The therapist asks the man, "What happened in your family of origin to lead you to fall in this hole?"

The spiritual director questions, "Where is God in this experience?"

The mentor says, "The last time I fell into a hole, I used a rope to crawl out."

The consultant says, "Here is a report that tells you why I think you fell into this hole. It offers three suggestions for programs on getting out of holes."

The pastor crawls into the hole with the man and says, "I want to be here with you through this difficult time."

When the coach arrives, she asks questions such as:

"What now? What is your goal?"

"What personal strengths can you use to achieve that goal?"

"What could you do to eliminate holes from your life?"

WHAT ELSE DO I NEED TO THINK ABOUT WHEN LOOKING FOR A COACH?
Coaches are flexible and willing to adapt to the needs of the client. But coaches are not chameleons. Just like every male firefly has his own unique flashing pattern to communicate his message to female fireflies, each coach has an individual style. This style will include both the content they work with and their relationship styles. Each coach adds value to a client's life in a way that is distinctive for that particular coach. Think about what you are seeking in a coaching relationship. Then reflect on the following questions:

1. What type of relational style will work for me? Coaches also have particular styles of relating and those do not shift dramatically from client to client. The coach who is typically gentle, kindly affirming and tenderly nudging the client forward, will probably not be the one to count on for a kick in the butt. Knowing if you want a coach who will mainly affirm you or will challenge you may be helpful. To consider this, think about the types of relationships in which you felt good about yourself, were able to communicate effectively, and experienced healthy growth. What characteristics contributed to these experiences?
2. Do I want individual or group coaching? Group coaching is often much cheaper than individual coaching. Group coaching works well when the group members share a common career (spiritual leaders, bankers), identity (mothers, writers), or goal (lose weight, manage homework).
3. Do I want my coaching sessions to take place in person, on the telephone, or via e-mail correspondence? Most coaches work either in person or on the telephone. Both kinds of sessions

offer benefits to the clients. Telephone sessions can give the coach and client a space without distractions. On the other hand, in-person coaching offers the warmth of personal presence and gives the coach the opportunity to read visual cues as well as vocal cues.

4. How frequently do I want to have sessions? Most clients meet with their coach one to four times a month. Frequency depends on the client's schedule and the nature of the coaching content (for example, clients with urgent goals may need more frequent sessions). Sessions last between 30 and 60 minutes. Session length is set by the coach and agreed upon by the client. Many coaches invite clients to contact them between sessions via telephone or e-mail.

5. How much do I want to pay? At this time, insurance companies rarely cover coaching sessions. Coaches offer their services for a wide array of fees, ranging between $150 to more than $1,000 per month. Check out the International Coach Federation's Web site (www.coachfederation.org) for suggestions on current fee ranges. Also, compare the fees of several coaches before choosing one.

6. Do I need to know the coach? Some clients want to meet with a coach who is familiar to them. Others prefer a stranger. It's best to have a coach who does not have a personal stake in your success (for example, a denominational official or a relative).

7. Do I need a specialized or general coach? Many coaches have a range of content or issues they are skilled at working with. Some coaches have a niche—a specialized area of coaching. Niches can include general population groups (women in transition), professions (spiritual leaders, lawyers), specific population groups (people who have attention deficit disorder; people who are lesbian, gay, bisexual, or transgendered), and topical groups (career, writing). Some coaches who have niches also have programs that they believe are proven ways to cope with the problems specific to the population they serve. At best, these coaches often work more like consultants—offering a client advice and direction based on a specific body of information. At worst, these coaches see only their product

and never the client. Their work becomes a sort of one-size-fits-all approach that often misses the particular needs of an individual. People who are seeking coaching need to ask coaches about their niches or any other special areas of expertise. Knowing this information can help a client find the right coach.

WHERE DO I FIND A COACH?

Once you know what you need from a coaching relationship, you can search for a coach. Here are some places to look:

1. Recommendations from family members, friends, colleagues, and acquaintances. Listen to the people you know and encounter; if someone you know and respect speaks about having a successful relationship with a coach, ask about their coach. Personal referrals can be the best source for finding a coach.

2. The International Coach Federation (ICF). The ICF is the largest nonprofit coaching organization. The membership meets yearly, publishes an online journal, and is committed to the study and improvement of the coaching profession. The ICF maintains a code of professional standards, including an accreditation process. It also manages one of the best Coach Referral Services. Find them online at www .coachfederation.org

3. The Christian Coaches Network. This association of Christian coaches provides a database of Christian coaches who have joined the network. The association also offers regular meetings and online resources. Find them online at www.christiancoaches.com

4. Coach training programs. Nearly every coach training program maintains a database of the coaches they have trained. Find a list of accredited coach training programs at the ICF Web site and search the links for more databases.

5. Denominational resources. Your local denomination may retain or recommend coaches. They may have a connection to an Employee Assistance Program (EAP). Ask your denominational representative if they can recommend a coach. Note that

it is difficult for a denominational representative to coach a spiritual leader because of his or her own agenda in the outcome.

6. Internet search. Use your search engine to search for a coach with the type of specialty you are looking for, such as "spiritual" and "coach" or "career" and "coach."

WHAT SHOULD I LOOK FOR IN A COACH?
Getting the right coach for you is an essential step in making your coaching relationship successful. Most coaches offer a free consultation, an opportunity for you to meet the coach either in person or on the telephone, experience a brief coaching conversation, and ask questions about the coach. Here are some questions you may want to ask a coach:

1. What is your background and experience? It might be helpful to know about

   - previous or additional vocational training and work experience;
   - coaching experience (years coaching, number and types of clients);
   - relevant personal information.

2. What is your coach training? Ask:

   - What point are you at in the training process?
   - Is your training program ICF accredited or part of an equivalent process?
   - How many hours of training do you have?
   - What type of continuing education have you done?

3. Are you a credentialed coach or are you in the process of being credentialed? If not, do you hold any other credentials?
4. Do you belong to any other coaching associations?
5. What specialized training, experience, or skill do you have?
6. What types of clients do you usually work with?
7. What is your coaching style?

8. What is your coaching philosophy?
9. What is the process you use for coaching? This might include:

- What does a session look like?
- How frequently do you meet with clients?
- What types of homework do you suggest?
- What is your availability between sessions?

10. Can you give me an example of a situation you worked on with a client and how it turned out?
11. What are your fees?
12. May I speak with any of your clients?

Being Coached

WHAT CAN I EXPECT FROM A COACHING RELATIONSHIP?
Each coaching relationship is unique and will look somewhat different. You can expect that your coach will abide by the International Coach Federation's Code of Ethics (available on the ICF Web site). Some of the behaviors and actions you can expect from your coach are listed below. Your coach will:

- Set and keep appropriate boundaries.
- Create a safe space.
- Listen to you.
- Respect you, your colleagues, and his or her other clients.
- Keep the content of your conversation confidential.
- Honor your words and stories as your truth.
- Focus on your needs and agenda.
- Provide accountability.
- Challenge you.
- Require you to participate in your growth.
- Speak honestly about self, qualifications, information, and resources.
- Refer you to other resources or professionals when appropriate.

Some behaviors and actions not tolerated in the coaching relationship include

- sexual relationships between coach and client;
- gossip about you or other people;
- obscenities, offensive language, offensive jokes;
- demeaning, abusive, or hurtful language toward you or other people;
- lying;
- exploiting the relationship for personal benefit.

Ending Well

HOW WILL I KNOW WHEN TO END THE COACHING RELATIONSHIP?
Coaching relationships can last anywhere from a few sessions to several years. The meetings can be regular or intermittent, taking place when the client needs them. Coaching relationships do not last forever. Here are some reasons that coaching relationships end:

1. The time is up. Some coaching relationships are contracted to last a specific amount of time. When the contracted time is over, clients may be able to contract for another set of sessions or the relationship may need to end.
2. The money runs out. If coaching is tied to personal or institutional budgets, coaching can end when the money is no longer available for this expense.
3. The goal is accomplished. Clients who tie their coaching relationship to a specific goal may decide to end the relationship when the goal is completed.
4. The client outgrows the coach. The client needs more support or different support than the coach is able to give. This may include needing a coach with a specific niche or attending therapy for a time.
5. The coach outgrows the client. The coach may move into a specialty that no longer fits for the client. In addition, the coach's fees may grow beyond the client's ability to pay.
6. The coach and client conflict. Some relationships do not work forever—or at all. When coach and client have different styles, it may be helpful for the client to seek a coach he or she can work with more effectively.
7. The client is not doing the work. Most coaches want to see their clients change, grow, and achieve their goals. If a client

regularly fails to do homework, show up for sessions, or pay their fees, the coach may choose to end the relationship.

HOW DO I END THE COACHING RELATIONSHIP?

I am profoundly grateful for every client I have worked with. Whether the client has stayed with me for three sessions or years of sessions, each one has shared a part of his or her journey with me. Their presence in my life and work is a great blessing to me. The title of William Shakespeare's play *All's Well That Ends Well* aptly sums it up. Both coach and client have the opportunity to end the coaching relationship well. My hope and prayer is to end the coaching relationship with grace and integrity—no matter the circumstances. As a coach, I have come to appreciate clients who end well. This includes three things: giving notice, communicating gratitude, and offering feedback.

1. Giving notice. I appreciate clients who let me know *before* they come to the final session that they intend to stop coaching. This provides both of us with the opportunity to complete unfinished business. This might include incomplete topics, unpaid fees, unaired grievances, or positive messages that need to be communicated.
2. Communicating gratitude. Every relationship—personal and professional—blesses us in some way. Even acrimonious associations offer lessons. Throughout the coaching relationship I want to communicate my gratitude, echoing Paul's words in Philippians, "I thank my God every time I remember you, constantly praying with joy in every one of my prayers for all of you, because of your sharing in the gospel from the first day until now" (Phil. 1:3-5). When a coaching relationship ends, it's an especially important time to express gratitude for what has been. What are you thankful for in the coaching relationship?
3. Offering feedback. I appreciate clients who tell me both what I have done well and what needs to be improved. This message might include

   - recognizing strengths of the coach;
   - affirming performance;
   - talking about what you needed more of (homework, direct questions, content);

- saying what you needed less of (advice, homework, content);
- speaking God's care.

Becoming a Professional Coach

When I began studies at Coach U, many of my classmates shared that they had been informally coaching family members and friends for years. I had a similar experience. When I saw life coach and author Martha Beck coaching someone on the Oprah show, I recognized the kind of work I was already doing and enjoying in my ministry.

Most people who become coaches experience both an internal and external call to this work. An internal call happens when we are drawn to something like magnet to metal. No matter how much we try to resist, this passion keeps popping up in our lives. An external call happens when other people recognize our giftedness for this work. Often, the work we are called to unites our strengths and the community's needs.

Once we decide to listen to our calling to become a professional coach, the rest of the path is relatively easy. Here are the steps:

1. Choose a coach training program. The International Coach Federation Web site lists the schools it accredits. Attending an accredited school is necessary for being credentialed by the ICF. Please note that not all coach training programs are accredited by the ICF. Many coach training programs offer their own certification process.

   The ICF Web site provides links to each of their accredited coach training schools' Web sites. As you study the various schools, think about:

   - What kind of a coach do I want to become? While some coach training programs offer training for general life coaching, others focus on specific niches such as business or executive coaching.
   - How does this coach training program connect to my current profession or the type of training I already have? Some training programs are geared to people from a specific field, such as therapists or business professionals.

- Do I want to end up with another degree as a result of this training? Not all coach training programs are connected with traditional college and university degree programs.
- What kind of a training experience do I want: in person or virtual? Much training is designed to accommodate professionals who are juggling full-time employment with their education. Virtual training usually takes place on telephone bridge calls and gathers people from all over the world. Additional work—such as homework assignments and testing—is done via e-mail and the Internet. In-person training can take place in a number (three to four per year) of intensive training sessions. It can also look more like a traditional degree program.
- What length of time can I dedicate to a training program?
- What can I afford to spend?

2. Find a coach. Every coach training program will require that you work with a professional coach. The ICF credentialing process requires that you do some coaching with a Master Certified Coach. Working with a coach from the beginning of one's training program can deepen the learning process.

3. Start coaching. Most coach training programs encourage students to begin coaching immediately. Student coaches often coach for reduced fees or bartered services. This is a helpful way to collect both hours and experiences.

4. Join professional coaching organizations. The main professional coaching organization to join is the International Coach Federation. Aside from that, many other professional nonprofit and for-profit coaching organizations offer professional development and networking meetings, coach referral services, and additional training. In addition, many professional coaching organizations also have local chapters and interest-based chapters. Some of the major organizations include:

- International Coach Federation, http://www.coachfederation.org
- Christian Coaches Network, http://www.christiancoaches.com
- International Association of Coaches, http://www.certifiedcoach.org

- Worldwide Association of Business Coaches,
  http://www.wabccoaches.com
- Professional Coaches and Mentors Association,
  http://www.pcmaonline.com
- Association for Coaching,
  http://www.associationforcoaching.com
- The International Consortium for Coaching in
  Organizations, http://www.coachingconsortium.org
- European Coaching Institute,
  http://www.europeancoachinginstitute.org
- Association for Professional and Executive Coaching and
  Supervision, http://www.apecs.org
- Global Body of Life Coaches,
  http://www.globalbodyoflifecoaches.com
- Coachville, http://www.coachville.com

5. Network. The best way to develop a coaching practice is to connect with people. Talk to people you already know and people you would like to get to know. Go to events where you can meet the kind of people you would like to coach or those who can connect you with the people you would like to coach. When you meet, don't talk incessantly about coaching! Conversation about coaching or coach training can be boring. Instead:

- Ask questions that help your conversation partner tell his or her story.
- Ask, "What are you passionate about?"
- Ask, "What do you dream of doing in life?"
- Share a story about how coaching has transformed your life.
- Share a story about how coaching is changing the lives of those you work with.
- Ask, "How can I support you?"
- Make proposals about how you can support one another.
- Connect your conversation partner with other people in your network.
- Ask, "Do you know anyone I need to meet?"
- Exchange a stack of business cards for referrals.

❇ Notes

Acknowledgments

Epigraph: Thomas O. Chisholm, "Great is Thy Faithfulness," *This Far By Faith: An African American Resource for Worship* (Minneapolis: Augsburg Fortress), 1999.

Epigraph: Bernie Taupin, "Mona Lisas and Mad Hatters," *Honky Chateau*, compact disc, © 1996 Island.

Introduction

1. LaShun Pace, "I Know I've Been Changed," *I Know I've Been Changed*, compact disc, © 2005 Malaco.
2. Joan Chittister, *Scarred by Struggle, Transformed by Hope* (Grand Rapids, MI: Eerdmans, 2003), 93.
3. Marc Gafni, *Soul Prints: Your Path to Fulfillment* (New York: Fireside, 2001), 8.
4. Ibid., 9.
5. Ibid., 114.
6. Mary Martha Kannass, (unpublished sermon, Hephatha Lutheran Church, Milwaukee, WI, March 8, 2006).
7. Ibid., (December 24, 2005).
8. Don E. Saliers, "Where Beauty and Terror Lie: The Poetics of Everyday Life," *Spiritus: A Journal of Christian Spirituality* 2, no. 2 (Fall 2002), 181–91.
9. Madeleine L'Engle, *Glimpses of Grace: Daily Thoughts and Reflections* (New York: HarperSanFrancisco, 1996), 68.

Part 1   Introduction

Epigraph: Jean Vanier, *Drawn into the Mystery of Jesus through the Gospel of John* (New York: Paulist Press, 2004), 47.

Epigraph: Eduardo Galeano, "The Upside-Down World," *The Progressive* 70, no. 2 (February 2006), 17.

1. Karen Casey, *Change Your Mind and Your Life Will Follow: 12 Simple Principles* (Boston: Conari Press, 2005), 109.

1   A Safe Space

Epigraph: J. R. R. Tolkien, *The Fellowship of the Ring* (Boston: Houghton Mifflin, 1954), 237.

1. Mary Martha Kannass, (unpublished sermon, Hephatha, Lutheran Church, Milwaukee, WI, April 17, 2005).
2. The same may be true in faith communities. Not every community can work for every person. As spiritual leaders, we may need to acknowledge that some relationships do not work. We may not be the right leader for this situation, this person, this congregation. In addition, some individuals may need to find a different leader or faith community. Admitting the difficulty and seeking solutions, though painful, can lead to a more healthy community.

2   A Place for Questions

Epigraph: Rainer Maria Rilke, *Letters to a Young Poet*, trans. M. D. Herter Norton (New York: Norton, 1954), 27.

Epigraph: Rochelle Melander and Harold Eppley, *Dancing in the Aisle: Spiritual Lessons We've Learned from Children* (Cleveland: United Church Press, 1999), 7.

1. See http://livingthequestions.com.
2. Heidi Hart, *Grace Notes: The Waking of a Woman's Voice* (Salt Lake City: University of Utah Press, 2004), 86.

3   Truth Telling

Epigraph: Martha Beck, *Breaking Point: Why Women Fall Apart and How They Can Re-Create Their Lives* (New York: Times Books, 1997), 290–91.

Epigraph: Marilynne Robinson, *Gilead* (New York: Farrar, Straus, and Giroux, 2004), 170.

1. Ann Braude, ed., "Virginia Ramey Mollenkott," *Transforming The Faiths of Our Fathers: Women Who Changed American Religion* (New York: Palgrave Macmillan, 2004), 69.
2. Martha Beck, *Breaking Point*, 291.
3. Martha Beck, *The Joy Diet* (New York: Crown, 2003), 29.
4. Wally Lamb, *I Know This Much Is True* (New York: HarperCollins, 1998).

5. Mary Martha Kannass (unpublished sermon, Hephatha Lutheran Church, Milwaukee, WI, January 19, 2003).

4   Acceptance

Epigraph: Cheri Huber, *There Is Nothing Wrong with You: Going Beyond Self-Hate* (Murphys, CA: Keep It Simple Books, 1993), 111.

1. Madeleine L'Engle, *The Ordering of Love: The New and Collected Poems of Madeleine L'Engle* (Colorado Springs, CO: ShawBooks, 2005), 138.

5   A Client-Centered Relationship

Epigraph: Rachel Naomi Remen, *My Grandfather's Blessings* (New York: Riverhead Books, 2000), 90.

6   Asset-Based Thinking

Epigraph: Jon Hassler, *Rookery Blues* (New York: Ballantine Books, 1995), 479.

1. Luther K. Snow, *The Power of Asset Mapping: How Your Congregation Can Act on Its Gifts* (Herndon, VA: Alban Institute, 2004), 46.

2. Marcus Buckingham and Donald O. Clifton, *Now, Discover Your Strengths* (New York: Free Press, 2001), 5.

3. Snow, 8.

4. In part 3, the chapter "Assessing Assets" offers tools for spiritual leaders to support one another and those they work with in discovering and using one's assets.

7   Experts and Seekers

Epigraph: Avi, "Fortune Cookie," *What Do Fish Have to Do With Anything? and Other Stories* (Cambridge, MA: Candlewick Press, 1997), 182.

8   The Power of Mutuality

1. Carter Heyward, *Saving Jesus from Those Who Are Right: Rethinking What It Means to Be Christian* (Minneapolis: Fortress Press, 1999), 61–62.

2. Ibid., 61.

3. Tim Pearson, coach, interview with the author, December 2, 2002. See Tim's Web site at http://www.TimPearson.net.

4. Heyward, 229n30.

5. G. K. Chesterton, *The Man Who Was Thursday: A Nightmare* (New York: Dodd, Mead and Company, 1908), 89.

9   Dual Roles and Relationships

Epigraph: David Heller, *Dear God: Children's Letters to God* (New York: A Perigee Book, 1987), 15.

1. Carter Heyward, *Touching Our Strength: The Erotic as Power and the Love of God* (New York: Harper and Row, 1989), 35.
2. Ibid.
3. Ibid.

10   Defined Boundaries

Epigraph: Dean Feldmeyer, *Viper Quarry: A Dan Thompson Mystery* (New York: Pocket Books, 1994), 2.

1. As noted in the introduction, this book defines spiritual leaders as pastors, lay congregational leaders, youth directors, educators, coaches, counselors, parish nurses, church musicians, church administrators, and anyone else who takes a professional or volunteer leadership role in the church or church-related organization.

11   Yours, Mine, and Ours

Epigraph: Byron Katie, *Loving What Is: Four Questions That Can Change Your Life* (New York: Harmony Books, 2002), 3.

1. Ibid.
2. Mary Martha Kannass, (unpublished sermon, Hephatha Lutheran Church, Milwaukee, WI, January 5, 2003).

12   The Power of Now

Epigraph: Eckhart Tolle, *The Power of Now: A Guide to Spiritual Enlightenment* (Novato, CA: New World Library, 1999), 28.

1. Ibid., 41.

13   An Action Focus

Epigraph: Coldplay, "Clocks," *A Rush of Blood to the Head*, compact disc, © 2002 Capitol.

14   Self-Care

Epigraph: Anne Lamott, *Operating Instructions: A Journal of My Son's First Year* (New York: Fawcett Columbine, 1993), 175.

1. Dar Williams, "The World's Not Falling Apart," *The Beauty of the Rain,* compact disc, © 2003 Razor and Tie.

2. John Bingham, *The Courage to Start: A Guide to Running for Your Life* (New York: Fireside, 1999), 101.

15   An Imperfect Beauty

Epigraph: Joan Anderson, *An Unfinished Marriage* (New York: Broadway Books, 2002), 31.

1. Stephanie Kallos, *Broken for You* (New York: Grove Press, 2004), 295.

16   A Spiritual Journey

1. John Steinbeck, *Travels with Charley: In Search of America* (New York: Penguin Books, 1962), 4.

Part 2   Introduction

Epigraph: *Reader's Digest New Complete Do-It-Yourself Manual,* (Pleasantville, NY: The Reader's Digest Association, 1991), 17.

17   Be a Fierce Presence

Epigraph: Rachel Naomi Remen, *My Grandfather's Blessings* (New York: Riverhead Books, 2000), 91, 102.

19   Affirm

Epigraph: Bingham, *The Courage to Start*, 130.

20   Practice Generosity

Epigraph: Janet Jackson, "What Have You Done for Me Lately," *Design of a Decade: 1986/1996*, compact disc, © 1995 A&M.

1. Robert H. Smith, *Matthew: Augsburg Commentary on the New Testament* (Minneapolis: Augsburg, 1989), 224.

21   Listen Well

Epigraph: Winston Churchill quoted in Jan Karon, *Patches of Godlight: Father Tim's Favorite Quotes* (New York: Viking, 2001).

1. *Lutheran Book of Worship* (Minneapolis: Augsburg, 1978), 157.

22   Prepare to Listen

Epigraph: Susan Howatch, *Ultimate Prizes* (New York: Knopf, 1989), 276.

23 Use Listening Tools

Epigraph: Amy Gash, *What the Dormouse Said: Lessons for Grown-ups from Children's Books* (Chapel Hill, NC: Algonquin Books of Chapel Hill, 1999), 111.

Epigraph: Kate DiCamillo, *Because of Winn-Dixie* (New York: Scholastic, 2000), 68.

1. Susan Scott, *Fierce Conversations: Achieving Success at Work and in Life, One Conversation at a Time* (Berkeley, CA: Berkeley Publishing Group, 2004), 104.

25 Prophesy

Epigraph: Jeanette Winterson, *Oranges Are Not the Only Fruit* (New York: Grove Press, 1997), 161.

26 Encourage Accountability

Epigraph: Rochelle Melander and Harold Eppley, *Our Lives Are Not Our Own: Saying "Yes" to God* (Minneapolis: Augsburg Fortress, 2003), 13.

27 Encourage Discernment

Epigraph: Elizabeth Watson quoted in Irene Allen, *Quaker Indictment* (New York: St. Martin's Press, 1998), 1.

Epigraph: André Gide quoted in Jan Karon, *Patches of Godlight: Father Tim's Favorite Quotes* (New York: Viking, 2001).

1. Gil Rendle and Alice Mann, *Holy Conversations: Strategic Planning as a Spiritual Practice for Congregations* (Herndon, VA: Alban Institute, 2003), 50.

2. Henriette Anne Klauser, *Write It Down, Make It Happen: Knowing What You Want—and Getting It* (New York: Fireside, 2000), 124.

3. This book contains a separate chapter on prayer, which I commend to you. In addition, I would encourage people to use whatever type of prayer supports them in their discernment process: mantras, written prayers, prayer walking, praying with beads, or spontaneous prayers.

28 Tackle the Tough Stuff

Epigraph: Rachel Naomi Remen, *My Grandfather's Blessings: Stories of Strength, Refuge, and Belonging* (New York: Riverhead, 2000), 169.

1. Patricia H. Davis, *Beyond Nice: The Spiritual Wisdom of Adolescent Girls* (Minneapolis: Fortress Press, 2001), ix.

2. For information on forming covenants see: Gil Rendle, *Behavioral Covenants in Congregations: A Handbook for Honoring Differences* (Herndon, VA: Alban Institute, 1998); Denise Goodman, *Congregational Fitness: Healthy Practices for Layfolk* (Herndon, VA: Alban Institute, 2000); Mary K. Sellon and Daniel P. Smith, *Practicing Right Relationship: Skills for Deepening Purpose, Finding Fulfillment, and Increasing Effectiveness in Your Congregation* (Herndon, VA: Alban Institute, 2004).

3. Susan Scott, *Fierce Conversations: Achieving Success at Work and Life One Conversation at a Time* (New York: Viking, 2002), xvi.

29   Offer Comfort

Epigraph: Rachel Naomi Remen, *My Grandfather's Blessings: Stories of Strength, Refuge, and Belonging* (New York: Riverhead, 2000), 168.

1. Joan Chittister, *Scarred by Struggle, Transformed by Hope* (Grand Rapids, MI: Eerdmans, 2003), 21.

2. Ibid., 28.

3. Mary Martha Kannass (unpublished sermon, Hephatha Lutheran Church, Milwaukee, WI, November 6, 2005).

4. Maia Wojciechowska, *A Single Light* (New York: Bantam Pathfinder, 1968), 33.

30   Practice Curiosity

Epigraph: Rachel Naomi Remen, *My Grandfather's Blessings: Stories of Strength, Refuge, and Belonging* (New York: Riverhead, 2000), 247.

31   Ask Questions and Offer Prompts

Epigraph: Zilpha Keatley Snyder, *The Changeling* (New York: Atheneum, 1970), 150.

32   Provide Models

Epigraph: Arnold Lobel, "The Elephant and His Son," *Fables* (New York: HarperTrophy, 1980), 32.

33   Remember Life Stories

Epigraph: Marilynne Robinson, *Gilead* (New York: Farrar, Straus and Giroux, 2004), 115.

34 Nudge

Epigraph: Madeleine L'Engle, *A Wrinkle in Time* (New York: Dell, 1962), 201.

1. Eugene Peterson, *The Message: The New Testament in Contemporary Language* (Colorado Springs, CO: NavPress, 1993), 32.

35 Pray

Epigraph: "Somebody prayed for me," no. 246, *This Far by Faith: An African American Resource for Worship* (Minneapolis: Augsburg Fortress, 1999).

1. Emily Saliers, "Get Out the Map," *Shaming of the Sun*, Indigo Girls, compact disc, © 1997 Sony.

36 Coach to Transform

Epigraph: Ann Patchett, *Bel Canto* (New York: HarperCollins, 2001), 300.

1. *Merriam-Webster's Collegiate Dictionary*, 11th ed. (Springfield, MA: Merriam-Webster, 2003).
2. Lance Secretan, "99% Inspiration," *Ode* (July-August, 2005), 38.
3. Ibid., 47.
4. In part three, "Creating a Healthy Foundation" includes a section on how to seek inspiration.
5. *Merriam-Webster's Collegiate Dictionary*, 11th ed.

37 Coach to Support

Epigraph: Katherine Paterson, *The Tale of the Mandarin Ducks* (New York: Codestar Books, 1990), 35.

38 Coach to Advise

Epigraph: Edna St. Vincent Millay quoted in Peter McWilliams, *Do It! Let's Get Off Our Buts* (Los Angeles: Prelude Press, 1991), 55.

1. Kathryn Shafer and Fran Greenfield, *Asthma Free in 21 Days: The Breakthrough Mindbody Healing Program* (New York: HarperSanFrancisco, 2000), 139. See also *Writing to Heal: A Guided Journal for Recovering from Trauma and Emotional Upheaval* by James W. Pennebaker and *Poetic Medicine: The Healing Art of Poem-Making* by John Fox.
2. See also chapter 44, "Recommend Resources."
3. See also chapter 32, "Provide Models."

4. I often recommend exercises from the book I wrote with my husband, Harold Eppley, *The Spiritual Leader's Guide to Self-Care* (Herndon, VA: Alban Institute, 2002).

39 Support Strategic Assessments

Epigraph: Robert Heinlein quoted in Peter McWilliams, *Do It! Let's Get Off Our Buts* (Los Angeles: Prelude Press, 1991), 240.

40 Strategize

Epigraph: Christian Nestell Bovee quoted in McWilliams, *Do It! Let's Get Off Our Buts*, 278.

1. Switchfoot, "This is Your Life," *The Beautiful Letdown*, compact disc, © 2000 Red Ink.
2. See chapter 43, "Network."

41 Address Difficult Behavior

Epigraph: Iona and Peter Opie, *I Saw Esau: The Schoolchild's Pocket Book* (Cambridge, MA: Candlewick Press, 1992), 37.

1. This list is adapted from Melander and Eppley, *The Spiritual Leader's Guide to Self-Care*, 92.
2. A UCLA study published in 2000 suggests that women respond to stress by "tending and befriending." In the midst of stress, women's bodies release the hormone *oxytocin*, the same calming hormone released during birthing and breastfeeding. This hormone leads women to respond to stress by tending to children and befriending others. In the process of tending and befriending, more oxytocin is released, further calming the stress. (See www.anapsid.org/cnd/gender/tendfend.html) Perhaps this is why women often respond to difficult behavior by calling up friends to talk through the situation.
3. Hezekiah Walker, "I Need You to Survive," *Family Affair Vol. 2: Live at Radio City Music Hall*, compact disc, © 2002 Verity.

42 Apologize

Epigraph: Marilynne Robinson, *Gilead* (New York: Farrar, Straus, and Giroux, 2004), 161.

1. Mary Martha Kannass (unpublished sermon, Hephatha Lutheran Church, Milwaukee, WI, December 4, 2005).

43   Network

1.   Sally Helgesen, *The Female Advantage: Women's Ways of Leadership* (New York: Doubleday, 1990), 26.

44   Recommend Resources

Epigraph: Oliver Wendell Holmes quoted in Jan Karon, *Patches of Godlight: Father Tim's Favorite Quotes* (New York: Viking, 2001).

Kate DiCamillo, *Because of Winn-Dixie* (New York: Scholastic, 2000), 100.

47   Bear Light

Epigraph: Jessy Dixon, "He Has Done Great Things," *Songs to Get You Through*, compact disc, © 1994 Fortress.

1.   Marilynne Robinson, *Gilead* (New York: Farrar, Straus and Giroux, 2004), 40.

Part 3   Introduction

1.   http://www.jsonline.com/news/state/aug05/351964.asp
2.   Emily Saliers, "Hammer and a Nail," *Nomads Indians Saints*, Indigo Girls, compact disc, © 1990 Sony.
3.   Ibid.

48   Accepting the Past

1.   Gina Berriault, *Women in Their Beds: New and Selected Short Stories* (Washington, DC: Counterpoint, 1996), 48.
2.   Joan Didion, *The Year of Magical Thinking* (New York: Knopf, 2005), 37.
3.   Ibid.
4.   Debbie Ford, *The Secret of the Shadow: The Power of Owning Your Whole Story* (San Francisco: HarperSanFrancisco, 2002), 83.
5.   Emily Saliers, "Deconstruction," *Become You*, Indigo Girls, compact disc, © 2002 Sony.

49   Completing Unfinished Business

Epigraph: Richard Carlson, *Don't Sweat the Small Stuff . . . and It's All Small Stuff* (New York: Hyperion, 1997), 19.

1.   For a more detailed treatment of forgiveness, see chapter 48, "Accepting the Past."

2. Martin E. P. Seligman, *Authentic Happiness: Using the New Positive Psychology to Realize Your Potential for Lasting Fulfillment* (New York: Free Press, 2002).

3. *Lutheran Book of Worship* (Minneapolis: Augsburg, 1978), 77.

50   Grieving Our Losses

Epigraph: Rachel Naomi Remen, *My Grandfather's Blessings: Stories of Strength, Refuge, and Belonging* (New York: Riverhead Books, 2000), 38.

1. Elizabeth Bishop, *The Complete Poems 1927–1979* (New York: Farrar, Straus Giroux, 1983), 178.

2. Joan Didion, *The Year of Magical Thinking* (New York: Knopf, 2005), 188–9.

3. Mary Martha Kannass (unpublished sermon, Hephatha Lutheran Church, Milwaukee, WI, November 6, 2005).

4. Bono, "Sometimes You Can't Make It on Your Own," *How to Dismantle an Atomic Bomb*, U2 © 2004 Interscope Records.

51   Creating a Healthy Foundation

1. Michele Weiner-Davis, *Change Your Life and Everyone in It* (New York: Fireside, 1995), 86.

2. Ibid.

52   Giving Permission

Epigraph: Joan Anderson, *A Walk on the Beach: Tales of Wisdom from an Unconventional Woman* (New York: Broadway, 2004), 217.

53   Assessing Assets

Epigraph: John Bingham, *The Courage to Start: A Guide to Running for Your Life* (New York: Fireside, 1999), 60.

1. Luther K. Snow, *The Power of Asset Mapping: How Your Congregation Can Act on Its Gifts* (Herndon, VA: Alban Institute, 2004), 5.

54   Identifying and Nurturing Passion

Epigraph: Coleman Barks, trans., *The Essential Rumi* (Edison, NJ: Castle Books, 1997), 41, 157.

1. Frederick Buechner, *Wishful Thinking: A Theological ABC* (New York: HarperCollins, 1973), 73.

2. Martha Beck, *Finding Your Own North Star: Claiming the Life You Were Meant to Live* (New York: Crown, 2001), 4.

3. Ibid.

4. Ibid., 5.

5. Martha Beck's book has an extensive testing tool related to this concept. See *Finding Your Own North Star*, chapters 1-3.

6. Anne Lamott, *Operating Instructions: A Journal of My Son's First Year* (New York: Fawcett Columbine, 1993), 48–49.

7. See Rachel Antony, Joel Henry, and Andrew Dean Norton, *The Lonely Planet Guide to Experimental Travel* (Oakland, CA: Lonely Planet, 2005). This innovative guide offers more than 40 travel experiments you can try. Spend 24 hours in an airport, use dice to determine your destination, or backpack in your own hometown. Any one of these travel experiments *could* change your life.

8. Coleman Barks, trans., *The Essential Rumi* (Edison, NJ: Castle Books, 1997), 157.

9. Jill Neimark, "The Making of a Healer," *Spirituality and Health* (June 2005), 48–52.

55   Midwifing Dreams

Epigraph: Friedrich Nietzsche quoted in Sara Ryan, *Empress of the World* (New York: Viking, 2001), 135.

1. Martha Beck, *Breaking Point: Why Women Fall Apart and How They Can Re-create Their Lives* (New York: Crown, 1997), 251.

2. Julie Connelly, "She Has a PhD in Perseverance Too," *AARP: The Magazine* (November and December 2005), 88.

3. Mandi Caruso, "Alive with Passion," *Spirituality and Health*, February 2006, 38.

4. Mary Martha Kannass (unpublished sermon, Hephatha Lutheran Church, Milwaukee, WI, December 18, 2005).

57   Visioning

Epigraph: Jan L. Richardson, *Night Visions: Searching the Shadows of Advent and Christmas* (Cleveland, OH: United Church Press, 1998), xvii.

1. Amy Ray, "Perfect World," *All That We Let In*, Indigo Girls, compact disc, © 2004 Sony.

2. Julia Spencer-Fleming, *Out of the Deep I Cry* (New York: Thomas Dunne Books, 2004), 84.

3. Gail Godwin, *Evensong* (New York: Ballantine Books, 1999), 12–13.

4. Madeleine L'Engle, *Walking on Water: Reflections on Faith and Art* (New York: Bantam Books, 1980), 13.

5. http://www.fi.edu/brain/exercise.htm

6. Julia Cameron, *Walking in This World: The Practical Art of Creativity* (New York: Jeremy P. Tarcher/Penguin, 2002), 11.

7. Ibid, 2.

8. Mary Catherine Bateson, *Full Circles, Overlapping Lives: Culture and Generation in Transition* (New York: Ballantine Books, 2000), 23.

9. C. S. Lewis, *The Lion, the Witch and the Wardrobe* (New York: Collier Books, 1950), 186.

10. Martha Beck, *Finding Your Own North Star: Claiming the Life You Were Meant to Live* (New York: Crown, 2001), 238.

11. Mary Oliver, "The Summer Day," *New and Selected Poems* (Boston: Beacon, 1992), 94.

58   Setting Goals

Epigraph: Paula Poundstone quoted in Peter McWilliams, *Do It! Let's Get Off Our Buts* (Los Angeles: Prelude Press, 1991), 312.

59   Transforming Messes and Mistakes

Epigraph: Susan Howatch, *The High Flyer* (New York: Knopf, 2000), 499.

1. Anne Lamott, *Bird by Bird: Some Instructions on Writing and Life* (New York: Pantheon, 1994), 21.

2. May Sarton, *The House by the Sea: A Journal* (New York: Norton, 1995), 53.

60   Overcoming Blocks

Epigraph: Madeleine L'Engle, *Walking on Water: Reflections on Faith and Art* (New York: Bantam Books, 1980), 96.

1. Martha Beck, *Finding Your Own North Star: Claiming the Life You Were Meant to Live* (New York: Crown, 2001), 321–322.

2. L'Engle, *Walking on Water*, 93.

3. Ibid., 98.

61   Making Meaning

Epigraph: Rachel Naomi Remen, *My Grandfather's Blessings: Stories of Strength, Refuge, and Belonging* (New York: Riverhead, 2000), 29.

1. Jonathan Haidt, *The Happiness Hypothesis: Finding Modern Truth in Ancient Wisdom* (New York: Basic Books, 2006), 147–49.

❁ Resources

Coaching and Communication Skills

The following books will support you in deepening your understanding of coaching and expanding your toolbox of skills.

Adams, Marilee G. *Change Your Questions Change Your Life: Discover the Power of Questions Thinking.* San Francisco: Berrett-Kohler, 2004.

Buzan, Tony, with Barry Buzan. *The Mind Map Book: How to Use Radiant Thinking to Maximize Your Brain's Untapped Potential.* New York: Plume, 1993.

Coach U, Inc. *Coach U's Essential Coaching Tools: Your Complete Practice Resource.* Hoboken, NJ: Wiley and Sons, 2005.

Collins, Gary R. *Christian Coaching: Helping Others Turn Potential into Reality.* Colorado Springs, CO: NavPress, 2001.

Cotrell, David, and Mark Layton. *The Manager's Coaching Handbook: A Practical Guide to Improving Employee Performance.* Dallas: Walk the Talk Company, 2002.

Crane, Thomas G. *The Heart of Coaching: Using Transformational Coaching to Create a High-Performance Culture.* San Diego: FTA Press, 2002.

Creswell, Jane. *Christ-Centered Coaching: 7 Benefits for Ministry Leaders.* St. Louis: Lake Hickory Resources, 2006.

Fairley, Stephen G., and Chris E. Stout. *Getting Started in Personal and Executive Coaching: How to Create a Thriving Coaching Practice.* Hoboken, NJ: Wiley and Sons, 2003.

Fitzgerald, Catherine, and Jennifer Garvey Berger, eds. *Executive Coaching: Practices and Perspectives.* Palo Alto, CA: Davies-Black, 2002.

Flaherty, James. *Coaching: Evoking Excellence in Others.* Burlington, MA: Elsevier, 1999.

Friedman, Edwin H. *Generation to Generation: Family Process in Church and Synagogue*. New York: Guilford Press, 1985.

Gerber, Robin. *Leadership the Eleanor Roosevelt Way: Timeless Strategies from the First Lady of Courage*. New York: Portfolio, 2002.

Gilbert, Roberta M. *Extraordinary Relationships: A New Way of Thinking About Human Interactions*. Minneapolis: Chronimed, 1992.

Goldsmith, Marshall, and Laurence S. Lyons, eds. *Coaching for Leadership: The Practice of Leadership Coaching from the World's Greatest Coaches*. San Diego: Pfeiffer, 2005.

Grodzki, Lynn, and Wendy Allen. *The Business and Practice of Coaching: Finding Your Niche, Making Money, and Attracting Ideal Clients*. New York: Norton, 2005.

Hargrove, Robert. *Masterful Coaching: Extraordinary Results by Impacting People and the Way They Think and Work Together*. San Diego: Pfeiffer, 1995.

Hudson, Frederic M. *The Handbook of Coaching: A Comprehensive Resource Guide for Managers, Executives, Consultants, and HR*. San Francisco: Jossey-Bass, 1999.

Keirsey, David. *Please Understand Me II: Temperment, Character, Intelligence*. Del Mar, CA: Prometheus Nemesis Book Company, 1998.

Kerr, Michael E., and Murray Bowen. *Family Evaluation: An Approach Based on Bowen Theory*. New York: Norton, 1988.

Kinlaw, Dennis C. *Coaching for Commitment*. San Diego, Pfeiffer, 1993.

Landsberg, Max. *The Tao of Coaching: Boost Your Effectiveness at Work by Inspiring and Developing Those Around You*. London: Profile Books, 2003.

Lindahl, Kay. *The Sacred Art of Listening: Forty Reflections for Cultivating a Spiritual Practice*. Woodstock, VT: SkyLight Paths, 2002.

Maisel, Eric. *Coaching the Artist Within: Advice for Writers, Actors, Visual Artists, and Musicians from America's Foremost Creativity Coach*. Novato, CA: New World Library, 2005.

Martin, Curly. *The Life Coaching Handbook: Everything You Need to be an Effective Life Coach*. Williston, VT: Crown House, 2001.

McGoldrick, Monica, and Randy Gerson. *Genograms in Family Assessment*. New York: Norton, 1985.

Morgan, Howard, Phil Harkings, and Marshall Goldsmith, eds. *The Art and Practice of Leadership Coaching: 50 Executive Coaches Reveal Their Secrets*. Hoboken, NJ: Wiley and Sons, 2005.

O'Neill, Mary Beth. *Executive Coaching with Backbone and Heart: A Systems Approach to Engaging Leaders with Their Challenges*. San Francisco: Jossey-Bass, 2000.

Peterson, David B., and Mary Dee Hicks. *Leader as Coach: Strategies for Coaching and Developing Others*. Minneapolis: Personnel Decisions International, 1996.

Rendle, Gil, and Alice Mann. *Holy Conversations: Strategic Planning as a Spiritual Practice for Congregations*. Herndon, VA: Alban Institute, 2003.

Scott, Susan. *Fierce Conversations: Achieving Success at Work and in Life, One Conversation at a Time*. New York: Berkley Publishing Group, 2002.

Sellon, Mary K., and Daniel P. Smith. *Practicing Right Relationship: Skills for Deepening Purpose, Finding Fulfillment, and Increasing Effectiveness in Your Congregation*. Herndon, VA: Alban Institute, 2005.

Snow, Luther K. *The Power of Asset Mapping: How Your Congregation Can Act on Its Gifts*. Herndon, VA: Alban Institute, 2004.

Starr, Julie. *Coaching Manual: The Definitive Guide to the Process, Principles, and Skills of Personal Coaching*. Upper Saddle River, NJ: Prentice Hall, 2002.

Wheatley, Margaret J. *Leadership and the New Science: Discovering Order in a Chaotic World*. San Francisco: Berrett-Koehler, 1999.

———. *Turning to One Another: Simple Conversations to Restore Hope to the Future*. San Francisco: Berrett-Koehler, 2002.

White, Daniel. *Coaching Leaders: Guiding People Who Guide Others*. San Francisco: Jossey-Bass, 2005.

White, Michael, and David Epston. *Narrative Means to Therapeutic Ends*. New York: Norton, 1990.

Whitmore, John. *Coaching for Performance: Growing People, Performance and Purpose*. London: Nicholas Brealey, 2002.

Whitney, Diana, and Amanda Trosten Bloom. *The Power of Appreciative Inquiry: A Practical Guide to Positive Change*. San Francisco: Berrett-Koehler, 2003.

Whitworth, Laura, Henry Kimsey-House, and Phil Sandahl. *Co-Active Coaching: New Skills for Coaching People toward Success in Work and Life*. Palo Alto, CA: Davies-Black, 1998.

Williams, Patrick, and Lloyd J. Thomas. *Total Life Coaching: 50+ Life Lessons, Skills, and Techniques to Enhance Your Practice . . . and Your Life*. New York: Norton, 2005.

Zeus, Perry, and Suzanne Skiffington. *The Complete Guide to Coaching at Work*. Roseville, Australia: McGraw-Hill Australia, 2000.

Personal Growth Books

When I run out of tools to offer my clients, I recommend a book. These personal growth books offer processes and programs for changing one's life.

Alston, John, and Lloyd Thaxton. *Stuff Happens (and then you fix it!): 9 Reality Rules to Steer Your Life Back in the Right Direction*. Hoboken, NJ: Wiley and Sons, 2003.

Anderson, Joan. *A Weekend to Change Your Life: Find Yourself after a Lifetime of Being All Things to All People*. New York: Broadway, 2006.

Beck, Martha. *Finding Your Own North Star: Claiming the Life You Were Meant to Live*. New York: Crown, 2001.

———. *The Joy Diet: Ten Daily Practices for a Happier Life*. New York: Crown, 2003.

Cameron, Julia. *The Artist's Way: A Spiritual Path to Higher Creativity*. New York: Jeremy P. Tarcher, 1992.

———. *The Vein of Gold: A Journey to Your Creative Heart*. New York: Jeremy P. Tarcher, 1996.

———. *Walking in this World: The Practical Art of Creativity*. New York: Jeremy P. Tarcher, 2002.

Ford, Debbie. *The Dark Side of the Light Chasers: Reclaiming Your Power, Creativity, Brilliance, and Dreams*. New York: Riverhead Books, 1998.

———. *The Secret of the Shadow: The Power of Owning Your Whole Story*. New York: HarperSanFrancisco, 2002.

Fortgang, Laura Berman. *Living Your Best Life*. New York: Jeremy P. Tarcher, 2001.

Fox, John. *Poetic Medicine: The Healing Art of Poem-Making*. New York: Jeremy P. Tarcher, 1997.

Gafni, Marc. *Soul Prints: Your Path to Fulfillment*. New York: Simon and Schuster, 2001.

Gregory, Danny. *The Creative License: Giving Yourself Permission to be the Artist You Truly Are*. New York: Hyperion, 2006.

Huber, Cheri. *There Is Nothing Wrong With You: Going Beyond Self-Hate*. Murphys, CA: Keep It Simple Books, 1993.

Kabat-Zinn, Jon. *Wherever You Go, There You Are: Mindfulness Meditation in Everyday Life*. New York: Hyperion, 1994.

Klauser, Henriette Anne. *Write It Down, Make It Happen: Knowing What You Want and Getting It*. New York: Fireside, 2000.

Kushner, Harold S. *Living a Life That Matters: Resolving the Conflict between Conscience and Success*. New York: Alfred A. Knopf, 2000.

Leider, Richard J., and David A. Shapiro. *Repacking Your Bags: Lighten Your Load for the Rest of Your Life*. San Francisco: Berrett-Koehler, 1995.

Lobenstine, Margaret. *The Renaissance Soul: Life Design for People with Too Many Passions to Pick Just One*. New York: Broadway Books, 2006.

McWilliams, Peter. *Do It! Let's Get Off Our Buts*. Los Angeles: Prelude Press, 1991.

Melander, Rochelle, and Harold Eppley. *The Spiritual Leader's Guide to Self-Care*. Herndon, VA: Alban Institute, 2002.

Morgenstern, Julie. *Time Management from the Inside Out: The Foolproof System for Taking Control of Your Schedule—and Your Life*. New York: Holt, 2000.

————. *Organizing from the Inside Out: The Foolproof System for Organizing Your Home, Your Office, and Your Life*. New York: Holt, 1998.

Pennebaker, James W. *Writing to Heal: A Guided Journal for Recovering from Trauma and Emotional Upheaval*. Oakland, CA: New Harbinger, 2004.

Pollan, Stephen M., and Mark Levine. *It's All in Your Head: Thinking Your Way to Happiness*. New York: Collins, 2005.

Richardson, Cheryl. *Take Time for Your Life: A Personal Coach's 7-Step Program for Creating the Life You Want*. New York: Broadway Books, 1998.

Sweet, Leonard. *Learn to Dance the Soul Salsa: 17 Surprising Steps for Godly Living in the 21st Century*. Grand Rapids, MI: Zondervan, 2000.

Terkel, Susan, and Larry Terkel. *Small Change: It's the Little Things in Life that Make a Big Difference*. New York: Jeremy P. Tarcher, 2004.

Narratives

In life's challenging moments, personal stories of transformation can offer hope and courage. For clients who need more than another exercise to complete, I send them to a memoir. These are some of my favorites.

Anderson, Joan. *A Year by the Sea: Thoughts of an Unfinished Woman.* New York: Doubleday, 1999.

———. *A Walk on the Beach: Tales of Wisdom from an Unconventional Woman.* New York: Broadway, 2005.

———. *An Unfinished Marriage.* New York: Broadway, 2003.

Andrew, Elizabeth J. *Swinging on the Garden Gate: A Spiritual Memoir.* Boston: Skinner House Books, 2000.

———. *On the Threshold: Home, Hardwood, and Holiness.* Cambridge, MA: Westview, 2005.

Ansay, A. Manette. *Limbo: A Memoir.* New York: William Morrow, 2001.

Armstrong, Karen. *Through the Narrow Gate: A Memoir of Spiritual Discovery.* New York: St. Martin's, 1981.

———. *The Spiral Staircase: My Climb Out of Darkness.* New York: Knopf, 2004.

Barr, Nevada. *Seeking Enlightenment Hat by Hat: A Skeptic's Path to Religion.* New York: Putnam's Sons, 2003.

Beck, Martha. *Leaving the Saints: How I Lost the Mormons and Found My Faith.* New York: Crown, 2005.

Becker, Suzy. *I Had Brain Surgery, What's Your Excuse? An Illustrated Memoir.* New York: Workman, 2004.

Bonomo, Carol. *The Abbey Up the Hill: A Year in the Life of a Monastic Day Tripper.* Harrisburg, PA: Morehouse, 2002.

Briggs, Carolyn S. *This Dark World: A Memoir of Salvation Found and Lost.* New York: Bloomsbury, 2002.

Cartledgehayes, Mary. *Grace: A Memoir.* New York: Crown, 2003.

Chittister, Joan. *Called to Question: A Spiritual Memoir.* New York: Sheed and Ward, 2004.

Cohen, Richard M. *Blindsided Lifting a Life Above Illness: A Reluctant Memoir.* New York: HarperCollins, 2004.

Crafton, Barbara Cawthorne. *The Sewing Room: Uncommon Reflections on Life, Love, and Work.* New York: Penguin, 1993.

Dawson, George, and Richard Glaubman. *Life Is So Good.* New York: Penguin, 2000.

DeSalvo, Louise. *Breathless: An Asthma Journal.* Boston: Beacon, 1997.

Donofrio, Beverly. *Looking for Mary (or, the Blessed Mother and me)*. New York: Viking Compass, 1998.

Dubner, Stephen J. *Turbulent Souls: A Catholic Son's Return to His Jewish Family*. New York: Avon, 1998.

Gallagher, Nora. *Things Seen and Unseen: A Year Lived in Faith*. New York: Knopf, 1998.

———. *Practicing Resurrection: A Memoir of Work, Doubt, Discernment and Moments of Grace*. New York: Knopf, 2003.

Grumbach, Doris. *Life in a Day*. Boston: Beacon, 1996.

Halpin, Brendan. *It Takes a Worried Man: A Memoir*. New York: Random House Trade Paperbacks, 2002.

Hampl, Patricia. *Virgin Time: In Search of the Contemplative Life*. New York: Ballantine, 1992.

Hart, Heidi. *Grace Notes: The Waking of a Woman's Voice*. Salt Lake City: University of Utah Press, 2004.

James, Nancy C. *Standing in the Whirlwind: The Riveting Story of a Priest and the Congregations that Tormented Her*. Cleveland: Pilgrim Press, 2005.

Kidd, Sue Monk. *The Dance of the Dissident Daughter: A Woman's Journey from Christian Tradition to the Sacred Feminine*. New York: HarperSanFrancisco, 1996.

———. *When the Heart Waits: Spiritual Direction for Life's Sacred Questions*. New York: HarperSanFrancisco, 1990.

Lamott, Anne. *Operating Instructions: A Journal of My Son's First Year*. New York: Anchor, 2005.

———. *Traveling Mercies: Some Thoughts on Faith*. New York: Pantheon, 1999.

———. *Plan B: Further Thoughts on Faith*. New York: Riverhead Books, 2005.

Linnea, Ann. *Deep Water Passage: A Spiritual Journey at Midlife*. New York: Pocket Books, 1993.

Lischer, Richard. *Open Secrets: A Memoir of Faith and Discovery*. New York: Broadway Books, 2001.

Mairs, Nancy. *Ordinary Time: Cycles in Marriage, Faith, and Renewal*. Boston: Beacon, 1993.

Mantel, Hilary. *Giving Up the Ghost: A Memoir*. New York: Holt, 2003.

Nafisi, Azar. *Reading Lolita in Tehran: A Memoir in Books*. New York: Random House, 2004.

O'Reilley, Mary Rose. *The Barn at the End of the World: The Apprenticeship of a Quaker, Buddhist Shepherd*. Minneapolis: Milkweed Editions, 2000.

Salzman, Mark. *True Notebooks*. New York: Knopf, 2003.

Sarton, May. *A Journal of a Solitude: The Intimate Diary of a Year in the Life of a Creative Woman*. New York: Norton, 1973.

Shea, Suzanne Strempek. *Songs from a Lead-Lined Room: Notes—High and Low—from My Journey through Breast Cancer and Radiation*. Boston: Beacon, 2002.

Shulman, Alix Kates. *Drinking the Rain: A Memoir*. New York: Penguin, 1995.

Smith, Jeffrey. *Where the Roots Reach for Water: A Personal and Natural History of Melancholia*. New York: North Point Press, 1999.

Swander, Mary. *Out of This World: A Journey of Healing*. New York: Penguin, 1995.

———. *The Desert Pilgrim: En Route to Mysticism and Miracles*. New York: Penguin, 2004.

Tan, Amy. *The Opposite of Faith: Memories of a Writing Life*. New York: Penguin, 2003.

Wallis, Joy Carroll. *The Woman Behind the Collar: The Pioneering Journey of an Episcopal Priest*. New York: Crossroad, 2004.

Welty, Eudora. *One Writer's Beginnings*. New York: Warner Books, 1983.

Weems, Renita J. *Listening for God: A Minister's Journey through Silence and Doubt*. New York: Touchstone, 1999.

Willims, Terry Tempest. *Leap*. New York: Vintage Books, 2000.

Winter, Miriam Therese. *The Singer and the Song: An Autobiography of the Spirit*. Maryknoll, New York: Orbis, 1999.

Zeppa, Jamie. *Beyond the Sky and the Earth: A Journey into Bhutan*. New York: Riverhead Books, 1999.

Inspiration

I once heard a young boy say, "When I get angry I go into a book. When I come out, it's like I start on a fresh page." These are some of the inspirational books I send clients to when they are seeking a fresh page in life.

Barks, Coleman, trans. with John Moyne. *The Essential Rumi*. Edison, NJ: Castle Books, 1995.

Blanchard, Bob, and Melinda Blanchard. *Live What You Love: Notes from an Unusual Life*. New York: Sterling, 2005.

Briehl, Susan, and Marty Haugen, eds. *Turn My Heart: A Sacred Journey from Brokenness to Healing*. Chicago: GIA, 2003.

Brussat, Mary Ann and Frederic Brussat. *Spiritual Literacy: Reading the Sacred in Everyday Life*. New York: Scribner, 1996.

———. *Spiritual RX: Prescriptions for Living a Meaningful Life*. New York: Hyperion, 2001.

Casey, Karen. *Change Your Mind and Your Life Will Follow: 12 Simple Principles*. Boston: Conari Press, 2005.

Chittister, Joan. *Scarred by Struggle, Transformed by Hope*. Grand Rapids, MI: Eerdmans, 2003.

Estes, Clarissa Pinkola. *Women Who Run with the Wolves: Myths and the Stories of the Wild Women Archetype*. New York: Ballantine, 1992.

Farrington, Debra K. *The Seasons of a Restless Heart: A Spiritual Companion for Living in Transition*. San Francisco: Jossey-Bass, 2005.

Frankl, Viktor E. *Man's Search for Meaning*. New York: Pocket Books, 1959.

Housden, Roger. *Ten Poems to Change Your Life*. New York: Harmony, 2001.

———. *Ten Poems to Open Your Heart*. New York: Harmony, 2002.

———. *Ten Poems to Set You Free*. New York: Harmony, 2003.

———. *Ten Poems to Last a Lifetime*. New York: Harmony, 2004.

Karr, Mary. *Sinners Welcome: Poems*. New York: HarperCollins, 2006.

L'Engle, Madeleine. *Glimpses of Grace: Daily Thoughts and Reflections*. New York: HarperSanFrancisco, 1996.

———. *Walking on Water: Reflections of Faith and Art*. New York: Bantam, 1980.

Malone, Nancy M. *Walking a Literary Labyrinth: A Spirituality of Reading*. New York: Riverhead Books, 2003.

McMillan, Kim, with Alison McMillan. *When I Loved Myself Enough*. New York: St. Martin's, 2001.

Morley, Janet. *All Desires Known: Inclusive Prayers for Worship and Meditation*. Harrisburg, PA: Morehouse, 1992.

Muller, Wayne. *Sabbath: Finding Rest, Renewal, and Delight in Our Busy Lives*. New York: Bantam, 2000.

Nouwen, Henri J. M. *Bread for the Journey: A Daybook of Wisdom and Faith*. New York: HarperCollins, 1997.

Oliver, Mary. *New and Selected Poems*. Boston: Beacon, 1992.

———. *New and Selected Poems Volume Two*. Boston: Beacon, 2005.

Palmer, Parker J. *Let Your Life Speak: Listening for the Voice of Vocation*. San Francisco: Jossey-Bass, 2000.

———. *The Active Life: A Spirituality of Work, Creativity, and Caring*. San Francisco: Jossey-Bass, 1990.

Remen, Rachel Naomi. *Kitchen Table Wisdom: Stories that Heal*. New York: Riverhead Books, 1996.

———. *My Grandfather's Blessings: Stories of Strength, Refuge, and Belonging*. New York: Riverhead Books, 2000.

Richardson, Jan L. *Sacred Journeys: A Woman's Book of Daily Prayer*. Nashville: Upper Room, 1995.

———. *Night Visions: Searching the Shadows of Advent and Christmas*. Cleveland: United Church Press, 1998.

———. *In Wisdom's Path: Discovering the Sacred in Every Season*. Cleveland: Pilgrim Press, 2000.

Rivers, Frank. *The Way of the Owl: Succeeding with Integrity in a Conflicted World*. New York: HarperSanFrancisco, 1996.

Roberts, Bruce B., Craig D. Rice, and Joe E. Smith. *Where in the World Is Integrity? The Challenge of Doing What Is Right*. Minneapolis: Augsburg Books, 2005.

Ruiz, Don Miguel. *The Four Agreements: A Practical Guide to Personal Freedom*. San Rafael, CA: Amber-Allen, 1997.

Rupp, Joyce. *Dear Heart, Come Home: The Path of Midlife Spirituality*. New York: Crossroad, 1996.

———. *The Cup of Our Life: A Guide for Spiritual Growth*. Notre Dame, IN: Ave Maria Press, 1997.

Vanier, Jean. *Becoming Human*. New York: Paulist Press, 1998.

———. *Drawn into the Mystery of Jesus through the Gospel of John*. New York: Paulist Press, 2004.

Whitmire, Catherine. *Plain Living: A Quaker Path to Simplicity*. Notre Dame, IN: Sorin Books, 2001.